ISRAEL'S ESCHATOLOGICAL ENEMY

ISRAEL'S ESCHATOLOGICAL ENEMY

The Identity of the King of Babylon in Isaiah 14:4–21

TIMOTHY ALLEN LITTLE

WIPF & STOCK · Eugene, Oregon

ISRAEL'S ESCHATOLOGICAL ENEMY
The Identity of the King of Babylon in Isaiah 14:4–21

Copyright © 2020 Timothy Allen Little. All rights reserved. Except for brief quotations in critical publications or reviews, no part of this book may be reproduced in any manner without prior written permission from the publisher. Write: Permissions, Wipf and Stock Publishers, 199 W. 8th Ave., Suite 3, Eugene, OR 97401.

Wipf & Stock
An Imprint of Wipf and Stock Publishers
199 W. 8th Ave., Suite 3
Eugene, OR 97401

www.wipfandstock.com

PAPERBACK ISBN: 978-1-7252-5689-7
HARDCOVER ISBN: 978-1-7252-5690-3
EBOOK ISBN: 978-1-7252-5691-0

Manufactured in the U.S.A.   04/28/20

To Angela,

whose sacrifice went unnoticed

by many, but whose sacrifice

made this project possible

Contents

List of Tables	ix
Acknowledgments	xi
Abbreviations	xiii
Chapter 1: Introduction	1
History of Interpretation	1
Need for This Dissertation	8
Thesis Statement	10
Chapter 2: The Genre of Isaiah 14	12
Mashal	15
Parodic Dirge	27
Conclusion	35
Chapter 3: The *Massa'* against Babylon—Isaiah 13:2—14:2	37
Preliminary Issues	38
Structure of Isaiah 13:2—14:27	42
Eschatology in Isaiah 13:2—14:2	65
Conclusion	98
Chapter 4: The King of Babylon	100
Questionable Criteria	101
Attributes of the King of Babylon	103
Activities of the King of Babylon	132
The Kings of Babylon	142
Conclusion	162
Chapter 5: Conclusion	163
Theological Implications	165
Areas for Further Study	165
Appendix 1: Summary of the Kings of Babylon	167
Bibliography	169

List of Tables

2.1	Comparison of "Royal Dirges" in the Old Testament and the Ancient Near East
2.2	Comparison between 2 Samuel 1 Dirge and Isaiah 14 Parody
3.1	Historical Setting of the *Massa'* against Babylon
3.2	The *Mas'ot* against the Nations
3.3	Inclusio between Isaiah 13:9–13
3.4	Reconstructed Stichography of Isaiah 13:20—14:2
3.5	Catchwords in Isaiah 13:18–22
3.6	Timeframe of the *Mashal* (Proverb)
3.7	Concluding Inclusios
3.8	Isaiah 14:24–27's Structural Connection to the *Massa'* against Babylon
3.9	Two Battles in Isaiah 13:2–22
4.1	Evaluation of Alexander the Great
4.2	Evaluation of Assur-uballit II
4.3	Evaluation of Belshazzar
4.4	Evaluation of Merodach-baladan
4.5	Evaluation of Nabonidus
4.6	Evaluation of Nebuchadnezzar
4.7	Evaluation of Sargon II
4.8	Evaluation of Sennacherib
4.9	Evaluation of Tiglath-pileser III

Acknowledgments

Particular thanks to the administration of Faith Baptist Bible College and Theological Seminary for encouraging me to complete this project and for assisting with the financial obligations. Doug Brown and Ken Rathbun eased my teaching load for a semester and regularly spurred me on to finish.

Mark McGinniss provided invaluable feedback throughout my PhD studies. Thank you for introducing me to Hebrew poetry and the Song of Songs. Your critical remarks were often not welcome at the time but provided a much better final product. Thank you, Mark, for investing in this project and me the last several years. I am a substantially different man because of your investment.

Finally, no one sacrificed more than my family. From maintaining the house and schooling the children to bringing me meals and keeping me healthy, my wife, Angela, sacrificed the most. There could not be a better עֵזֶר. My children regularly prayed for me as I went to the office to write. They also provided an occasional respite from studies into dart guns, Legos, and cuddles.

Abbreviations

ABD	*Anchor Bible Dictionary.* 6 vols. Edited by David Noel Freedman. New York: Doubleday, 1992
ACW	*Ancient Christian Writers.* 1946–
ANET	*Ancient Near Eastern Texts Relating to the Old Testament.* 3rd ed. Edited by James B. Pritchard. Princeton: Princeton University Press, 1969
ANF	*Ante-Nicene Fathers.* 10 vols. Edited by Alexander Roberts and James Donaldson. Reprint, Peabody, MA: Hendrickson, 1994
BETS	*Bulletin of the Evangelical Theological Society*
BHS	*Biblica Hebraica Stuttgartensia.* 5th ed. Edited by Karl Elliger and Wilhelm Rudolph. Stuttgart: Deutsche Bibelstiftung, 1997
ConJ	*Concordia Journal*
GTJ	*Grace Theological Journal*
HALOT	*The Hebrew Aramaic Lexicon of the Old Testament.* 5 vols. Edited by Ludwig Koehler and Walter Baumgartner. Translated and edited by M. E. J. Richardson. Leiden: Brill, 1994–2000
KTU	*Die keilalphabetischen Texte aus Ugarit.* Edited by M. Dietrich et al. AOAT 24/1. Neukirchen-Vluyn, 1976. 2nd ed. of *KTU: The Cuneiform Aphabetic Texts from Ugarit, Ras Ibn Hani, and Other Places.* Edited by M. Dietrich et al. Münster, 1995

Abbreviations

NIDOTTE	*New International Dictionary of Old Testament Theology & Exegesis*. 5 vols. Edited by Willem A. VanGemeren. Grand Rapids: Zondervan, 1997
NPNF^1	*Nicene and Post-Nicene Fathers,* Series 1. 14 vols. Edited by Philip Schaff. Reprint. Peabody, MA: Hendrickson, 1994
NPNF^2	*Nicene and Post-Nicene Fathers,* Series 2. 14 vols. Edited by Philip Schaff. Reprint. Peabody, MA: Hendrickson, 1994
SC	*Sources Chrétiennes*. Paris: Cerf, 1948–
TDOT	*Theological Dictionary of the Old Testament*. 15 vols. Edited by G. Johannes Botterweck et al. Grand Rapids: Eerdmans, 1974–2015
SCJ	*Stone-Campbell Journal*

Chapter 1

Introduction

ISAIAH 14:4B–21 DESCRIBES A ruler who is only identified as the "king of Babylon." Keown concludes, "No modern scholar is able to identify הילל בן־שחר [shining one, son of the dawn]."[1] This dissertation proposes that the king of Babylon referred to in Isaiah 14 is Israel's eschatological enemy.[2]

HISTORY OF INTERPRETATION

Before the modern period, Nebuchadnezzar was usually identified as the king of Babylon, but Isaiah 14:12–14 referred to Satan. Since the Reformation, scholars have presented a broad smattering of views which have been

---

1. Keown, "History of the Interpretation of Isaiah 14:12–15," 139.

2. Isaiah and the people of Israel would have known the king of Babylon as an eschatological foe who opposed them and God. Some have identified Israel's eschatological enemy as the antichrist. Karrer, for example, connects antichrist to New Testament passages and explains that the antichrist is the "immanent eschatological opponent of God" (Karrer, "Antichrist," 81–82). Hubbard extends the idea to the Old Testament and even Isaiah 14 (Hubbard, "Antichrist," 68–70). Ryken claims antichrist is not an eschatological person but an idea which, "lives on beyond the first century, to the present and to the eschaton, wherever the nature and message of Christ are refuted in the service of fraudulent demands for absolute loyalty" (Ryken, *Dictionary of Biblical Imagery*, 34). See also Jervis, "Antichrist," 27–28. Antichrist concerns New Testament studies (1 John 2:18, 22; 4:3; 2 John 7). Isaiah 14 describes an eschatological enemy of Israel. Whether this person should be associated with a New Testament idea of antichrist steps outside of Isaiah 14 and the purpose of this publication.

fueled by higher criticism, archaeology, and history. This section details some of this history.

Jewish Interpretation

The Babylonian Talmud referred to Isaiah 14:12–14 four times. Nebuchadnezzar is explicitly described as the king of Babylon two times,[3] and is the implied referent the other two times.[4] The LXX translators also believed Nebuchadnezzar was the king of Babylon as revealed in their translation of Isaiah 14:20.[5]

Church Fathers

Several early church fathers believed Isaiah 14:12–14 referred to Satan. Origen states, "And how could we possibly accept, as spoken of a man, what is related in many passages of Scripture, and especially in Isaiah, regarding Nebuchadnezzar? For he is not a man who is said to have 'fallen from heaven,' or who was 'Lucifer,' or who 'arose in the morning.'"[6] Thus, Origen claimed the shining one (הילל) was the devil, named Lucifer. Tertullian also believed Isaiah 14 referred to Satan.[7] Augustine recognized a historical referent in Isaiah 14, but thought Isaiah 14:12–14 referred to Satan. He states, "For example, what is said in Isaiah, 'How he is fallen from heaven, Lucifer, son of the morning!' and the other statements of the context which, under the figure of the king of Babylon, are made about the same person, are of course to be understood of the devil."[8] This citation reveals that Augustine believed the shining one (הילל) was a proper name, Lucifer. Augustine

---

3. b. Šabb. 149b; b. Ḥul. 89b.

4. b. Ḥag. 13a; b. Pesaḥ. 94b. These texts are the same. Keown recognizes three references to Nebuchadnezzar in the Talmud (Keown, "History of the Interpretation of Isaiah 14:12–15," 26–27). Shipp also recognizes three references to Nebuchadnezzar (Shipp, *Of Dead Kings and Dirges*, 13). Interestingly their lists of three differ. Keown misses the reference in b. Ḥag. 13a (Keown's omission could be intentional because it is the same as b. Pesaḥ. 94b), and Shipp misses the clear reference in b. Šabb. 149b.

5. See ch. 4.

6. Origen, *First Principles* 4.22 (ANF 4:372). See also Origen, *Against Celsus* 6.43 (ANF 4:593); *First Principles* 1.5 (ANF 4:258–59).

7. Commenting on Isaiah 14:13–14 he stated, "This must mean the devil" (Tertullian, *Against Marcion* 5.27 [ANF 3:466]).

8. Augustine, *On Christian Doctrine* 3.37 (NPNF[1] 2:573).

refers to Satan as Lucifer as if it were an established theological truth. For example, in his commentary on John, Augustine states, "A certain one was named Lucifer, who fell; for he was an angel and became a devil; and concerning him the Scripture said, 'Lucifer, who did arise in the morning, fell.' And why was he *Lucifer*? Because being enlightened, he gave forth light."[9] Concerning Augustine, Keown remarks, "This is the accepted origin of the devil as far as Augustine is concerned."[10] By the time of Augustine, the church had predominantly accepted that Isaiah 14:12–14 referred to Satan. Not all of the church fathers, however, believed these verses referred to Satan. Aphrahat, Theodoret of Cyrus, and Chrysostom apply Isaiah 14:13–14 to Nebuchadnezzar.[11]

Hippolytus of Rome claimed the king of Babylon in Isaiah 14 was the antichrist. He stated, "That these things, then, are said of no one else but that tyrant, and shameless one, and adversary of God, we shall show in what follows."[12] He then quotes extensively from Isaiah 10:12–17; 14:4–21; and Ezekiel 28:2–10. Hippolytus then connected these quotes with Daniel 7 and the little horn.

Medieval Scholars

Medieval scholars interpreted Isaiah 14 consistently with the church fathers before them.[13] Gregory the Great alluded to verse 13 when he wrote, "For in the day of their death the just man does 'fall to the South,' and the unjust

---

9. Augustine, *On the Gospel of St. John* 3.7 (*NPNF*[1] 7:21; emphasis original).

10. Keown, "History of the Interpretation of Isaiah 14:12–15," 58.

11. Aphrahat writes, "Now Nebuchadnezzar said:—*I will ascend to heaven and exalt my throne above the stars of God and sit in the lofty mountains that are in the borders of the North*. Isaiah said concerning him :—*Because thy heart has thus exalted thee, therefore thou shalt be brought down to Sheol, and all that look upon thee shall be astonished at thee*" (Aphrahat, *Demonstrations* 5.4 [*NPNF*[2] 13:353, emphasis original]). Theodoret states, "For instance, Nabuchodonosor, the arrogant tyrant, who raised up the golden image and called on all to adore it, saying: *I will exalt my throne above the stars. I will ascend above the height of the clouds*" (Theodoret, *On Divine Providence* [*ACW* 49:152, emphasis original]). See also Theodoret of Cyrus, *Commentary on Isaiah* 14:4–30 (SC 295:84–100). Chrysostom explains, "Hear, for instance, what the prophet says of a barbarian king, when seized with this frenzy. 'I will exalt,' saith he, 'my throne above the stars of heaven'" (Chrysostom, *Homily XI*.4 [*NPNF*[1] 9:414]).

12. Hippolytus, *Treatise on Christ and Antichrist* 15–25 (*ANF* 5:207–9).

13. For a fuller history, see Keown, "History of the Interpretation of Isaiah 14:12–15," 62–72. There has been little study of medieval exegesis of Isaiah 14.

'to the North,' in that both the just man in favour of the Spirit is brought to joy, and the sinner, together with the apostate Angel, who said, *I will sit also upon the mount of the testimony, in the sides of the North*, is cast away in his frozen heart."[14] Gregory casually referenced this verse and applied it to Satan. Anselm of Canterbury represents the medieval assumption of Satan's sin to be "like God." While he does not cite Isaiah 14 directly, Satan's sin "to be like God" provides the foundation for a theological discussion between this teacher and student.[15] Aquinas believed Nebuchadnezzar was the king of Babylon, though he applied Isaiah 14:12–14 "in a spiritual sense to the devil."[16]

Post-Reformation Scholarship

Since the Reformation, there has been a great variety of interpretations of Isaiah 14. Luther rejected a Satanic interpretation: "This is not said of the angel who once was thrown out of heaven but of the king of Babylon, and it is figurative language."[17] Calvin similarly resolutely rejected a Satanic interpretation:

> The exposition of this passage, which some have given, as if it referred to Satan, has arisen from ignorance; for the context plainly shows that these statements must be understood in reference to the king of the Babylonians. But when passages of Scripture are taken up at random, and no attention is paid to the context, we need not wonder that mistakes of this kind frequently arise. Yet it was an instance of very gross ignorance to imagine that *Lucifer* was the king of devils, and that the Prophet gave him this name. But as these inventions have no probability whatever, let us pass by them as useless fables.[18]

Not all Protestants, however, followed Luther and Calvin's exegesis. Keown lists many post-Reformation exegetes who continued the church fathers' interpretation.[19]

---

14. Gregory the Great, *Morals on the Book of Job*, 2:48 (emphasis original).
15. Anselm of Canterbury, *Complete Philosophical and Theological Treatises*, 223–24.
16. Wilken et al., *Isaiah*, 179–80.
17. Luther, *Lectures on Isaiah*, 140.
18. Calvin, *Commentary on the Book of the Prophet Isaiah*, 442 (emphasis original).
19. Keown, "History of the Interpretation of Isaiah 14:12–15," 76–94.

Modern Scholarship

Modern scholarship has produced an assortment of views that can be divided into three categories: a historic king, a symbolic king, and Satan.[20] Some scholars believe the king of Babylon is a historic king. Some of these argue for Nebuchadnezzar.[21] Others believe he is Tiglath-pileser III,[22] Sargon II,[23] Sennacherib,[24] Assur-uballit II,[25] Merodach-baladan,[26] Nabonidus,[27] Belshazzar,[28] Alexander the Great,[29] a historic king,[30] or an unknown historic king.[31] Others believe Isaiah 14 originally referred to the "king of Assyria" (e.g., Sargon II) and a later redactor changed it to "king

---

20. Some authors take multiple views. For example, some believe the king of Babylon is a historic king, but Isaiah 14:12–14 refers to Satan.

21. Bultema, *Commentary on Isaiah*, 162; Day, *Yahweh and the Gods and Goddesses of Canaan*, 182; Wildberger, *Isaiah 13–27*, 55.

22. Hayes and Irvine, *Isaiah*, 227; Brangenberg III, "Re-Examination," 91.

23. Gallagher, *Sennacherib's Campaign to Judah*, 87–90; Ginsberg, "Reflexes of Sargon in Isaiah," 49; Shipp, *Of Dead Kings and Dirges*, 165–66; Roberts, *First Isaiah*, 207–13; Sweeney, *Isaiah 1–39*, 237.

24. Erlandsson, "Burden of Babylon," 8; Martin, "Isaiah," 1061; Vanderburgh, "Ode on the King of Babylon," 120.

25. Auvray, *Isaïe 1–39*, 163.

26. Smith, *Isaiah 1–39*, 311; Watts, *Isaiah 1–33*, 204.

27. Chisholm says, "The king of Babylon taunted here may be Nabonidus (the official king of Babylon when it fell), Belshazzar (who was functioning as king at the time; see Dan. 5:1), or even Nebuchadnezzar" (Chisholm, *Handbook on the Prophets*, 51). Clements explains, "This was intended to be Nabonidus . . . it is evidently not simply one ruler, but the whole tyrannical rule which he represented" (Clements, *Isaiah 1–39*, 141). See also Goldingay, *Isaiah*, 102; Jahnow, *Das hebräische Leichenlied*, 242.

28. Without citation, Cobb claims an "old explanation" connects Belshazzar to this prophecy. Cobb, "Ode in Isaiah XIV," 26.

29. Torrey, "Some Important Editorial Operations," 116–17.

30. Similar to the unknown king view, these authors claim the king of Babylon is a historic king, but they do not specify which king. For example, Frame states, "Scripture does not narrate the fall of Satan and his angels, but Isaiah 14:3–21 and Ezekiel 28:2–19 deal with the defeat of the kings of Babylon and Tyre, respectively, using imagery suggesting analogies with the fall of Satan" (Frame, *Systematic Theology*, 775n5). Frame's purpose is not to discover to which king the prophecy refers, but rather to explain that it does not refer to Satan. See also Geisler, *Systematic Theology*, 743; Grudem, *Systematic Theology*, 413; Alden, "Lucifer, Who or What?," 35–39; Grogan, "Isaiah," 104; Seitz, *Isaiah 1–39*, 131; Smith, *Isaiah 1–39*, 431; Steveson, *Commentary on Isaiah*, 118; Vine, *Isaiah*, 55; Lowth, *Isaiah*, 90.

31. Gray, *Isaiah I–XXXIX*, 251; Motyer, *Prophecy of Isaiah*, 142; Prinsloo, "Isaiah 14:12–15^," 436; Tucker, "Book of Isaiah 1–39," 158.

of Babylon," applying it to a different king (e.g., Nebuchadnezzar).[32] All of these views agree that the king of Babylon was an historic figure.

Some scholars believe the king of Babylon is a symbolic, ideal, representative, or eclectic king. Alexander explains, "Equally useless is the question whether by the king of Babylon we are to understand Nebuchadnezzar, Evilmerodach, or Belshazzar. The king here introduced is an ideal personage, whose downfall represents that of the Babylonian monarchy."[33] This view is little different from the historic king view, purporting the king of Babylon is a historic group of people who were characterized by pride. Others claim he is a poetic fiction. Webb explains, "The king of Babylon here, like Babylon itself in chapter 13, is a representative figure, the embodiment of that worldly arrogance that defies God and tramples on others in its lust for power."[34] Thus for Webb, this king is fictitious and serves a proverbial function to warn readers of arrogance.

Others do not identify the king of Babylon but believe Isaiah 14:12–14 refers to Satan.[35] For example, Akin explains, "The *helel* of Isaiah 14:12 (lit. 'shining one') is translated 'morning star' (NIV) or 'Day Star' (ESV)

---

32. This view has many differences because authors must identify the first king (e.g., an Assyrian king) and the second king (e.g., a Babylonian king). Blenkinsopp, *Isaiah 1–39*, 286; Younger, "Recent Study on Sargon II," 319; Childs, *Isaiah*, 123; Herbert, *Book of the Prophet Isaiah*, 102; Jensen, "Helel Ben Shaḥar," 340; Scott, "Book of Isaiah," 258–59; Skinner, *Book of the Prophet Isaiah*, 120; Kaiser, *Isaiah: 13–39*, 30–31; Bailey, "Expository Articles," 172; Bost, "Le Chant Sur La Chute d'un Tyran En Esaïe 14," 8; Van van Keulen, "On the Identity of the Anonymous Ruler," 122–23; Nielsen, *There is Hope for a Tree*, 160–61.

33. Alexander, *Prophecies of Isaiah*, 289. See also Young, *Book of Isaiah*, 1:435; Mackay, *Study Commentary on Isaiah*, 345. Ironside is difficult to categorize. He explains, "The 'king of Babylon' seems to be used here as a synonym for all Gentile powers that . . . have taken part in the persecution of God's ancient people. (Ironside, *Expository Notes on the Prophet Isaiah*, 87). Because Ironside uses "synonym" instead of "symbolize," he seems to have in mind a very large group of people (eclectic view).

34. Webb, *Message of Isaiah*, 83. See also Erdman, *Book of Isaiah*, 50; Leupold, *Exposition of Isaiah*, 255; Arnold, *Who Were the Babylonians?*, 11; Buksbazen, *Prophet Isaiah*, 197; Oswalt, *Book of Isaiah*, 314; Tate, "Satan in the Old Testament," 468; Keown, "History of the Interpretation of Isaiah 14:12–15," 95.

35. Akin, *Theology for the Church*, 257; Archer, "Isaiah," 622; Bertoluci, "Son of the Morning," 2; Bultema, *Commentary on Isaiah*, 167; Carman, "Falling Star and the Rising Son," 221–231; Chafer, *Satan*, 51; Chafer, *Systematic Theology*, 7:284–85; Criswell, *Isaiah*, 116; Dickason, *Angels*, 135–140; Jennings, *Studies in Isaiah*, 179; Pentecost, *Things to Come*, 423; Enns, *Moody Handbook of Theology*, 307–8; Barackman, *Practical Christian Theology*, 237.

or 'Lucifer' (NKJV) and is rightly understood by many as a reference to Satan."[36]

Some authors believe Isaiah 14 refers to a historic king of Babylon who is an antitype of Satan and a type of the antichrist. Delitzsch explains, "A retrospective glance is now cast at the self-deification of the king of Babylon, in which he was the antitype of the devil and the type of antichrist."[37] Ryrie agrees, "The fall of the king of Babylon is an antitype of the previous fall of Satan and a type of the future fall of antichrist."[38]

Others believe the king of Babylon is the antichrist, but Isaiah 14:12–14 refers to Satan.[39] McCune explains:

> The context of Isaiah 14 is eschatological, pointing to a time when Yahweh will again move to fulfill Israel's national election, settle her in her own land, and make her the head nation of the world. . . . The perspective of the account is one in which Israel looks back over the Tribulation, from which she has just emerged, and takes up a taunt (*mashal*) against her greatest enemy ever—the antichrist, the eschatological king of Babylon. In recounting this taunt of the Babylonian king, the prophetic description briefly turns to a parenthetical matter—the energizer of this eschatological king, Satan (vv. 12–14)—before returning to the original subject matter (v. 15).[40]

MacArthur and Mayhue agree, "While referring to the future king of Babylon, Isaiah 14:4–21 seems also to allude to Satan in the same manner as Ezekiel."[41] Hassler also agrees with this position, "The burden concerning Babylon (Isa 13:1—14:27) awaits a solely eschatological fulfillment (with 14:13–14 being a historical allusion)."[42]

Some claim the king of Babylon is the eschatological enemy of Israel and call him the antichrist. Newton explains:

---

36. Akin, *Theology for the Church*, 257.
37. Delitzsch, *Biblical Commentary on the Prophecies of Isaiah*, 312.
38. Ryrie, *Basic Theology*, 164.
39. McCune, *Systematic Theology of Biblical Christianity*, 377; Hassler, "Isaiah 13:1—14:27," 152; MacArthur and Mayhue, *Biblical Doctrine*, 704; Sorenson, *Understanding the Bible*, 425–26; McClain, *Greatness of the Kingdom*, 195, cf. 480; Jacobs, "Eschatological Significance of Babylon," 140–47.
40. McCune, *Systematic Theology of Biblical Christianity*, 377.
41. MacArthur and Mayhue, *Biblical Doctrine*, 704.
42. Hassler, "Isaiah 13:1—14:27," 4.

> In the fourteenth of Isaiah, Antichrist is again called the Assyrian. "The Lord of hosts hath sworn, saying, Surely as I have thought, so shall it come to pass; and as I have purposed, so shall it stand: That I will break the Assyrian *in my Land*, and upon my mountains tread him under foot: then shall his yoke depart from off them, and his burden depart from off their shoulders" —*i.e.*, the shoulders of Israel.
>
> In the same chapter he is also called "the King of Babylon," and "Lucifer" (the Bringer of Light), because he will blasphemously assume the character of Christ as the bright and morning star.[43]

Newton retained the translation "Lucifer" but applied it to the antichrist, an eschatological enemy of Israel, rather than Satan. He also identifies the "Mount of the Congregation" in Isaiah 14:13 as the temple where this man will offer sacrifices, but that is the extent of his exegesis.[44] Pink quotes Newton at length but does little to develop Newton's idea: "Verses 9 to 20 contain a striking portrait of the lofty arrogance and fearful doom of the Man of Sin."[45]

Conclusion

The Targums and early church thought Nebuchadnezzar was the king of Babylon, though there were dissenters like Hippolytus of Rome. After Augustine, the church broadly concluded that Isaiah 14:12–14 referred to Satan. The Reformers rejected this interpretation about Satan but retained the Nebuchadnezzar view. As modern scholarship pursued a historic king that met the description of Isaiah 14, the views multiplied.

NEED FOR THIS DISSERTATION

Isaiah 13–14 has been the focus of at least seven dissertations in the last fifty years. Erlandsson claimed Isaiah wrote Isaiah 13–14 in 701 BC to encourage Judah not to trust Babylon because it would be destroyed in 689 BC.[46] Erlandsson never states explicitly, but strongly hints that Sennacherib

---

43. Newton, *Aids to Prophetic Enquiry*, 122 (emphasis original).
44. Newton, *Aids to Prophetic Enquiry*, 123.
45. Pink, *Antichrist*, 240.
46. Erlandsson, *Burden of Babylon*, 164–65.

is the king of Babylon.[47] Keown focused on a history of interpretation and concluded, "The king need not be identified. He represents the evil oppressor of any age."[48] Bertoluci examined the mythological allusions in Ezekiel 28 and Isaiah 14, concluding that both passages transcend "the earthly realm . . . and portray the fall of the chief angel Satan from heaven and his role in the controversy between good and evil."[49] Gosse purports a long evolutionary development to Isaiah 13:1—14:23 and concludes that Babylon is figurative.[50] Fry produced a detailed exegetical study of Isaiah 13:1—14:27 with the intent "to understand more clearly the form and function of the 'Oracle Concerning Babylon' within the development of the Isaianic tradition."[51] He does not develop the identity of the king of Babylon, but he seems to take a representative view.[52] Zapff examined the redaction history of Isaiah.[53] Shipp focused on the mythological and genre implications in Isaiah 14 concluding: "It is possible that Sargon II is the king referred to in both 14:4b–21 and vv. 28–32."[54] These dissertations do not come to the same conclusion as this study.

Hassler, however, comes very close to this dissertation's thesis, claiming Isaiah 13–14 is eschatological. His dissertation, however, is primarily historical and intertextual/theological: "The current writer will investigate the past historical record and progressive revelation in order to identify a potential time (or times) of fulfillment."[55] This dissertation, on the other hand, focuses on the genre, structure, and language used in the oracle (*massa'*). Hassler looks back in time with the benefit of history and progressive revelation to demonstrate that Isaiah 13–14 is eschatological. This dissertation claims each generation could have recognized exegetically that Isaiah 13–14 awaited a future fulfillment.

---

47. Erlandsson, *Burden of Babylon*, 112–13, 122, 141.

48. Keown, "History of the Interpretation of Isaiah 14:12–15," 147.

49. Bertoluci, "Son of the Morning," 11.

50. Gosse, *Isaïe 13,1–14,23*, 273–74.

51. Fry, "'Oracle Concerning Babylon,'" 2.

52. Fry explains, "Gosse rightly asserts that the basic message of the first two poems of the 'Oracle Concerning Babylon' is an affirmation of God's [sic] sovereignty over the evil that the city of Babylon and the king of Babylon have come to represent" (Fry, "'Oracle Concerning Babylon,'" 26).

53. Zapff, *Schriftgelehrte Prophetie*.

54. Shipp, *Of Dead Kings and Dirges*, 162.

55. Hassler, "Isaiah 13:1—14:27," 2–3.

Furthermore, Hassler still retains the historical allusion to Satan in Isaiah 14:13-14: "He might be the king of Babylon spoken of throughout the taunt song, since he experiences a fall (Isa 14:4, 12), weakens the nations (vv. 4-6, 12, 16-17), and exhibits pride (vv. 11, 13-14). But verses 13-14 do not seem to convey the thoughts of a mere human being."[56] This dissertation rejects this historical allusion and claims even 14:13-14 refers to Israel's eschatological enemy.

The history of interpretation above demonstrated that a few authors have claimed that Isaiah 14 refers solely to Israel's eschatological enemy. All of these authors, however, create a theological synthesis rather than an exegetical argument. This dissertation fills this gap in the scholarship and creates an exegetical argument that the king of Babylon in Isaiah 14 is the eschatological enemy of Israel.

THESIS STATEMENT

The primary claim of this study is that the king of Babylon is the eschatological enemy of Israel. This thesis is argued through an analysis of the genre, context, and content of Isaiah 13-14.

The second chapter analyzes the genre of Isaiah 14. Mackay believes that a proverb (*mashal*) is a comparison, and the lesson to be learned is, "Don't be like this guy."[57] Attempting to identify the king, according to Mackay, moves beyond the text.[58] This dissertation argues that this kind of proverb creates a comparison with a *real person*, not a typological, symbolic, or representative individual. While Mackay's application is correct, his interpretation is unlikely.

Because Isaiah 14:4b-21 is part of the larger oracle (*massa'*) against Babylon in 13:1—14:27, chapter three analyzes 13:2—14:4a, 22-27. This structural analysis argues that the *massa'* is one unit, and the whole *massa'* is eschatological except the Assyrian sign in 14:24-27. It provides one of the strongest arguments in favor of an eschatological interpretation. The third chapter also analyzes chapter 13, demonstrating that there are two eschatological battles. The Lord is leading a holy army to destroy the whole earth, and the Medes are involved in a localized skirmish with Babylon.

---

56. Hassler, "Isaiah 13:1—14:27," 124.
57. Mackay, *Study Commentary on Isaiah*, 341-42.
58. Mackay, *Study Commentary on Isaiah*, 345.

INTRODUCTION

While Isaiah 13:14—14:2 theoretically could have been fulfilled already, the final section of chapter 3 contends that it has not been fulfilled.

Chapter 4 examines the *mashal* (Isa 14:4b-21) and argues that no historic king meets the criteria of the king of Babylon. When suggesting a potential king of Babylon, scholars highlight the points of continuity and deemphasize or spiritualize the points of discontinuity. This dissertation produces a list of criteria primarily from Isaiah 14:4b–21 by which each potential king of Babylon can be compared. While some kings come closer than others, no historic king can exegetically assume the Isaiah 13–14 king of Babylon title.

Chapter 2

The Genre of Isaiah 14

As articulated in the introduction, some scholars believe the king of Babylon in Isaiah 14 is a symbolic, ideal, eclectic, or representative king. Webb explains, "The king of Babylon here, like Babylon itself in chapter 13, is a representative figure, the embodiment of that worldly arrogance that defies God and tramples on others in its lust for power."[1] Buksbazen similarly states, "Apparently 'the king of Babylon' is not any particular historical figure, but the personification of all the wickedness, arrogance and cruelty of the Babylonian empire. We might even go a step further and say that the king of Babylon personifies all the self-deification and self-glorification of the godless governments of all ages."[2] Tate agrees, "The portrayal of the tyrant is paradigmatic. If I may adapt a statement about the hero figure from the mythologist Joseph Campbell, this is 'the tyrant of a thousand faces.' His name is Legion, and his kind has plagued the history of humanity."[3] According to these authors, the king of Babylon is not a specific king but a poetic fiction created by Isaiah to teach kings (or people) a lesson, namely, be humble.

Some claim support for this view comes from the genre. Isaiah 14:4b states, "And you will lift up this proverb (משל) concerning the king of Babylon." They correctly argue that a proverb is a comparison, and the lesson to be learned is, "Don't be like this guy." Mackay, for example, explains:

---

1. Webb, *Message of Isaiah*, 83. See also Erdman, *Book of Isaiah*, 50; Leupold, *Exposition of Isaiah*, 255; Arnold, *Who Were the Babylonians?*, 11.
2. Buksbazen, *Prophet Isaiah*, 197.
3. Tate, "Satan in the Old Testament," 468.

> In 14:4 [Isa 14:4–21] is described as a "proverb," though modern translations prefer "taunt." Neither is quite right because in English we have no term that covers the same range of meaning as the Hebrew *māšāl*. It originally referred to a pithy comparison that brought out the underlying realities of a situation, and so provided guidance for the conduct of others. In that respect it is very similar to our word "proverb." But it could also be used for a more extended comparison (and so is like our "parable"). However, when the lesson to be learned is negative, and particularly in the phrase "take up a *māšāl* against . . .," then what is said inevitably criticizes the subject of the proverb and, once his fate is evident, may be equivalent to a "byword" (Jer. 24:9) or a "taunt." *Nevertheless these renderings obscure the fact that the basic idea is that of comparison.* This poem is *not a satirical funeral oration* regarding the King of Babylon, with cheap and unworthy jibes. Rather *it is a piece of instructional literature that vividly and ironically treats the King of Babylon as an object lesson in how not to behave.* In this way it also functions as a powerful statement of how Yahweh can, and does, overturn those who vaunt themselves and entertain thoughts of their own invincibility.[4]

According to this view, since Isaiah 14:4b–21 is a proverb (*mashal*), attempting to identify the king would be eisegetical. Mackay mentions a few possible kings but then concludes:

> More probably, however, *the prophet does not have any particular king in mind*. Isaiah had been made aware that, after the Assyrian threat had passed, Babylon would emerge as the dominant power opposing the kingdom of God and seemingly thwarting his purposes. But the imperial power of Babylon, though desolating Jerusalem, would not endure either. Its collapse epitomizes the destiny of all forces hostile to Yahweh and his people. Indeed it foreshadows the doom of Satan himself. *Ultimately it does not matter what the identity of Babylon or its king is. They stand for all who set themselves against God,* and they face a common destiny of disgrace and defeat.[5]

According to Mackay, Isaiah has created a poetic fiction which serves as an object lesson to warn future rulers that they should "not be like this guy." The identity of the king of Babylon is not relevant; what is relevant is one's humility.

---

4. Mackay, *Study Commentary on Isaiah*, 341–42 (emphasis added).
5. Mackay, *Study Commentary on Isaiah*, 345 (emphasis added).

Mackay's application, while correct, does not conclude the discussion concerning the the identity of the king of Babylon. Shipp, for example, believes the king of Babylon is Sargon II, but he also claims, "The dirge provides a particularly suitable vehicle for the *mashal* as 'cosmic exemplar.' It provides a warning to all would-be tyrants that their fall and shame will exactly correspond to the heights and glory to which they aspire."[6] Thus, according to Shipp, the king is Sargon II, but the application is the same as the representative view.

The proverb works best, however, with a physical ruler rather than a poetic fiction. Mackay, for example, lacks clarity when he claims the king of Babylon serves as an "object lesson."[7] If the king serves as an object lesson, one would expect him to be an actual ruler living in either the past, present, or future. The representative view is also unlikely because the Isaiah 14 king is a specific king (the king *of Babylon*), not a general king (a king). Isaiah uses the fate of the most arrogant ruler of all the ages to teach others the folly of pride.

The genre of Isaiah 14 is more complex than just the proverb. Goldingay claims, "The poem is a funeral dirge sung for a king."[8] Childs claims Isaiah 14 is not a real funeral dirge, but a parody of the funeral dirge.[9] Westermann, however, rejects the funeral dirge assessment, stating, "This Isaianic text is not called a dirge. Rather it is described as a 'taunt' (v 3 [sic])."[10] Thus, there are three elements which this chapter analyzes: the proverb (*mashal*), dirge, and parody.

A *mashal* is a proverb which, according to Waltke, "pertains to function, not to content."[11] Thus, a *mashal* can be used with a wide variety of genres.[12] Isaiah 14 is written in the form of a parodic dirge. The *mashal* uses the dirge genre to teach the reader a lesson in humility. The dirge form is

---

6. Shipp, *Of Dead Kings and Dirges*, 42.

7. Mackay, *Study Commentary on Isaiah*, 342.

8. Goldingay, *Isaiah*, 102.

9. Childs states, "Moreover, the mocking is shaped into a parody of a conventional funeral dirge, such as one finds in David's lament over the death of Saul and Jonathan (2 Sam. 1:17ff.)" (Childs, *Isaiah*, 126).

10. Westermann, *Lamentations*, 4. The "taunt" to which Westermann refers is the genre marker, *mashal* (משל), found in Isaiah 14:4. Furthermore, the genre marker *masha*, is found in verse 4, not verse 3.

11. Waltke, *Book of Proverbs*, 56.

12. Landes also claims that a משל is "not characterized by a more or less fixed literary form" (Landes, "Jonah," 138).

normally quite solemn, lamenting the death of an individual (e.g., 2 Sam 1:17–27, David laments the death of Saul and Jonathan). Isaiah 14, however, makes a parody of the solemn funeral dirge. By using this genre, Isaiah heightens the humiliation of the king of Babylon. Instead of mourning the Babylonian king's death, there is rejoicing (14:7–8). Thus, Isaiah 14:4b–21, as a parodic dirge, will be sung in the future to celebrate the death of Israel's enemy. As a *mashal*, it warns the reader of the folly of arrogance.

MASHAL

This section analyzes the *mashal* genre and contends that an eschatological interpretation of Isaiah 14 coalesces with this genre label. First, the origin of the *mashal* is discussed; then this section inspects six characteristics of the *mashal*. There is one foundational characteristic of a *mashal*, the comparison. The remaining five characteristics—enigmatic, nonspecific genre, human, future, and concrete—may or may not apply. Each characteristic is first explained and then applied to Isaiah 14.

Concerning terminology, *mashal* seems to have acquired the status of a genre label in scholarly writing; the plural, however, lacks a consensus.[13] The terms *mashal* (sing.) and *meshalim* (pl.) are used here.

Concerning translating *mashal*, Mackay noted that "modern translations prefer 'taunt'" as a translation of *mashal* in Isaiah 14:4.[14] Hassler follows Herbert and Barrick in translating *mashal* as "taunt song."[15] One, however, taunts the living, not the dead. If one believes the king of Babylon is living at the time of this taunt's composition, then it could be a good translation. The king of Babylon, however, is deceased at the time of Israel's proclaiming this *mashal*, making this label inadequate.

This dissertation prefers translating *mashal* in Isaiah 14:4 as a "proverb." Wildberger explains concerning משל, "The word actually means 'likening, comparison;' ... it can be used as a neutral term, 'saying, proverb,' but can also be used in the special technical sense of a 'mocking saying';

---

13. Curkpatrick uses *mashal* and *mashalim* (Curkpatrick, "Between Mashal and Parable," 61). Shipp uses the terms *mashal* and *mĕšālîm* (Shipp, *Of Dead Kings and Dirges*, 35). Niditch uses *mashal* and *mashal* (pl.) (Niditch, *Folklore and the Hebrew Bible*, 74). Thus, *mashal* seems widely agreed upon as a technical term but the plural still lacks a consensus.

14. Mackay, *Study Commentary on Isaiah*, 341.

15. Hassler, "Isaiah 13:1—14:27," 40; Herbert, "'Parable' (Māšāl) in the Old Testament," 180; Barrick, "Eschatological Significance of Leviticus 26," 103.

the מָשָׁל is the one who speaks mocking words (Num. 21:27; see also Isa 28:14)."[16] Wildberger reads a text's specific genre into משל. *Meshalim* employ several genres.[17] More specifically, Isaiah 14:4b-21 is a "mocking lament." But translating משל as a "mocking lament" communicates the kind of *mashal* (its specific genre), and therefore reads the specific genre into משל. "Proverb" is an adequate translation of *mashal*.[18]

Origin and Definition

The word *mashal* is a transliteration of the Hebrew משל. This Hebrew root possesses two semantic ranges, "to rule" and "to create a proverb; to liken." HALOT states that משל I means, "to formulate an expression, show a parable," and משל II means, "to rule."[19] Schmidt claims משל I and II build off the meaning, "to stand."[20] Whybray asserts the foundational meaning is משל II, "to rule," and משל I can be understood as "powerful words."[21] Haupt believes the "primary connotation of both verbs is 'to shine.'"[22] He explains "Heb. *môšēl*, ruler, is a person who *shines*, i. e. is *eminent*, distinguished. This meaning is preserved in Arab. *máṯula*, to be eminent; *maṯîl* means not only *like*, similar, but also *distinguished*, excellent."[23]

Eissfeldt criticizes those who combine the roots, claiming:

> This derivation makes the same mistake as the two previously mentioned: it wants to reduce the two divergent meanings of משל

---

16. Wildberger, *Isaiah 13–27*, 50.

17. See "Broad Genre Use" below.

18. Much can also be argued for translating *mashal* "parable," but New Testament studies have made this term too encumbering. For discussion see Blomberg, *Interpreting the Parables*, 29–69. The English proverb is known for its brevity, so translating *mashal* "proverb" is not without its difficulties either. See Wildberger, *Isaiah 13–27*, 50. Interestingly, the LXX translates משל θρῆνος (lamentation).

19. HALOT, "משל I," 2:647.

20. Schmidt, *Studien zur Stilistik der alttestamentlichen Spruchliteratur*. Schmidt draws a parallel with the Arabic *mṯl*. Haupt, however disagrees, "Arab. *máṯula = aqáma* is a transposed doublet of *ṯámala*, and this is identical with Heb. *Šamár*" (Haupt, "Hebrew MAŠÁL," 140).

21. Whybray, *Proverbs*, 13. Curkpatrick is sympathetic to this connotation (Curkpatrick, "Between Mashal and Parable," 58). Robertson continues to purport this view, Robertson, *Christ of Wisdom*, 10n7.

22. Haupt, "Hebrew MAŠÁL," 140.

23. Haupt, "Hebrew MAŠÁL," 140 (emphasis original).

by abstract thinking alone, ignoring whether or not the places where the word appears make that derivation probable or not, and without considering the occurrence of משל in other Semitic languages.[24]

Eissfeldt believes one cannot make an exegetical case for combining משל I and II, and the attempts to build off some Semitic root have failed.[25] A full analysis of משל I and II falls outside the scope of this dissertation. The prevailing scholarly consensus has followed Eissfeldt in distinguishing the two words. Eissfeldt plausibly proposes:

> It is also possible that משל 'rule' and משל 'be like' have nothing to do with each other and were originally somehow differentiated in terms of sound. Through the written form, many verbal subtleties and nuances can not be reproduced and have, therefore, blurred and become equal to each other.[26]

Beyse also argues for two separate roots: "The verbal root *mšl* occurs in the OT with two different semantic domains which etymologically represent two distinct roots. (a) The denominative verb *māšāl* I (qal and piel), 'formulate an expression,' derives from *māšāl*, 'saying, proverb.' . . . (b) *mšl* II, 'rule,' derives from Proto-Sem. *mšl."[27] The root that concerns this dissertation is משל I.

---

24. "Diese Herleitung begeht denselben Fehler wie die beiden vorher genannten: sie will die beiden divergierenden Bedeutungen von משל durch abstraktes Denken allein aufeinander zurückführen, ohne darauf zu achten, ob die Stellen, an denen das Wort vorkommt, diese Ableitung wahrscheinlich machen oder nicht, und ohne auf das Vorkommen der Radikale משל in den übrigen semitischen Sprachen einzugehen" (Eissfeldt, *Der Maschal im Alten Testament*, 2). McKane similarly theorizes, "It is perhaps better to be content with a simple review of the total field of usage and to say that 'to rule' is confined to Hebrew, whereas 'to be like' is distributed throughout the Semitic languages, and that there is no evidence either in Hebrew or the other Semitic languages that *māšāl* has any connection with the meaning 'to rule'" (McKane, *Proverbs*, 25–26).

25. Eissfeldt proceeds to dismantle the various views of those who have tried to combine the words (Eissfeldt, *Der Maschal im Alten Testament*, 2–6).

26. "Möglich ist aber auch, daß משל „herrschen" und משל „gleich sein" von Haus aus nichts miteinander zu tun haben, auch ursprünglich lautlich irgendwie differenziert waren und erst durch die schriftliche Fixierung, die so manche lautliche Feinheiten und Nuancen nicht wiedergeben konnte und daher verwischen mußte, einander gleich geworden sind" (Eissfeldt, *Der Maschal im Alten Testament*, 4).

27. Beyse, "מָשָׁל," *TDOT* 9:64–67. See also HALOT, "משל I," 2:647; NIDOTTE, "משל," 2:1134–37. Herbert firmly states, "There is no certain connexion between these two words" (Herbert, "'Parable' (Māšāl) in the Old Testament," 180). See also Landes, "Jonah," 139.

Comparison

The primary idea of a *mashal* is a comparison. Wilson states, "The root meaning of the vb. seems to be, be like, be equal to; the basic idea of comparison apparently underlies most uses of the vb. and nom."[28] Schöpflin agrees, "A משל arises from a comparison."[29] Johnson claims understanding *mashal* as a comparison is foundational to understanding its broad use."[30] Thus, the function of a *mashal* is to create a comparison by which the reader is exhorted to live a certain way.

A comparison may manifest itself explicitly or implicitly. Schöpflin explains:

> The comparison may, first of all, consist in the analogical as well as in the contrastive relationship between two figures. If an analogy is established, there will be a comparison—be it expressed explicitly by comparison particles, be it implicitly—in the shape of pictoriality, whereby the statement in question can be encoded in a more or less extensive context of images.[31]

Thus, according to Schöpflin, an explicitly stated, analogical comparison uses a comparative particle.[32] If the comparison is implicit, then more imagery is required. Genesis 10:9 contains an explicitly stated, analogical comparison: "He [Nimrod] was a mighty hunter before the Lord; therefore, it has been said, 'Like Nimrod a mighty hunter before the Lord.'"[33] Like an

---

28. Wilson "משל," *NIDOTTE* 2:1134.

29. "Ein משל entsteht durch einen Vergleichsvorgang." Schöpflin, "משל—Ein Eigentümlicher Begriff Der Hebräischen Literatur," 22. See also Molnár-Hídvégi, "Paths Not Taken," 88; Suter, "*Māšāl* in the Similitudes of Enoch," 198; Curkpatrick, "Between Mashal and Parable," 59; Landes, "Jonah," 139.

30. Johnson, "מָשָׁל," 3:162.

31. "Der Vergleich kann zunächst sowohl einem Analogie- als auch in einem Kontrastverhältnis zweier Größen bestehen. Wird eine Analogie hergestellt, so erscheint der Vergleich—sei er explizit ausgedrückt durch Vergleichspartikel, sei er implizit—in Gestalt von Bildhaftigkeit, wobei die betreffende Aussage in einem mehr oder minder umfangreichen Bildzusammenhang verschlüsselt sein kann" (Schöpflin, "משל—Ein Eigentümlicher Begriff Der Hebräischen Literatur," 22–23).

32. See Genesis 10:9 below.

33. All translations are the author's unless otherwise noted. משל is not explicitly used here, but a comparison between 1 Samuel 10:12 and 1 Samuel 19:24 demonstrates the word משל does not need to be there. First Samuel 10:12 states, "Therefore it became a proverb [משל] 'Is Saul also among the prophets?" Similarly, 1 Samuel 19:24 states, "Therefore they say, "Is Saul also among the prophets?" McKane explains, "In I Sam. 19.24 the same saying is not stated to be a *māšāl* but is introduced by the formula 'Therefore they say'. Since we

English simile, this proverb employs the comparative particle and could be quoted and applied to mighty hunters. Bandstra explains, "Apparently this group [mighty hunters] was a well-known saying that had application to a certain type of person."[34] McKane agrees, "Nimrod has become a model or paradigm of the superlative hunter, and so when you want to say that a man is an outstanding hunter you establish his resemblance to the 'model' Nimrod."[35] This comparison is analogical. A simple comparative particle creates the analogy and no imagery is used.

At other times, the comparison is implicit and not stated explicitly.[36] Polk explains, "In fact, the core element in the 'basic meaning,' the idea of comparison (which seems to follow so directly from the root meaning of *mšl*, 'to be like'), is often *not* there at all as a formal feature, but only comes into play implicitly as the effect of certain features that *are* present formally."[37] For

---

know from I Sam. 10.12 that this saying is a *māšāl*, we can conclude that wherever a saying is introduced by 'Therefore they say' or a similar formula it is a popular proverb, even although it is not designated a *māšāl*" (McKane, *Proverbs*, 27). See also Wenham, *Genesis 1-15*, 223; Hamilton, *Book of Genesis*, 339; Mathews, *Genesis 1—11:26*, 451.

34. Bandstra, *Genesis 1-11*, 531.

35. McKane, *Proverbs*, 27.

36. Some *meshalim*, Suter explains, do not make a clear comparison, "There are a number of cases in which the *māšāl*/likeness/comparison is not integral to the genre itself but rather serves as an organizing principle for a particular unit–a rhetorical function" (Suter, "*Māšāl* in the Similitudes of Enoch," 199). See also Herbert, "'Parable' (*Māšāl*) in the Old Testament," 180. Suter appeals to "the oracles of Balaam in Numbers 23-24, Psalms 49 and 78, Job's peroration in Job 27-31, and the taunt-songs in Isaiah 14, Micah 2, and Habakkuk 2" (Suter, "*Māšāl* in the Similitudes of Enoch," 199n28). See also Herbert, "'Parable' (*Māšāl) in* the Old Testament," 180. Suter, however, is only drawing the distinction between the explicit and implicit *meshalim*. Suter continues discussing the different implicit *meshalim* in the succeeding pages, explaining how there are implicit comparisons.

Concerning the Balaam *maśot* and passages in Job. Wilson explains, "The use of *māšāl* in the prophetic literature introduces a further nuance of meaning. . . . The construction is especially evident in the Balaam narrative, where it occurs no less than 7x (Num 23:7, 18; 24:3, 15, 20, 21, 23). Elsewhere it appears 3x in the Latter Prophets (Isa 14:4; Mic 2:4; Hab 2:6) and twice in Job (27:1; 29:1). The lack of certain meaning of *māšāl* in these contexts is illustrated by the variety of translations employed: oracle, prophecy, discourse, parable, and taunt. With the exception of the passages in Job, these constructions introduce prophetic warnings. The use seems a logical extension from the use of *māšāl* as a negative example. The contexts in Job are difficult and the meaning of *māšāl* less certain, but it may be that some aspect of warning or admonition characterizes those passages as well" (Wilson, *NIDOTTE* 2:1135). Concerning the Balaam *maśot*, Landes agrees (Landes, "Jonah," 143). Thus, these negative examples are implicit comparisons and still contain the comparative nuance.

37. Polk, "Paradigms, Parables, and Měšālîm," 568 (emphasis his).

example, 1 Kings 20:11 states, "So the king of Israel answered and said, 'Tell him, "Let not the one who puts on his armor boast like the one who takes it off."'" The comparison is not explicitly stated, but implied. McKane explains, "This is Ahab's reply to Ben Hadad, and it means that a victory should not be celebrated before it is won."[38] Ahab created an implicit comparison *mashal* to accuse Ben Hadad of celebrating a victory before it is won. The readers/listeners must put the proverbial pieces together and make the comparison for themselves.[39] Because an implicit proverb requires intellectual action on the part of the reader, it can be enigmatic as well.[40]

Isaiah 14, similarly, contains an implicit comparison. The reader must engage the text and apply it to one's own life. The implicit comparison, however, reveals nothing concerning the identity of the king of Babylon. One could claim the king is Nebuchadnezzar, Sargon II, the antichrist, or whoever, but the application of the *mashal* is the same: "Don't be like that guy!"[41]

An Enigma

Because an implicit comparison requires the reader to make the comparison, a *mashal* can be enigmatic. McKane explains:

> The "proverb" may initially present a barrier to understanding, but when it is intuited it throws a brilliant light on the situations which it fits. The function of the riddle is to mystify and baffle; it is deliberately enigmatic. Some "proverbs" are characterized by ambivalence; it is possible to assign a literal, pedestrian meaning to them, while they also have a proverbial potential.[42]

Curkpatrick agrees, "*Meshalim* are resistant to transparent interpretation. They reflect the moral and social incongruities of life from which they are created as similes, yet resist clear analogical resolution as 'mere similes.'"[43] Niditch explains, "I suggest that a good *mashal*—whether a say-

---

38. McKane, *Proverbs*, 29.

39. Polk explains, "That is to say, the *reader* makes the comparison; it is not that the popular proverb *is* one" (Polk, "Paradigms, Parables, and Měšālîm," 569; emphasis his).

40. See "An Enigma" below.

41. Johnson, "משׁל," 166.

42. McKane, *Proverbs*, 23.

43. Curkpatrick, "Between Mashal and Parable," 61. Curkpatrick later explains further, "The *mashal* creates both clarity and density, evoking the familiar while allowing the complexity of the familiar to generate paradox in a metonymic oscillation between specific

ing, a symbolic action, or a symbolic story—was designed to be oblique, testing the listener's capacity to make sense, allowing for various interpretations and levels of meaning; it is indirect communication through analogies."[44] Thus, the *mashal* possesses an enigmatic quality that requires participation on the part of the reader.

Exegetically, משל (proverb) and חידה (riddle) occur together in Psalm 49:5; 78:2; Ezekiel 17:2; and Habakkuk 2:6; as well as in Wisdom of Solomon 8:8 and Ecclesiasticus 39:3.[45] The riddle is by nature enigmatic. Because these two words are used in parallel, the argument that *meshalim* are enigmatic is strengthened. Psalm 78:2, for example, states, "I will open my mouth in a proverb (משל); I will gush forth ancient riddles (חידה)."[46] In this passage, משל is parallel with חידה. The חידה is a riddle and conveys what the psalmist wishes to teach, a משל.[47]

The enigmatic character of *meshalim* is even clearer in Ecclesiastes 12:9, "Furthermore, because Qohelet was wise, he still taught (למד) the people knowledge; and he pondered (אזן), sought out (חקר), and set in order (תקן), many proverbs (משלים)." Niditch explains, "Eccl 12:9 describes Koheleth the wise man as 'weighing' or 'testing' or 'proving,' ('zn), 'searching out' (ḥqr), and 'making straight' (tqn; that is 'arranging' or 'figuring out the indirect') many *mashal*'s [sic]."[48]

---

reference (clarity) and endless reference (dissemination of specific reference)" (62).

44. Niditch, *Folklore and the Hebrew Bible*, 82.

45. Tate, *Psalms 51–100*, 281.

46. The parallel משל and חידה is found in Psalm 49 as well. Niditch explains, "Ps 49:5 (v. 4 in the English) associates the *mashal* with the *ḥidah*, and the 'opening up' of the latter with music" (Niditch, *Folklore and the Hebrew Bible*, 75).

47. The משל concerns the application (comparison idea) and חידה concerns the work of the sage/psalmist where he resolves the riddle. Tate explains, "Riddles use words that belong to common knowledge but which conceal special meanings known only to those who know how to solve the riddle. The riddle connotes ambiguity and mystery, often revealing a 'paradox of reality.' Thus, Ps 78 deals with the paradox of Israel's inability to trust God's great acts of deliverance, despite the long-continued and repeated nature of those acts" (Tate, *Psalms 51–100*, 281). Thus, the psalmist's explanation of the riddle creates a משל (comparison), teaching the audience a lesson, "Don't be like them!"

Ross sees more continuity between the terms in the wisdom tradition but functionally makes the same observation, "The psalmist wants their attention because he is resolved to open his mouth . . . and instruct the people with parables and riddles. The 'parable' (מָשָׁל; s.v. Ps. 49:4) is a teaching based on analogy, and the 'riddle' (חִידָה; s.v. Ps. 49:4) is the unfolding of the mysterious ways of God. Such insights and analyses are the marks of wisdom" (Ross, *Commentary on the Psalms*, 654).

48. Niditch, *Folklore and the Hebrew Bible*, 75. Seow states, "The assertion is that

The multiple interpretations of Isaiah 14 argue for its enigmatic nature.[49] As a *mashal*, it invites the reader to examine their own life, recognizing their lowly state as a mere human, and be humble.

Broad Genre Use

A *mashal* is a broad literary category and can be used in several different genres. Curkpatrick explains, "*Mashal* maintains its 'root meaning' of 'likeness, pattern, rule' through diverse kinds of utterance ('prophetic oracle,' 'allegory,' 'riddle,' 'taunt,' 'solemn declaration,' 'didactic poem'), effecting a sense of enigma, even as it generates interpretation."[50] Evidence for the broad genre use of a *mashal* comes from the book of Proverbs. Niditch explains, "References to the *mashal* (pl.) of Solomon preserved in the Book of Proverbs, are rubrics appearing to refer to material that follows them, but this biblical book contains a mixed bag of literature and thus does not help to focus on a definition of the genre."[51]

Human *Mashal* and the "Taunt"

Isaiah 14 is patterned after a human *mashal* where, according to Polk, the point of comparison is "not just the thing signified but the signifier itself. They have themselves been made a sort of speech-act, a metaphor, a parable."[52] Other uses of the human *mashal* include Ezekiel 14:7–8:

---

his work was typical of a sage" (Seow, *Ecclesiastes*, 392). See also Krüger, *Qoheleth*, 210. Commenting on the three verbs which describe Qoheleth's work, Ogden explains, "Important information about aspects of the process whereby the tradition was preserved and handed on lies within these three verbs" (Ogden, *Qoheleth*, 226).

49. Amzallag and Avriel make too much of the enigmatic nuance of משל in Isaiah 14, "In this form of *māšāl*, the meaning is hidden in a riddle. It remains to be discovered by the audience, and success depends on the listener's/reader's intelligence, understanding, wisdom, and knowledge of the language" (Amzallag and Avriel, "Cryptic Meaning of the Isaiah 14 *Māšāl*," 645).

50. Curkpatrick, "Between Mashal and Parable," 59.

51. Niditch, *Folklore and the Hebrew Bible*, 74. There is broad scholarly consensus that a משל is a broad category. See Suter, "*Māšāl* in the Similitudes of Enoch," 196; Jeremias, *Parables of Jesus*, 20; Herbert, "'Parable' (Māšāl) *in* the Old Testament," 180.

52. Polk, "Paradigms, Parables, and Měšālîm," 577. Polk uses Isiaha 14 as an illustration of the human משל.

> For any man from the house of Israel, or from the strangers who sojourn in Israel, who separates himself from me and raises up his idols in his heart and puts a stumbling block of iniquity in front of himself, then comes to the prophet to seek for himself concerning me, I, the Lord, will answer him by myself. (8) I will set my face against that man and I will make him a sign (אות) and a proverb (משל), and I will cut him off from the midst of my people. Then you will know that I am the Lord.

Here the Lord will cut off the individuals who take up idols and inquire of the Lord. The man, then, becomes a *mashal*. Concerning Ezekiel 14, Polk explains:

> Typically, the people who become a *māšāl*-byword have fallen from high to low estate and find themselves the objects of horror and astonishment, being spat at, ridiculed, taunted, and abhorred. In fact, they have become a paradigm—archetypes of a bad fate and, in that a bad fate was understood as the consequence of moral turpitude, a bad life.[53]

Niditch agrees, "The human *mashal* is an icon or exemplar who becomes part of the tradition to be stylized, remembered, analogized, and cited."[54] Isaiah 14, similarly, is a human *mashal*.

The Future *Mashal*

Human *meshalim* can refer to individuals in the past, present, or future. The Ezekiel 14 *mashal* above describes an individual who sins a certain way. This *mashal* is future. Micah 2:4 similarly states, "In that day one will lift up a proverb (משל) against you." Habakkuk 2:6 also states, "Will not all these lift up a proverb against him." In Isaiah 14, the *mashal* is future. The remnant of Israel will return to the land, reflect upon the king of Babylon's fate, and speak this *mashal* against him.

Concreteness and the General Proverb

The previous five characteristics have demonstrated how Isaiah 14 *could be interpreted* as an eschatological ruler, but they have not eliminated other

---

53. Polk, "Paradigms, Parables, and Měšālîm," 577. Niditch agrees, Niditch, *Folklore and the Hebrew Bible*, 76.

54. Polk, "Paradigms, Parables, and Měšālîm," 577.

possible interpretations. This sixth characteristic not only allows for an eschatological interpretation, but also argues against the representative view.

McKane believes the first proverbs were concrete analogies. He uses Genesis 10:9 as an illustration, "Like Nimrod the mighty hunter before the Lord." This proverb is concrete; the point of comparison is a physical man, Nimrod. Concerning these first proverbs, McKane states:

> These are "proverbs" in that they have a special kind of concreteness in virtue of which their meaning is open to the future and can be divined again and again in relation to a situation which calls for the "proverb" as apt comment. A "proverb" can be generalized and the generalization does some justice to it, but it forecloses the meaning and destroys the hermeneutical openness which derives from its original concreteness.[55]

Putting McKane's evolutionary origin of proverbs aside, most proverbs are general, not concrete.[56] Proverbs 10:5 states, "One who gathers in summer is a prudent son; One who sleeps in harvest is a son who brings shame." The proverb is general; it does not refer to a specific person like the Genesis 10:9 proverb.

McKane makes a distinction between the degrees of concreteness, stating the more concrete proverbs are more effective. He uses 1 Samuel 24:14, "From evil men evil issues," as an illustration and states:

> Although "From evil men evil issues" has a certain concreteness and is a model with a representative potential, it is not highly concrete, and no effort is needed to grasp the resemblance between

---

55. McKane, *Proverbs*, 23.

56. Concerning the history of a *mashal*, Eissfeldt, McKane, et al. believe the *mashal* evolved over time, consisting first of simple proverbs and finally becoming longer parables and short stories. See Eissfeldt, *Der Maschal im Alten Testament*, 43. McKane illustrates how the משל changed through an analysis of the short proverbs in the Old Testament to the broad genres in the book of Proverbs (McKane, *Proverbs*, 27–33). See also Niditch, *Folklore and the Hebrew Bible*, 71–80; Polk, "Paradigms, Parables, and Měšālîm," 566.

Von Rad disagrees, claiming the proverbial literature originated in "school wisdom." Von Rad states, "The period whose literary heritage we shall examine begins with the emergence of school wisdom in the early monarchy. The existence of an older clan wisdom need not be contested in principle; its existence is, indeed, even highly probable. It is, however, a phenomenon that is so difficult to define that our examination takes no notice of it as an independent factor. Besides, the acceptance of a connection between it and school wisdom has proved to be questionable. . . . We accept the material as it is presented by the collectors, and we are justified in understanding it, in that form, as school wisdom" (Von Rad, *Wisdom in Israel*, 11–12).

the model and the generalization, "There is a harmony between character and action." The effectiveness of a *māšāl* derives from its concreteness and from the circumstance that a model of a general truth stimulates the imagination and clamours for attention, as a matter-of-fact statement would not.[57]

While Proverbs 10:5 may not be as concrete as Genesis 10:9, it still contains concreteness and can be effective.

McKane's different degrees of concreteness may be better understood as a difference in specificity. Curkpatrick does not differentiate the degrees of concreteness: "The *mashal*'s use of earthy, sensual subject matter for intensification, maintains a metonymic oscillation between new theological images and their opaque, material subject matter."[58] The Genesis 10:9 proverb concerning Nimrod is specific; whereas, Proverbs 10:5 is not specific. A *mashal*, however, must contain some level of concreteness by which a reader might draw a comparison.

Up to this point, a *mashal* does not *have to* relate to a physical person, but *it could*. Some could claim that the king of Babylon is not a specific king just like the Proverbs 10:5 "son" is not a specific son. There are two reasons, however, why Isaiah 14 likely refers to a physical person. First, it is a human *mashal*. Just as the Ezekiel 14 idolater would become a physical example of the dangers of idolatry, so also does the king of Babylon become an example of the dangers of pride.

The second reason concerns the prepositional phrase "of Babylon." General proverbs have unspecified nouns (1 Sam 24:14, "from *evil men*;" Prov 10:5, "a *wise son*;" 20:8, "A *king* who sits on the throne of judgment;" 22:29, "He will stand before *kings*"). These general proverbs refer not to a specific king or person, but to a general king or person. The addition of the construct chain "of Babylon," however, makes the representative view unlikely. Isaiah is not referring to a general, representative king; he is referring to a specific king, the king of Babylon. There would be no point in adding the construct phrase "of Babylon" if Isaiah did not have a specific king in mind.

Oswalt recognizes the concreteness of a *mashal*, but still defends the representative king view:

---

57. McKane, *Proverbs*, 28.

58. Curkpatrick, "Between Mashal and Parable," 60. Polk connects the enigmatic character of a משל to its concreteness (Polk, "Paradigms, Parables, and Měšālîm," 568–69). Eissfeldt states, "A general truth, which is what we are concerned with, is normally made clear with pictures or example." (Eissfeldt, *Old Testament*, 83).

The attempt to identify a precise historical figure is probably futile. Isaiah is using a concrete representation to discuss the nature and end of human pride. . . . That Tiglath-pileser as well as Sargon and Sennacherib styled themselves as "kings of Babylon" would make it easier for Isaiah to have patterned his representative figure after these great tyrants, but there is no indication that he has one particular person in mind.[59]

According to Oswalt, the king of Babylon is a concrete representation of potentially three Assyrian rulers. Oswalt's position is illogical. If the king of Babylon *symbolizes* three kings, then he is not a concrete person but a representative king.

Conclusion

This section has analyzed a *mashal* and demonstrated that it allows for an eschatological ruler. First, a *mashal* is a comparison that requires self-evaluation on the part of the reader. Some comparisons are explicitly stated with a comparative particle, but most are implicit, requiring the reader/listener to think about the *mashal*, correctly identify the comparison, and then apply it to one's life. The author wants the reader/listener to think about the *mashal*, and the enigmatic nature of the *mashal* forces the reader to think. Isaiah 14 fits both of these categories. The representative view correctly identifies the perlocutionary effect of Isaiah 14; it serves as a warning not to exalt oneself in pride. The representative view, however, fails to distinguish between the function of Isaiah 14 and its content.

This section has also argued that a *mashal* is a broad literary category which can be used in several different genres, including a prophecy or lament. Isaiah 14 is a human *mashal* where the king of Babylon serves as a paradigm or exemplar to the reader/listener. The *mashal* is not restricted to a past time frame but can also be prophetic. Ezekiel 14:7–8, Micah 2:4, and Habakkuk 2:6 serve as other future *meshalim*. Isaiah 14 is a specific human *mashal* making the representative view unlikely. There are many general *meshalim* in the Bible but a general *mashal* does not give details concerning the referent (i.e., king *of Babylon*).

This eschatological enemy of Israel, the most villainous king of all earthly kings, serves as a "cosmic exemplar" to every man (and every earthly ruler), not to be puffed up in pride.

---

59. Oswalt, *Book of Isaiah*, 314.

PARODIC DIRGE

Not only is Isaiah 14 a *mashal*, but it is more specifically a parodic dirge. Second Samuel 1:17 states, "Then David lamented (ויקנן) with this lamentation (קינה) over Saul and Jonathan his son." Isaiah 14 is a parody of the royal funeral dirge exemplified in 2 Samuel 1. This section analyzes the dirge genre and explains how Isaiah 14 is a parody of the solemn funeral dirge.

Lament or Dirge

English translators regularly translate קינה in 2 Samuel 1:17 as "lamentation."[60] This translation fits well with the mourning and sorrow which David exemplifies and encourages in the lament to follow. This translation, however, should not be confused with the "lament" genre created by form critics. Longman, explaining the form critic lament genre, claims there are three kinds of laments: individual, communal, and royal.[61] He recognizes seven elements to a lament: 1) Invocation, 2) Plea to God for help, 3) Complaints, 4) Confession of sin or an assertion of innocence, 5) Curse of enemies (imprecation), 6) Confidence in God's response, and 7) Hymn or blessing.[62] Longman notes that most laments are found in the Psalter and that Lamentations is a communal lament.[63] Longman's "lament" does not correspond, however, with the lament in 2 Samuel 1. Saul and Jonathan are dead, and David is calling on the people of Israel to mourn. There is no confession of sin, curse of enemies, confidence in God's response, or hymn or blessing.

Berlin draws a distinction between biblical laments (2 Sam 1) and what modern form critics have called laments (Longman's definition). She explains,

> The term modern form critics have most consistently applied to Lamentations and to similar biblical poems in the book of Psalms is *communal lament*. This designation is a modern invention, not a biblical term, and was first applied to Psalms, most consistently to Pss 44, 60, 74, 79, 80, 83, 85, 90, 94, 123, and 137. Note that the term *qinah* does not occur in these psalms, and they are not funeral dirges. . . . There are a number of characteristic elements of

---

60. See KJV, NKJV, NASB, NRSV, ASV, HCSB, and ESV.
61. Longman, "Lament," 198.
62. Longman, "Lament," 200.
63. Longman, "Lament," 203.

a communal lament, but the sine qua non [sic] is the appeal for deliverance. This makes the communal lament quite different from a biblical *qinah*. A *qinah* is an outpouring of grief for a loss that has already occurred, with no expectation of reversing that loss; a communal lament is a plea to prevent a calamity or to reverse it.[64]

Second Samuel 1:17 is a biblical lament, not a lament in the form critical sense.

Form critics have created a different genre category to encompass the biblical lament of 2 Samuel 1:17. Berlin seems to use the terms *qinah*, biblical lament, and dirge synonymously. Westemann contrasts the lament of distress with the lament of the dead.[65] Jahnow called it a *Leichenlied* or "corpse song."[66] The term used to describe the biblical lament (*qinah*) in this dissertation is dirge.[67]

Isaiah 14 among the Dirges

Isaiah 14 is not specifically labeled a קינה (*qinah*, dirge), but not every dirge contains this label.[68] Shipp writes, "Most scholars up to the present have assumed that Isaiah 14:4b–21 is a *qînāh*."[69] Westermann disagrees. He claims there are no dirges proper in the Hebrew canon.[70] He analyzes the pieces of dirges found in the Old Testament and ancient Near Eastern texts and formulates the following motifs for dirges:

> An opening cry of ah!, alas!, or the equivalent; a mournful cry as such (sometimes with direct address of the deceased); a summons to mourn (sometimes even addressed to inanimate objects); a proclamation that a death has occurred (sometimes with reference to the mode of death); a comparing of the former with the

---

64. Berlin, *Lamentations*, 24 (emphasis original).

65. Westermann states, "The fundamental distinction between a lament for the dead and a lament of distress is not to be overlooked. They are in their origin and in their nature different phenomena. The lament for the dead god or king . . . is not to be found [in the Psalms]" (Westermann, *Lamentations*, 167).

66. Jahnow, *Das hebräische Leichenlied*.

67. "Dirge" seems to be the prevailing scholarly translation as well. See HALOT "קִינָה I," 3:1097; Fleischer, "קִינָה," *TDOT* 13:17–23; Westermann, *Lamentations*; Shipp, *Of Dead Kings and Dirges*.

68. Fleischer, "קִינָה," *TDOT* 13:23.

69. Shipp, *Of Dead Kings and Dirges*, 51.

70. Westermann, *Lamentations*, 1–2.

The Genre of Isaiah 14

present state of affairs (the contrast motif), including a eulogizing of the deceased; a description of the mourner's pain or of the general state of misery; reference to the effect all this is having on the bystanders; questions expressing bewilderment at what has happened.[71]

Concerning Isaiah 14, Westermann states, "This Isaianic text is not called a dirge. Rather it is described as a 'taunt' (v 3 [sic]). Of the motifs characteristic of the dirge it makes use of only the contrast motif."[72] Westermann's analysis fails to take into account the parodic nature of Isaiah 14.[73]

Several of the motifs Westermann mentions are found in Isaiah 14. First, Westermann claims dirges begin with "an opening cry of ah!, alas!, or the equivalent." Isaiah 14:4 begins with "How (איך) the oppressor has ceased." While "How" (איך) may not be the characteristic "Woe" (הוי), it is used in 2 Samuel 1:17 and Ezekiel 26:17, two texts which are explicitly described as dirges (קינה). Second, Westermann mentions a dirge contains "a summons to mourn (sometimes even addressed to inanimate objects)." In Isaiah 14:8, inanimate objects (trees) are rejoicing (parodic element, the opposite of mourning) over the death of the tyrant. Third, Westermann states that a dirge references "the effect all this is having on the bystanders." Isaiah 14:16–17 mentions the contemplations of bystanders. Fourth, Westermann acknowledges there may be "questions expressing bewilderment at what has happened." The contemplations of the bystanders in Isaiah 14:16–17 are questions expressing their bewilderment. Westermann admits Isaiah 14 contains the contrast motif. Thus, five of Westermann's motifs can be found in Isaiah 14.

Shipp builds off Westermann's work, analyzes additional ancient Near Eastern texts, and concludes, "There were two types of dirges extant in the ancient Near East: one characterized by memory of the deceased and intended to eulogize him or her; and another, a liturgical dirge intended to ensure the safe and proper descent of the deceased king to the underworld and legitimate the new king on his throne."[74] Concerning Shipp's common (nonroyal) dirge, he found three broad sections: (1) eulogy of the deceased,

---

71. Westermann, *Lamentations*, 2.

72. Westermann, *Lamentations*, 4.

73. Shipp correctly recognizes that differences would be expected in the parodies (Shipp, *Of Dead Kings and Dirges*, 60).

74. Shipp, *Of Dead Kings and Dirges*, 66.

(2) lament proper, and (3) jussive prayers on behalf of the deceased.[75] Shipp's points of similarity are too general to be helpful. One would expect to find these characteristics in any eulogy for the deceased. Furthermore, the element that is found in ancient Near Eastern texts but not found in the Old Testament is the prayers on behalf of the dead. But this omission is expected. David would not say a prayer "to hasten and bless the journey" of dead Saul and Jonathan for theological reasons.

Shipp's analysis of the royal dirge yielded six thematic points of correspondence which are illustrated in Table 2.1. There are two problems with Shipp's methodology. First, Shipp demonstrated a great deal of selectivity with his texts. He failed to include 2 Samuel 1 and other biblical texts in his analysis. Claiming that the biblical texts are not complete does not exempt him from including them in his analysis.[76] Second Samuel 1 is a royal dirge but only contains the "lament" theme from Shipp's analysis. Second, his last two themes, sacrifice for/by king and new king proclaimed, are tenuous. Shipp's text selection is too narrow to make a definitive case with only 50 percent clearly supporting his analysis.

---

75. Shipp, *Of Dead Kings and Dirges*, 52–53.

76. Shipp agrees with Westermann's claim that "there are no complete *qînôt* in the Hebrew Bible and that only 2 Sam 3:33–34 and Jer 38:22—along with 2 Sam 1:19–27 and Jer 9:16–21, which are 'artistic imitations' of true dirges in Westermann's view—even come close to being true dirges" (Shipp, *Of Dead Kings and Dirges*, 51).

The Genre of Isaiah 14

Table 2.1. Comparison of "Royal Dirges" in the Old Testament and the Ancient Near East[77]

	Command to go down	Lament	Rousing Underworld Dwellers	Rephaim/ Dead Kings	Sacrifice For/By King	New King Proclaimed
KTU 1.161	✓	✓ (objects- footstool, table- cry)	✓	✓	✓	✓
Death of Ur-Nammu	✓	✓ (performed by king)	✓	✓ (7, ishib, lumah, gutug who had died greet king)	✓	(lacking)
Isa. 14:4b–21	✓ (past tense)[1]	✓ (trees of Lebanon rejoice; parody of dirge)		✓	✓ (slaughter-place [מִטְבֵּחַ] for his sons)	✓ (offspring *not* called out)
Ezek. 32:18–32	✓	✓ (a lament [קִינָה], command to [נְחֵה])	✓	✓	(no sacrifice; kings and armies are slain)	(lacking)

✓ = Meets criterion

[1] Vv. 11 and 15.

An additional characteristic of the dirge is meter. Longman explains, "In general, this term describes poetry in which the first colon of a parallel line is longer than the second. According to an older way of describing meter, the first colon has three beats, while the second has two."[78] According to Watson, this 3 + 2 pattern "is known as the *qinah* metre [and] is frequent in laments (*qinah* = 'lament') though it is also found elsewhere."[79] Kugel claims there is no such thing as Hebrew meter, much less a *qinah* meter. He states, "Perhaps Hebrew had some sort of meter of its own, but it [is] now irretrievably lost."[80] The purpose of this dissertation is not to legitimize or delegitimize the existence of Hebrew meter. If there is Hebrew meter

77. Shipp, *Of Dead Kings and Dirges*, 65.
78. Longman, "Lament," 199.
79. Watson, *Classical Hebrew Poetry*, 98. See also Fleischer, "קִינָה," TDOT 13:23.
80. Kugel, *Idea of Biblical Poetry*, 190. Alter agrees, Alter, *Art of Biblical Poetry*, 8.

and, by extension, *qinah* meter, then it is found in Isaiah 14. Concerning Hebrew meter and Isaiah 14, Fleischer confidently states:

> Budde published the fundamental studies of *qînâ* meter, showing that a *qînâ* is characterized by alternation between bicola and tricola. This criterion together with the introductory *ēkâ* (or *ēk*, 2 S. 1:19b; Ezk. 26:17) is used to identify texts not explicitly so designated as *qînôṭ*, especially Lam. 1–5 and Isa. 14:4–21. More ambitious attempts based solely on meter to discover yet more *qînôṭ* succeed only at the price of radical emendation, and should be treated skeptically.[81]

Fleischer deems Isaiah 14 a dirge based upon the *qinah* meter and other signs of the dirge (i.e., אִיךְ). This section has demonstrated that five of Westermann's characteristics and four of Shipp's thematic elements are present in Isaiah 14. Furthermore, the LXX translated משל, θρῆνος (lament), indicating the LXX translators believed Isaiah 14 was a lament. Thus, Isaiah 14 is very likely a dirge.[82]

Parody

While Isaiah 14 is a funeral dirge, it is more accurately a parody of this genre. Concerning a definition of parody, Abrams and Harpham explain, "A parody imitates the serious manner and characteristic features of a particular literary work, the distinctive style of a particular author, or the typical stylistic and other features of a serious literary genre, and deflates the original by applying the imitation to a lowly or comically inappropriate subject."[83] The dirge is a "serious literary genre" which is applied to a "comi-

---

81. Fleischer, "קִינָה," *TDOT* 13:23.

82. Concerning the genre of Lamentations, Berlin states, "Literary works are often of mixed genre, and new ones are continually evolving" (Berlin, *Lamentations*, 24). Isaiah 14, likewise, is of mixed genre. Even though it does not contain all the characteristics of the dirge, it has several of them and should still be labeled a dirge. Furthermore, variations from the traditional dirge should be expected because Isaiah 14 is also a *mashal* and a parody.

83. Abrams and Harpham, *Glossary of Literary Terms*, 41. A parody, according to Shaw, is "any humorous, satirical, or burlesque imitation of a person, event, or serious work of literature" (Shaw, *Concise Dictionary of Literary Terms*, 202). In the case of Isaiah 14, the dirge is a "serious work of literature." Yee explains, "Parody, then, is the literary imitation of another literary work, but 'with a difference.' The 'difference' of parody lies in the degree, manner, or purpose of 're-creating and exaggerating the fictional imaginative world of its model'" (Yee, "Anatomy of Biblical Parody," 568). Yee also explains, "[It is] the literary imitation of an established form or style" (565). Shipp also agrees, "parody

cally inappropriate subject," death.[84] Stern defines a parody and practically described the parody in Isaiah 14 without even referencing it:

> A literary parody requires the parodic work to be an imitation of another recognizable and known literary work or genre (whether transmitted in writing or orally), and it requires the parodic work to be a travesty of the work or genre parodied, that is, a deliberately inappropriate and intentionally outrageous comic imitation—a presentation, for example, in which content and style not only clash but violate the very rules of generic decorum.[85]

Isaiah 14 is a recognizable genre, the dirge. It is a travesty of the dirge because instead of evoking feelings of sadness, it evokes feeling of joy. The "content and style" in Isaiah 14 clash and "violate the very rules of generic decorum."

There are several reasons why an author may employ parody. Lelièvre analyzed ancient parodies and explored the idea that "parody implies humour."[86] He found, however, that some ancient parodies do not have

---

relies on the unexpected or humorous 'misuse' or an established form" (Shipp, *Of Dead Kings and Dirges*, 43).

Lelièvre creates an explanation based on the Greek origin: "What then is the basic meaning which παρῳδή in itself conveys? The ᾠδή element is at any rate prima facie sufficiently straightforward: ἀείδειν 'to sing' is naturally used of verse composition—though parody ultimately comes to include prose. παρά may be said to develop two trends of meaning, being used to express such ideas as nearness, consonance, and derivation as well as transgression, opposition, or different. . . . On this analogy our word would indicate that parody is something sung—or composed—conformably to an original but with a difference, and this idea can be seen to lie behind the two main techniques used by the ancient parodists" (Lelièvre, "Basis of Ancient Parody," 66).

84. Isaiah 14 is called an irony by some (Holladay, "Text, Structure, and Irony," 633–45; Van Wyk, "Isaiah 14:4b–21," 240–47; O'Connell, "Isaiah 14:4b–23," 406–18). Isaiah 14, however, is more accurately a parody. O'Connor explains the relationship between irony and parody, "Ironic devices, as we know, include the pun, paradox, understatement, peripety, dramatic contrasts, conscious naivete, and the unknowing or unknowledgeable narrator. Parody is a form of irony, of simulation, saying one thing and partly intending another. . . . It is serio-comic, and praises while it condemns. As with other devices or forms of irony, when employed intelligently and affirmatively, parody makes more lucid the reader's sense of a style or a subject" (O'Connor, "Parody as Criticism," 248). The two words are sometimes used synonymously: Hannoosh, "Reflexive Function of Parody," 116; Lasch, "Achieving Parody," 13–14.

85. Stern, "Alphabet of Ben Sira," 424–25.

86. Lelièvre, "Basis of Ancient Parody," 70. Shipp shows that ancient parodies predated the Greeks. He analyzes K 1351, a Neo-Assyrian memorial stele, and Ezekiel 32:18–32 and claims Isaiah 14 is a similar parody of the funeral dirge (Shipp, *Of Dead Kings and*

humor: "There is no humorous intention here [Hermogenes], and further examples of nonhumorous uses of the terms from Olympiodorus, Zonaras, later rhetoricians, and others are to be found."[87] The parody creates some humor, but its purpose is not solely to entertain. Yee explains, "Humor is the chief result of the incongruity between form and content in parody, which raises the expectation for X and gives Y. Parodic humor ranges from simple comedy to satire to complete scorn or derision. . . . In this case [Isa 14], the parody becomes a vehicle for *social criticism*."[88] The Isaiah 14 parody mocks the king of Babylon. Yee explains elsewhere, "Parody can, however, be satirical, as in Isaiah 14, which uses the dirge form to mock and condemn the tyrant."[89] Israel will mock and condemn the king of Babylon by declaring this proverb when they are regathered (Isa 14:1–2).[90]

Yee presents six points of correspondence between Isaiah 14 and 2 Samuel 1, showing that Isaiah 14 is likely a parody of the solemn funeral dirge (see Table 2.2).

Dirges, 43–47).

87. Lelièvre, "Basis of Ancient Parody," 71.
88. Yee, "Anatomy of Biblical Parody," 568 (emphasis his).
89. Yee, "Anatomy of Biblical Parody," 566.
90. Yee correctly understands the genre and purpose of the parody, "The *Sitz im Leben* of the form is a funeral setting and its purpose is to extol the *life* of the deceased in magnanimous terms. Parodying the dirge form, Isaiah 14 appears not after the death of a hero but during the life of a tyrant. The dirge parody now functions as prophecy, announcing the certain death of an oppressive ruler as if it had already taken place. The *Sitz im Leben* of the dirge is transformed from a funeral setting to gatherings of the tyrant's oppressed and resentful subjects, who taunt him behind his back. The purpose of the form now is to mock the tyrant relentlessly for his arrogance and his repression and to foretell his *death* and the death of his children" (Yee, "Anatomy of Biblical Parody," 581; emphasis original).

Table 2.2. Comparison between 2 Samuel 1 Dirge and Isaiah 14 Parody[91]

	2 Samuel 1	Isaiah 14
Rhetorical Introduction Announcing Death	2 Sam 1:19—How (אֵיךְ) have the mighty fallen!	Isaiah 14:4b—How (אֵיךְ) the tyrant has ended, the tyranny has ended!
Suppression of News of Death from Enemies	2 Sam 1:20—Tell it not in Gath, Proclaim it not in the streets of Ashkelon; Lest the daughters of the Philistines rejoice, Lest the daughters of the uncircumcised exult.	Isa 14:7—The whole earth is calm and quiet; they break forth into singing.[1]
Description of Nature at the Person's Death	2 Sam 1:21—Mountains of Gilboa, no dew and no rain, upon you or the fields of heights.	Isa 14:8–11—Even the junipers rejoice because of you, the cedars of Lebanon. "Since you were laid low, no longer does the hewer come up against us."
Description of the Person's Exploits	2 Sam 1:22–23—The sword of Saul did not turn back, and the sword of Saul did not return empty.	Isaiah 14:5–6—[He] struck the people in rage, blows without ceasing; that governed the nations in anger, persecution without respite.
Call of Mourners to Weep	2 Sam 1:24–25—Daughters of Israel, weep for Saul.	Isa 14:16–17—Those who see you stare at you, they speculate about you, "Is this the man . . ."
Expression of the Singer's Personal Grief	2 Sam 1:26–27—"Distress has come to me because of you, my brother Jonathan."	Isa 14:18–21—All the kings of the nations, all of them lie honorably, each in his own tomb. But you are cast from your grave.

[1] Yee has no correspondence to Isaiah 14 here. Yee places 14:7 under "Description of Nature at the Person's Death."

CONCLUSION

The first genre marker analyzed in this chapter was the *mashal* (proverb). The primary idea behind a *mashal* is a comparison. Isaiah 14 contains an implicit comparison requiring the reader to engage the text and apply it to one's own life. One could claim the king is Nebuchadnezzar, Sargon II, or an eschatological enemy of Israel, but the function of the *mashal* is the same: "Don't be like that guy!" Next, it was argued that a *mashal* is enigmatic.

91. Adapted from Yee, "Anatomy of Biblical Parody," 569–86.

Because a *mashal* requires the reader to make the comparison, there may be some initial confusion which the reader must clarify. The *mashal* is also a broad genre category employing many different genres, including allegory, riddle, or lament. Isaiah 14 is a prophetic human *mashal*. Finally, while some *meshalim* are more concrete than others, they all have their foundation in the real world. The representative king view is unlikely because the king of Babylon is a specific king, not an indefinite one (i.e., "a king"). There would be no point in adding the construct phrase "of Babylon" if Isaiah did not have a specific king in mind.

Second, it was argued that Isaiah 14 is a parodic dirge. To start, the dirge was defined, then, using Shipp's and Westermann's categories for dirges, this section argued that Isaiah 14 shares many similarities with dirges. Because Isaiah 14 is in the form of a dirge, it is more likely that the point of comparison is a real physical ruler rather than a representative king who would never be eulogized. Finally, the parody was defined and it was illustrated that Isaiah parodied the solemn royal dirge to mock the tyrant who will one day oppress the whole world.

Chapter 3

The *Massa'* against Babylon—Isaiah 13:2—14:2

THE STRUCTURE AND CONTENT of the *massa'* (oracle, burden) against Babylon argue that the Babylon of Isaiah 13:2–22 and the regathering of Israel in 14:1–2 are still future. Isaiah 14:22–23 concludes the section of the *massa'* against Babylon, and 14:24–27 contains a short-term sign which validates the long-term prophecy in 13:2—14:23. This chapter is divided into three sections. This first section contends that interpreting Isaiah 13–14 eschatologically fits within the broader context of Isaiah.

The second section analyzes the structure of Isaiah 13:2—14:27. First, a structural analysis of Isaiah 13:2-13 asserts that והיה ("And it will be . . .") divides the *massa'*. Next, the structure of Isaiah 13:14—14:3a reveals the eschatological timeframe of the *mashal* (Isa 14:4b–21). Finally, the structure of Isaiah 14:22–27 contests that it is part of the Babylon *massa'*, and 14:24–27 is a short-term sign.

The third section argues that Isaiah 13:2—14:2 is eschatological. First, the two battles in Isaiah 13:2-22 are differentiated, and the regathering of Israel in Isaiah 14:1–2 is analyzed. An exegetical analysis of these passages and a comparison with history reveals Isaiah 13:2—14:2 has not yet been fulfilled. Because Isaiah 13:2—14:2 is still future, the king of Babylon must also be future.

Israel's Eschatological Enemy

PRELIMINARY ISSUES

Three preliminary issues provide the foundation for the eschatological interpretation which follows: genre, historical setting, and the macro structure.

Genre

Isaiah 13:1 is explicitly described as a "burden" (משא, henceforth *massa'/ masot*).[1] The meaning "burden" comes from the literal use of the word as found in Exodus 23:5 where a donkey carries a משא, and Numbers 4:15 where the responsibilities of the Kohathites are משא.[2] Instead of a literal burden to carry, the *massa'* in Isaiah 13–23 is a metaphoric "burden"; it is difficult to carry because it concerns destruction and doom. This genre works well in an eschatological text. Gehman agrees, claiming that a *massa'* "suggests the idea of catastrophe, destruction, threat, punishment, or the judgment of God and carries with it sublime ominousness."[3] Some scholars believe the *massa'* is a distinct genre, but, as evidenced in Isaiah 13–23, *massa'* is a broad label that employs different, more specific genres like the *mashal* in Isaiah 14:4b–21.[4]

Historical Setting

The historical setting of Isaiah 13–14 is difficult to discern. Sometimes Isaiah included historical references (e.g., Isa 6:1), but there are none present in Isaiah 13–14.[5] The destruction of Assyria functions as a short-term sign to validate the long-term Babylonian prophecy in Isaiah 13:2—14:23.[6] This

---

1. Oswalt claims, "The precise meaning of *maśśā'*, 'burden,' is not clear" (Oswalt, *Book of Isaiah*, 298n1). See also, Kaiser, *Isaiah: 13–39*, 1. משא appears to be a metaphoric use of the literal "burden." Jeremiah 23:33 uses משא as a pun, adding further evidence to this meaning. See Erlandsson, *Burden of Babylon*, 65.

2. Gehman, "'Burden' of the Prophets," 110.

3. Gehman, "'Burden' of the Prophets," 110.

4. Smith agrees, "It seems that it is not possible to talk about a consistent genre of 'oracles against foreign nations' in Isaiah 13–23 as a distinct literary phenomenon with a unique structure and purpose" (Smith, *Isaiah 1–39*, 288). For more discussion of the *massa'*, see Weis, "A Definition of the Genre Massa."

5. Smith, *Isaiah 1–39*, 288–89.

6. See "Function of Isaiah 14:24–27" below.

analysis fits the historical situation of eighth-century Isaiah.[7] Therefore, the prophecy must have been given *before* the Isaiah 37 annihilation of Sennacherib's army. A debatable argument can also be made that this prophecy was declared *after* the Isaiah 39 visit of Merodach-baladan's emissaries.[8] In an effort to encourage Hezekiah to trust in the Lord and not foreign alliances, Isaiah declares this *massa'* against Babylon.

Table 3.1. Historical Setting of the Massa' against Babylon

Isaiah 38	Hezekiah becomes deathly sick and is healed
Isaiah 39	Merodach-baladan sends envoy to Hezekiah
Isaiah 36	Assyria invades Israel
Isaiah 13–14	Isaiah prophesies Babylon's future destruction and Assyrian sign
Isaiah 37	Hezekiah trusts the Lord and the Assyrian army is destroyed

The *Massa'* against Babylon among the *Mas'ot* against the Nations

Isaiah 13 begins a new major section in the book of Isaiah. Chapters 11 and 12 are eschatological in nature, focusing on Israel's regathering and subsequent praise of the Lord. The Isaiah 13–14 *massa'*, according to Oswalt, follows "naturally upon the vision of Immanuel as ruler of the kingdoms."[9] The eschatological interpretation of Isaiah 13–14, though Oswalt disagrees with it, better asserts the theme of Immanuel as ruler of the kingdoms

---

7. Because the object of the prophecy is Babylon, not Assyria, most higher critics believe the text has been redacted. Childs summarizes several views (Childs, *Isaiah*, 122–23). According to Roberts, "The attribution to Isaiah, son of Amoz, is apparently to give the oracle the authority of the great eighth-century prophet, though the contents of the following oracle seem to reflect the concerns of a period a century later than the time of Isaiah of Jerusalem" (Roberts, *First Isaiah*, 197). Mackay correctly explains, "Such criticism is generally based on a denial that genuine information about the future was divinely disclosed to the prophet. That is a modern, rationalistic preconception which was certainly not shared by the prophets themselves. They knew they possessed divinely revealed information (cf. 41:21–29)" (Mackay, *Study Commentary on Isaiah*, 319). Gehman explains, "In considering the word משׂא, it is important, therefore, to bear in mind that the prophet does not speak for himself, but is the mouthpiece of God" (Gehman, "'Burden' of the Prophets," 108).

8. One would think Hezekiah would have been warier of a Babylonian envoy had Isaiah already prophesied against Babylon and its king.

9. Oswalt, *Book of Isaiah*, 298.

because the Lord asserts his authority over the whole world (Isa 13) and over the earth's greatest king (Isa 14).

Each *massa'* can be easily identifiable by the introductory מַשָּׂא. Oswalt correctly explains, "Chapters 13–23 form one of the most easily recognized units in the book of Isaiah because of the recurrence of the word *maśśā'*, 'burden' (RSV, NIV 'oracle'), throughout."[10]

The organization of the *massa'*, however, is elusive. Mackay believes the Babylon prophecy is first because of its "length and significance."[11] Kaiser sees no discernible structure except that the first *massa'* is against Babylon, "the great capital city as the seat of world power," and the last against Tyre, "the leading merchant city of the ancient world."[12] Roberts and Childs discuss redaction theories but fail to explain the text in its received form.[13]

Motyer presents a compelling structural analysis of the *mas'ot* (see Table 3.2). He makes the following observations: (1) There are two series of *mas'ot*—the first series addresses five specific cities, and the second series uses four enigmatic titles (one specific city—Tyre);[14] (2) Babylon begins each series and the people of God (Israel/Jerusalem) are fourth in each series; and (3) Geographically, Israel and Judah are in the middle. Motyer explains:

> One feature of the structure bears on the meaning of the whole: in each case the people of God, occupying the fourth place in the lists, are surrounded by the peoples of the world. In the first list these are Babylon to the north, Philistia to the west, Moab to the east and Egypt to the south. In the second list they are Babylon to the north, Edom to the south, Arabia to the east and Tyre to the west. Their position makes them vulnerable. Where will they seek security? But their position also makes them central—central to the way the Lord runs the world and very much at the centre of his eschatological world-view.[15]

---

10. Oswalt, *Book of Isaiah*, 298. See also Kaiser, *Isaiah: 13–39*, 1. Disagreement exists concerning the terminus of the *mas'ot* against the nations. Blenkinsopp believes they continue to ch. 27, Blenkinsopp, *Isaiah 1–39*, 271.

11. Mackay, *Study Commentary on Isaiah*, 318.

12. Kaiser, *Isaiah: 13–39*, 4.

13. Childs, *Isaiah*, 122–23; Roberts, *First Isaiah*, 197.

14. There are some oddities which Motyer discusses as well. For example, the *massa'* against Damascus primarily concerns Israel; there are two "Woes" in 17:11, 18:1; the countries are not exactly north, south, east, west; etc. (Motyer, *Prophecy of Isaiah*, 132–34). Smith finds Motyer's structure "attractive" as well (Smith, *Isaiah 1–39*, 290).

15. Motyer, *Prophecy of Isaiah*, 132. This structure is debated. Goldingay, for example, places Tyre in the north. Goldingay also sees 17:12–14 as the foci and describes the entire

Thus, Israel and Judah are in the middle, and being in the middle has advantages and disadvantages. One disadvantage is security, which fits the overall theme of Isaiah 7–39. Erlandsson explains, "The 'Prophecy against Babylon' . . . speaks about the futility of putting ones [sic] hope in Babylon. JHWH will Himself take pity on His people and crush proud Assyria. Babylon itself will very shortly lie in ruins (13:19–22)."[16] Oswalt also correctly states, "One central theme runs through chs. 7–39—the trustworthiness of God. . . . Ahaz trusts Assyria and the promised result is destruction. Hezekiah trusts God and Assyria is destroyed. Between these two segments come the chapters under consideration here. They are united by this common theme: the God of Israel is the Lord of the nations."[17] Babylon was the most tempting ally against an impending or ongoing Assyrian invasion, so Babylon is the first nation over whom Isaiah demonstrates God's superiority. What better way to demonstrate God's superiority over Babylon and her king than give an account of its eschatological destruction by the very army of God? After describing the fate of Babylon, Isaiah then turns to the other nations surrounding Israel in whom they may errantly trust.[18]

---

section as "the fate of many nations" (Goldingay, *Isaiah*, 91–95). Oswalt claims, "The 'oracles' have no geographical ordering" (Oswalt, *Book of Isaiah*, 298). Though later Oswalt sees a possible inclusio based upon geography, "The recognition that Babylon was at the eastern end of the civilized world while Tyre was at the west . . . suggests a bracketing effect" (Oswalt, *Book of Isaiah*, 299). Smith finds Motyer's proposal "attractive" (Smith, *Isaiah 1–39*, 290). Motyer's analysis provides a plausible but debatable explanation of the macro structure of the Babylon *massa'* which fits the thematic structure of Isaiah 7–39.

16. Erlandsson, "Burden of Babylon," 7.

17. Oswalt, *Book of Isaiah*, 297. Young also agrees, "The flowering tree of 13–23 has its roots in chapter 7. Indeed, this chapter is foundational for an understanding of what is to follow. In this great seventh chapter two basic thoughts are presented in seed form. First there is to be deliverance for God's people through Immanuel, the Son of the virgin. . . . At the same time, the world powers were to come more and more upon the horizon, for they would increase in strength and power until they had accomplished God's purposes with them" (Young, *Book of Isaiah*, 1:412).

18. Oswalt, *Book of Isaiah*, 330.

Table 3.2. The Mas'ot against the Nations[19]

Series 1		Series 2	
13:1—14:27	Babylon	21:1–10	Desert by the Sea (Babylon)
14:28–32	Philistia	21:11–12	Silence (Edom)
15:1—16:14	Moab	21:13–17	Evening (Arabia)
17:1—18:7	Damascus/Israel	22:1–25	Valley of Vision (Jerusalem)
19:1—20:6	Egypt	23:1–18	Tyre

Most of the authors quoted above ascribe to a historic fall of Babylon. The theme of God's superiority over the nations, however, works better with the eschatological view. God asserts his authority over the kingdoms of men (13:4) by individually leading an army (13:4) that purges sinners, the arrogant, and Babylon from the land (13:11, 19). God demonstrates his superiority over earth's greatest kingdom and greatest king.

STRUCTURE OF ISAIAH 13:2—14:27

Widespread agreement exists concerning the beginning of the *massa'*, but there is widespread disagreement concerning its conclusion. Isaiah 13:1 introduces the *massa'* against Babylon, and Isaiah 14:28 introduces the *massa'* against Philistia. The intervening text (13:2—14:27) is the focus of this study. There are four major sections of the *massa'*: Isaiah 13:2–13 describes the worldwide eschatological destruction by the Lord; 13:14—14:2 explains Babylon's destruction and Israel's regathering; 14:3–23 introduces the *mashal* (14:3–4a), includes the *mashal* (14:4b–21), and concludes the *massa'* against Babylon (14:22–23); and the final section is a sign (14:24–27) to validate the *massa'*. Thus, the *massa'* is a complete unit.

This structural analysis argues for a complete eschatological interpretation and discounts the partial historic fulfillment and partial eschatological expectation view. Smith, for example, believes 13:1–16 is eschatological, but 13:17—14:23 refers to Merodach-baladan.[20] By demonstrating that the *massa'* is structured as a whole, the evidence in favor of a complete eschatological interpretation is strengthened.

---

19. Motyer, *Prophecy of Isaiah*, 132.
20. Smith, *Isaiah 1–39*, 294–95, 303.

Isaiah 13:2–13

BHS indents verses 9 and 17, understanding the two "Behold!" (הנה) interjections as providing structure to the *massaʾ*. There is much to be said for this view. It creates three balanced stanzas. The first stanza contains thirteen lines, the second fourteen, and the third twelve, for a total of thirty-nine lines (and an average of thirteen lines per stanza). Thematically, this view has merits as well. Skinner takes this view, and states:

> Chap. xiii falls into three main divisions. A subdivision of each into two nearly equal strophes is possible, though less clearly marked.
> i. vv. 2–8. A magnificently poetical description of the impending attack. . . .
> ii. vv. 9–16. The meaning of judgement. . . .
> iii. vv. 17–22. The fate of Babylon[21]

Knoblet adds a few subdivisions to Skinner's divisions, but Knoblet essentially follows Skinner.[22]

The structure of Isaiah 13 lacks scholarly consensus. Some scholars support the division after verse 8, but almost all believe there is a division after verse 16. For example, Goldingay, Motyer, and Smith have only two sections to the entire chapter (2–16 and 17–22).[23] Childs, Blenkinsopp, Steuernagel, and Watts also recognize the division between 16–17: 2–5, 6–16, and 17–22.[24] Mackay and Brueggemann see four total sections (2–5, 6–8, 9–16, and 17–22) with two main sections (2–16 and 17–22).[25] Clements is very similar (2–3, 4–5, 6–8, 9–16, and 17–22).[26] Marti and Scott add several other sections, but also recognize the divisions between 8–9 and 16–17 (2–4, 5–8, 9–12, 13–16, 17–19, and 20–22).[27] There are few who vary from the 16–17 division. Os-

---

21. Skinner, *Book of the Prophet Isaiah*, 113. Dillman takes this structure as well (Dillmann, *Der Prophet Jesaia*, 125–26).

22. Knoblet, "Investigation of Isaiah Thirteen," 39.

23. Goldingay, *Isaiah*, 97–98; Motyer, *Prophecy of Isaiah*, 135; Smith, *Isaiah 1–39*, 295.

24. Childs, *Isaiah*, 124–25; Mackay, *Study Commentary on Isaiah*, 321–32; Watts, *Isaiah 1–33*, 195; Blenkinsopp, *Isaiah 1–39*, 274–76; Steuernagel, *Einleitung in das Alte Testament*, 487.

25. Mackay, *Study Commentary on Isaiah*, 321–32; Brueggemann, *Isaiah*, 115–22. One minor difference is that Brueggemann separates 22b as its own unit.

26. Clements, *Isaiah 1–39*, 133–38. Leupold's only difference is that he breaks 17–22 into two sections: 17–19 and 20–22 (Leupold, *Exposition of Isaiah*, 240–49).

27. Marti, *Das Buch Jesaja*, 117–22; Scott, "Book of Isaiah," 255–58.

Israel's Eschatological Enemy

walt, however, has two sections—1–18 and 19–22[28]—as does Young—1–8 and 9–22.[29] Alexander has 1–9, 10–18, and 19–22.[30] While there are some variations among these scholars, none of them see a division between 13–14.

There are six reasons why there should be a major break after Isaiah 13:13. First, "Therefore" (עַל־כֵּן) functions as a structural marker and concludes the first major section in verse 13.[31] Motyer seems to see a minor division after verse 13 when he states, "This verse forms the summary and conclusion."[32] Second, there is an inclusio which sets Isaiah 13:9–13 off as a unit.[33] Five words are repeated in 13:13: (1) day, (יוֹם), (2) Lord (יהוה), (3) wrath (עברה), (4) fierce (חרון), and (5) anger (אף) (see Table 3.3).

Table 3.3. Inclusio between Isaiah 13:9–13

9a. Behold, the day[1] of the Lord[2] is coming with cruelty,	הִנֵּה יוֹם[1]־יְהוָה[2] בָּא אַכְזָרִי	9a
9b. And wrath,[3] and fierce[4] anger[5]	וְעֶבְרָה[3] וַחֲרוֹן[4] אָף[5]	9b
...	...	
13c. In the wrath[3] of the Lord[2] of hosts,	בְּעֶבְרַת[3] יְהוָה[2] צְבָאוֹת	13c
13d. And in the day[1] of his fierce[4] anger[5]	וּבְיוֹם[1] חֲרוֹן[4] אַפּוֹ[5]	13d

Third, the agents and manners of destruction are vastly different. Isaiah 13:2–13 describes (1) an angelic army (2) which is led by the Lord, and they (3) destroy the earth and nearly all in it. Isaiah 13:14–22 describes (1) a Median army, (2) whose leader is unstated, and (3) they take no prisoners,

---

28. Oswalt, *Book of Isaiah*, 301.

29. Young, *Book of Isaiah*, 408, 439.

30. Alexander, *Prophecies of Isaiah*, 268. Alexander's division between 9–10 is bewildering.

31. עַל־כֵּן also occurs in 13:7 and concludes the first minor section (2–8). Fry also recognizes the structural function of עַל־כֵּן: "The formula עַל־כֵּן, 'therefore,' introduces verse 13, which like verse 10 describes the effects that Yahweh's coming will have on the cosmos. The introductory formula עַל־כֵּן indicates that this new material is a consequence of what has come before, Yahweh's coming to punish and stop the evil of the world (verse 11)" (Fry, "'Oracle Concerning Babylon," 69). He later states, "Line 13a concludes Yahweh's speech (11a–13a) in the first person" (70).

32. Motyer, *Prophecy of Isaiah*, 139. See also Oswalt, *Book of Isaiah*, 307.

33. Concerning Isaiah 13:13, Erlandsson explains, "[It] resumes the wrath terminology from v. 9 and links up with the term יוֹם in v. 6, imparting to the description of Yahweh's day in vs. 6–13 a well designed unity" (Erlandsson, *Burden of Babylon*, 116). Erlandsson seems to ignore verse 9.

plunder houses, rape women, and dash children. These battles are different.[34] Fourth, first person verbs, found exclusively in Isaiah 13:3 and 11–13a, form an inclusio marking Isaiah 13:2–13 off as a unit. Isaiah 13:14–22, however, contains no first-person verbs.[35] Fifth, the Lord's "anger" (אף) is mentioned three times in Isaiah 13:2–13, occurring in the beginning (3), middle (5, 9), and at the end (13), but it is not mentioned at all in Isaiah 13:14–22.

The sixth and most important reason why there is a major division after Isaiah 13:13 is the presence of והיה ("And it will be . . .") in 13:14. This is the most important point because והיה occurs again in Isaiah 14:3, marking the second major division of the *massa'* against Babylon. והיה sometimes introduces a new section.[36] והיה by itself does not constitute a sufficient reason for a division. Its use, coupled with the previous five points, makes a substantive argument in favor of a major division after Isaiah 13:13. Erlandsson also correctly observes that והיה is functioning structurally in Isaiah 13: "With the coordinating expression והיה (v.14) begins a description (vs. 14—18) which links up with the description of war in vs.2—5 and consequently the description of the day of Yahweh in vs.6—13 is enclosed, the whole forming a kind of 'ring composition.'"[37] This observation is missed by most commentators, resulting in a plethora of interpretations concerning the structure of Isaiah 13–14.

Dividing Isaiah 13 between verses 13–14 is not without historic precedent. Cheyne divides chapter 13 into two sections, 2–13, "The Divine judgment upon the world," and 14–22, "The first act in the world judgment."[38] Bredenkamp does as well, "Only from V. 14 on does the text focus on Babel."[39] As already demonstrated, Erlandsson also recognizes a division between verses 13–14.[40]

---

34. See "The Battle" section below.

35. There is a 1cs suffix in Isaiah 13:17 but there are no first-person verbs.

36. cf. Isa 7:18, 10:12, 20, 11:10, 11, and 14:3 (note the Masoretic *p^{e}tûḥā'* after 7:17, 10:19 11:9, 10 and the *s^{e}tûmā'* after 10:11, 14:2).

37. Erlandsson, *Burden of Babylon*, 116. Erlandsson's "ring composition" is rejected and a response to it can be found below.

38. Cheyne, *Prophecies of Isaiah*, 82–85. Kuenen sees three sections: 2–8, 9–13, 14–22 (Kuenen, *Historisch-kritische Einleitung in die Bücher des Alten Testaments*, 2:84).

39. "Erst von V.14 an verdichtet sich das Gericht auf Babel" (Bredenkamp, *Der Prophet Jesaia*, 92).

40. Erlandsson divides Isaiah 13 into four sections: 2–5, 6–13, 14–18, and 19–22 (Erlandsson, *Burden of Babylon*, 114).

Israel's Eschatological Enemy

Isaiah 13:14—14:2

Scholars are divided concerning the structure of Isaiah 13:14—14:2. Some believe the text should be divided after either Isaiah 13:16 or 13:18.[41] Others believe Isaiah 14:1 either concludes the *massa'* in Isaiah 13 and introduces a new section, or just connects the *massa'* to the *mashal*. For example, Blenkinsopp comments, "Both compositions [the Babylonian oracle (13:1) and *mashal* (14:4–21)] are followed by brief passages in prose (14:1–2, 22–23), part of an ongoing commentary or series of commentaries in evidence throughout the entire book."[42] Hayes and Irvine see little continuity between chapters 13–14.[43] Smith explains, "There is no way to determine if the prophet originally spoke 14:1–2 in conjunction with the Babylon oracles here in chaps. 13–14, but is it [sic] likely that these verses were editorially placed here at the time when the author put these oracles in their present order."[44] Thus, Smith believes Isaiah edited the *mas'ot* and put this section here.[45] Smith's view is not very different from the critical views that associate Isaiah 14:1–2 thematically with Isaiah 40–55.[46]

Scholars vary substantially concerning the function of Isaiah 14:1–2. Childs explains, "The editorial effect of this unity is to anticipate the full significance for Israel of God's sovereignty over the nations, which will receive its extended development in chapters 40–55."[47] Clements argues that the purpose is "to present a fitting conclusion for the sequence of prophecies regarding Judah and Babylon by showing that in the end it will all result in a happy

---

41. As stated above, Smith sees a division at 13:16 (Smith, *Isaiah 1–39*, 294–95; 303). Erlandsson divides the text at 13:18 (Erlandsson, *Burden of Babylon*, 116).

42. Blenkinsopp, *Isaiah 1–39*, 278.

43. Hayes and Irvine, *Isaiah*, 226–29.

44. Smith, *Isaiah 1–39*, 305.

45. Smith is noncommittal concerning the fulfillment of 14:1–2. He puts forth a couple theories, then explains, "All that is required for people to understand this prophecy is for some Israelites to be in exile" (Smith, *Isaiah 1–39*, 306). Then later he states, "This prophecy should be connected to God's grand eschatological transformation of the hearts of mankind (2:1–5; 11:10–16; 19:18–25)" (307).

46. Childs presents the critical view: "Both the language used and the concepts developed are closely akin to those of chapters 40–55, which is further evidence against the position of those who defend a late eighth-century context for these chapters" (Childs, *Isaiah*, 126). The only difference is that Smith believes Isaiah was the editor instead of a later redactor.

47. Childs, *Isaiah*, 126.

and blessed future for Israel."⁴⁸ Blenkinsopp claims Isaiah 14:1–2 "confer[s] a degree of thematic unity on the compilation by viewing historical events from the perspective of the restored post-disaster community."⁴⁹ Wildberger believes a later redactor is applying the destruction of Babylon to Israel.⁵⁰

The multiplicity of views is largely the result of scholars failing to discern structural clues in the text. Since והיה ("And it will be . . .") is functioning structurally in Isaiah 13:14, then it is most likely functioning structurally again in Isaiah 14:3. Thus the first two major divisions of the oracle are Isaiah 13:2–13 and 13:14—14:2. This section first argues for a section division after Isaiah 13:18; second, that there is continuity between Isaiah 13:22 and 14:1; and finally, a division between Isaiah 14:2 and 14:3.

Section Division after Isaiah 13:18

Just like Isaiah 13:2, Isaiah 13:14 begins with a great deal of ambiguity. Fry agrees with this analysis, "Verses 14–22 also echo the movement of vv 2–5 from obscurity to clarity. They reveal the military nature of the scene gradually at the same time as they withhold and bring into question the identity of the invader."⁵¹ Erlandsson also recognizes the similarities between Isaiah 13:14 and 13:2: "With the coordinating expression והיה (v.14) begins a description (vs. 14—18) which links up with the description of war in vs.2—5 and consequently the description of the day of Yahweh in vs.6—13 is enclosed, the whole forming a kind of 'ring composition.'"⁵² Erlandsson is correct concerning the structural use of והיה and the ambiguity in 2–5 and 14–18, but misses the extent of the connection. Erlandsson's "ring composition" is difficult to maintain for four reasons. First, the details of Isaiah 13:2–5 and Isaiah 13:14–18 do not correspond. In Isaiah 13:2–13, God's army is engaged in a "holy war," but the Medes are doing unholy things as they conquer in Isaiah 13:14–22. Unless one believes angels, who are engaged in holy war, will be dashing children into pieces and raping women, the battle transpiring in Isaiah 13:14–17 is different from the battle in Isaiah 13:2–5.⁵³

---

48. Clements, *Isaiah 1–39*, 138.
49. Blenkinsopp, *Isaiah 1–39*, 281.
50. Wildberger, *Isaiah 13–27*, 14.
51. Fry, "'Oracle Concerning Babylon,'" 74.
52. Erlandsson, *Burden of Babylon*, 116.
53. This point is argued in the "Two Battles" section below.

Israel's Eschatological Enemy

The second reason Erlandsson's division is difficult to maintain is because he incorrectly applies the pronouns in Isaiah 13:16–17 to 13:11. He explains:

> In the section vs.14—18 a definite people is mentioned who wage this war, namely the Medes (v.17). With a הנני "look" it is announced that Yahweh intends to arouse this people to strife against the proud sinners. The identity of these proud sinners is not indicated in vs.14—18. This description of the scourge of war gives no concrete information as to the land or race which is afflicted. It speaks only of "them" (עליהם v.17) as well as in v.16 (עליהם עיניהם בתיהם and עלליהם נשיהם). The suffixes of these words refer back to the proud and godless tyrants in v.11. There is no possibility of escaping the Medes. Nothing can awaken compassion in them and they do not accept bribes (v.17f.).[54]

It is more likely that the pronouns refer to those fleeing in verses 14–15 because they are the near referent. The real questions are: "Who is fleeing?" and "Who is pursuing?" The ambiguity in Isaiah 13:14–16 resembles the ambiguity in 13:2–5; except here the pursuers and fleers are announced as the Medes and the Babylonians.

The third reason Erlandsson's division is difficult to maintain is because he places too much emphasis on the 3fs והיתה (And it [f.] will be ...") in 13:19.[55] Isaiah 13:14–18 describes the destruction of Babylon's people, and Isaiah 13:19–22 describes the destruction of Babylon. Erlandsson is correct; there is a transition in Isaiah 13:18, and it is a self-contained unit (concerning the city of Babylon). But Isaiah 13:19–22 still connects to the destruction in Isaiah 13:14–18 (concerning the people of Babylon).

The fourth reason is the catchword צבי (gazelle, splendorous). Watson explains, "A secondary function [of keywords] is *to indicate the structure* of a poem. Finally, such words may function as *catchwords* linking separate verses or stanzas."[56] In Isaiah 13:14, the peoples flee like a scared gazelle (צבי); then in Isaiah 13:19, Babylon is described as splendorous (צבי).[57] The people (14–18) and the city (19–22) are צבי.

---

54. Erlandsson, *Burden of Babylon*, 117.

55. "As in vs.14–18 the account opens with the verb היה and is in itself clearly a self-contained unit" (Erlandsson, *Burden of Babylon*, 118).

56. Watson, *Classical Hebrew Poetry*, 288 (emphasis his).

57. צבי occurs only eight times in Isaiah (Isa 4:2; 13:14, 19; 23:9; 24:16; 28:1, 4, 5), making it likely that it is functioning structurally here.

The Massa' against Babylon—Isaiah 13:2—14:2

The destruction described in chapter 13 starts with a worldwide description of God destroying the armies of the world on the day of the Lord. The focus shifts at Isaiah 13:14 to a more specific description. The Median conquest is described, first, on a human level in Isaiah 13:14–18 and, second, on a metropolitan level in Isaiah 13:19–22.[58] While the king of Babylon goes out to war against the Lord (13:2–13), the Medes attack his home country mercilessly (13:14–22).[59]

Continuity between Isaiah 13:22 and 14:1

Hayes and Irvine claim "Isaiah 14:1–27 is a complete text."[60] There are three exegetical reasons, however, why there is continuity between Isaiah 13:22 and 14:1: (1) the traditional division of the text; (2) the כי clause in Isaiah 14:1; and (3) the structural continuity between Isaiah 13:19–22 and 14:1–2.

The first argument in favor of continuity between Isaiah 13:22 and 14:1 is the traditional division of the text. There are no Masoretic division markers after 13:22. The last Masoretic $s^e\underline{t}ûmā'$ or $p^e\underline{t}ûḥā'$ was after Isaiah 12:6, thus 13:1 begins a new section in the book of Isaiah. There is not another $s^e\underline{t}ûmā'$ or $p^e\underline{t}ûḥā'$ through all of chapter 13 until the $s^e\underline{t}ûmā'$ after 14:2.[61] 1QIsa^a has a full paragraph break after Isaiah 14:2. Thus, there is some traditional evidence for a division after Isaiah 14:2, but no support for a division after 13:22.

Second, Isaiah 14:1 most likely begins with a contrastive כי. The NIV does not translate the כי, treating it like an asseverative and, potentially, treating Isaiah 14:1 as a new section.[62] The NASB translates it temporally ("When"), and the NLT interprets it as a contrast ("But"). Young believes it is causal, "In the previous chapter we learned that, because of her sin, Babylon must and will fall. Now, the prophet gives us a second reason: Babylon must perish *because* it was the purpose of God to raise and exalt

---

58. Fry agrees with this structural analysis, "But these verses, in their vivid description of utter destruction and desolation, function as an appropriate poetic conclusion to the first poem's third strophe, which in vv 14–18 focuses on the taking and pillaging of the city and in vv 19–22 describes the result of that action" (Fry, "'Oracle Concerning Babylon,'" 86). Unfortunately, Fry does conclude with 13:22 and claims 14:1 is a new poem (87).

59. These two battles are described in more detail below.

60. Hayes and Irvine, *Isaiah*, 227.

61. 1QIsa^a does have a full paragraph break after 13:16.

62. Joüon and Muraoka, *Grammar of Biblical Hebrew*, 580.

His people."⁶³ Smith rejects the causal interpretation, claiming כי is either "a contrast with Babylon's fate ('but') or as having a temporal significance ('when' as in NASB)."⁶⁴ All of these views, except the asseverative, evidence some connection between 13 and 14.

Erlandsson makes a linguistic and intertextual argument in favor of the contrastive כי:

> This section opens with the words כי ירחם יהוה, which provide an effective contrast to לא ירחם in 13:18. If 13:2–18 is considered to be a judgment on Israel's enemies, it serves, at the same time, as a proclamation of salvation for Israel, which in a more immediate manner continues in 14:1–2. Once more will Israel be chosen (בחר) and be permitted to take possession of its own land and אדמת יהוה, as it is also called (cf. Hos 9:3). Furthermore, ירחם in 14:1 is contrasted with לא ירחם in 9:16 in the same way as רחמה in Hos. 2:3 is contrasted with לא רחמה in Hos. 1:6.⁶⁵

Thus, the relationship between Isaiah 13:22 and 14:1 is that of a contrast. There is a transition between these two verses, but it is not a completely new poem as Fry suggests.⁶⁶ There is a reversal in fortunes which takes place at the same *time*. *When* Babylon is destroyed, *then* Israel is restored.

---

63. Young, *Book of Isaiah*, 431 (emphasis mine). See also, Wolf, *Interpreting Isaiah*, 112; Mackay, *Study Commentary on Isaiah*, 337; Webb, *Message of Isaiah*, 80.

64. Smith, *Isaiah 1-39*, 306.

65. Erlandsson, *Burden of Babylon*, 119. Brueggemann agrees "As Babylon knows a great reversal from pride to nullification, so commensurately, Israel knows a great reversal from suffering to compassion and closeness" (Brueggemann, *Isaiah*, 123). Roos agrees as well, "The opening כִּ of explanation of v. 1 suggests a link between 13.22 and 14.1. In contrast to the preceding verses, Isa 14.1–2 inserts Israel positively in the context by point to a reversal of fortunes" (Roos, "Babylon in the Book of Isaiah," 27). Beuken also recognizes the continuity between 13:22 and 14:1 (Beuken, "Common and Different Phrases for Babylon's Fall," 54).

66. Fry claims it is functioning as a contrast *and* introduces a new poem. He states, "The first poem (Isa 13:2–22) of the 'Oracle Concerning Babylon' focuses on the manifestation of Yahweh's indignant anger coming to punish the wicked in the invasion and destruction of Babylon on Yahweh's Day. The second poem of the oracle (Isa 14:1–23) focuses on the positive results of the terrible event, a reversal in the fortunes of God's people and their oppressors. Yahweh has compassion on Israel and reverses the roles of oppressed and oppressor (14:1–2) resulting in the singing of a taunt, introduced by 14:3–4c, and directed against the fallen king of Babylon" (Fry, "'Oracle Concerning Babylon,'" 87). Muilenburg demonstrates that כי can begin a poem, Muilenburg, "Linguistic and Rhetorical Usages of the Particle כי," 149–50. He also argues, however, it can function 25 other ways including contrastively, "The word is often used adversatively to denote a striking contrast." Muilenburg, "Linguistic and Rhetorical Usages of the Particle כי., 139." The analysis below supports a contrastive כי.

The Massa' against Babylon—Isaiah 13:2—14:2

A structural analysis of Isaiah 13:19—14:2 supports the conclusion that the כִּי is contrastive and the division between chapters 13-14 is not a major break in the *massa'*. Because the *BHS* editors and several English translations treat Isaiah 14:1-2 as prose, this section first argues that verses 1-2 are poetry. Then the structure is examined. This analysis argues that the fall of Babylon, regathering of Israel, and *mashal* against the king of Babylon happen at the same *time* which supports an eschatological interpretation of the *mashal*.

Isaiah 14:1-2 is Poetry

The stichography of 14:1-2 in *BHS* is prose. The NKJV, KJV, NASB, ESV, and NLT have followed the stichography of *BHS* and segmented 14:1-2 as prose.[67] The NIV, however, has segmented 14:1-2 as poetry and 14:3-4a as prose.[68] Table 3.4 presents the stichography of *BHS* for 13:20-22 and a reconstructed stichography of 14:1-2.[69] The analysis below argues for established line forms, repetition, word pairs, and even tricola.[70]

---

67. Gray mixes the poetry and prose, "It requires some audacity to detect poetry in vv.[3, 4a]; and v.[2a] would yield but a poor distich 4: 4, even if the last clause were omitted. But v.[1a, b, d, e] are as a matter of fact two distichs (3: 3) of lines parallel in sense, and [1c] a monostich of 3 accents: v.[2b, c] is 3: 3 or 3: 2" (Gray, *Isaiah I-XXXIX*, 244-45).

68. This dissertation agrees with the NIV's stichography (1984 and 2011).

69. Watts agreed with the stichography presented below (Watts, *Isaiah 1-33*, 201). Fry's stichography seems to support the two tricola as well (Fry, "'Oracle Concerning Babylon,'" 87-88.)

70. Concerning the presence of tricola, Watson claims that a "tricolon is only found in true verse so that its presence is an almost unequivocal pointer to poetry" (Watson, *Classical Hebrew Poetry*, 53).

Table 3.4. Reconstructed Stichography of Isaiah 13:20—14:2

20	לֹא־תֵשֵׁב לָנֶצַח	וְלֹא תִשְׁכֹּן עַד־דּוֹר וָדוֹר
	וְלֹא־יַהֵל שָׁם עֲרָבִי	וְרֹעִים לֹא־יַרְבִּצוּ שָׁם׃
21	וְרָבְצוּ־שָׁם צִיִּים	וּמָלְאוּ בָתֵּיהֶם אֹחִים
	וְשָׁכְנוּ שָׁם בְּנוֹת יַעֲנָה	וּשְׂעִירִים יְרַקְּדוּ־שָׁם׃
22	וְעָנָה אִיִּים בְּאַלְמְנוֹתָיו	וְתַנִּים בְּהֵיכְלֵי עֹנֶג
	וְקָרוֹב לָבוֹא עִתָּהּ	וְיָמֶיהָ לֹא יִמָּשֵׁכוּ׃
14:1	כִּי יְרַחֵם יְהוָה אֶת־יַעֲקֹב	וּבָחַר עוֹד בְּיִשְׂרָאֵל	וְהִנִּיחָם עַל־אַדְמָתָם
	וְנִלְוָה הַגֵּר עֲלֵיהֶם	וְנִסְפְּחוּ עַל־בֵּית יַעֲקֹב׃
2	וּלְקָחוּם עַמִּים	וֶהֱבִיאוּם אֶל־מְקוֹמָם
	וְהִתְנַחֲלוּם בֵּית־יִשְׂרָאֵל	עַל אַדְמַת יְהוָה	לַעֲבָדִים וְלִשְׁפָחוֹת
	וְהָיוּ שֹׁבִים לְשֹׁבֵיהֶם	וְרָדוּ בְּנֹגְשֵׂיהֶם׃

Watson cites Isaiah 14:1–2 as an illustration of a specific kind of word pair, the break-up of stereotypical phrases.[71] Isaiah 14:2 states, "The peoples take them and bring them to their place." Normally peoples would take Israel and bring them (deport them) to a foreign land. According to Watson, the stereotypical phrase is broken up with the peoples returning Israelites back to Israel. This continues in the next tricolon where the "house of Israel will possess (נחל) them on the ground of the Lord as slaves and female slaves." Normally Israel would be dispossessed (נחל) from the ground of the Lord and be slaves and female slaves to another people. Thus, according to Watson, this stereotypical phrase is broken up. This dissertation, however, argues below that a stereotypical interpretation of Isaiah 14:1–2 is unlikely. Watson admits that "[Break-up of stereotype phrases] is related to indicator 10, 'word-pairs.'"[72] Thus, this is more accurately a word-pair which is still evidence of poetry.

Continuity between Isaiah 13:20–22 and 14:1–2

Three additional observations support the conclusion that Isaiah 14:1–2 is poetry. The first point of continuity concerns the structure. Isaiah 13:20–22

---

71. Watson, *Classical Hebrew Poetry*, 47, 52. Watson errantly includes verse 3, but the stereotypical phrase is not found in verse 3.

72. Watson, *Classical Hebrew Poetry*, 52.

The Massa' against Babylon—Isaiah 13:2—14:2

and 14:1–2 both contain twelve cola. Isaiah 13:20 and 14:1 both begin without a vav, but then vavs precede each *description*. This structure is more apparent in 13:20–22 because a vav precedes each colon. This structure continues in 14:1–2. The first description begins with the conjunction כי and the succeeding nine descriptions are all preceded by a vav. The tricolon in verse 2 is one *description* of the restoration (not three, thus only one vav).

The second point of continuity concerns Isaiah 13:22b and the tricolon in 14:2. Isaiah 13:22b pertains to the timeframe of the destruction, not a description of the destruction. Thus, comparing the *descriptions* of the destruction/restoration sections, the first colon of both sections does *not* have a vav, but the next nine *descriptions* begin with a vav (note again the tricolon in 14:2 is one *description*). One potential difficulty with this explanation is the ABC structural tricolon in verse 2.[73] This tricolon, however, balances out Isaiah 13:22b (the timeframe of the destruction) creating twelve cola from 13:20–22 and twelve cola from 14:1–2 (see Table 3.4).

Catchwords are the third point of continuity. The first and third verbs in Isaiah 14:1a–c are functioning as catchwords. The first verb (ירחם—"he will have compassion") contrasts with the Medes who do not show compassion toward the fruit of the womb (Isa 13:18b). This catchword illustrates that Isaiah 14:1–2 connects not only with 13:19–22, but also 13:14–18. The entire *massa'* is one unit. The third verb (והניחם—"and he will make them rest") introduces a theological concept which is repeated in Isaiah 14:3a.[74] Therefore, the first word (ירחם—"he will have compassion") points back to Isaiah 13:18b and the third verb (והניחם—"and he will make them rest") points forward to Isaiah 14:3a (see Table 3.5).

---

73. Watson explains, "The structural tricolon is a set of three lines which exhibit no parallelism, strictly speaking, but are linked in some way" (Watson, *Classical Hebrew Poetry*, 182). The three lines, however, seem linked thematically. Kugel explains concerning parallelism, "To state the matter somewhat simplistically, biblical lines are parallelistic not because B is meant to be parallel of A, but because B typically *supports* A, carries it further, backs it up, completes it, goes beyond it" (Kugel, *Idea of Biblical Poetry*, 52; emphasis original). Kugel explains this is true of bicola and tricola (Kugel, *Idea of Biblical Poetry*, 52). The tricolon in Isaiah 14:2 builds upon itself. The most emphatic colon is the last one where the children of Israel acquire male and female servants.

74. For a discussion of והניחם, see "Extent of the Regathering" below.

Table 3.5. Catchwords in Isaiah 13:18–22

וּקְשָׁתוֹת נְעָרִים תְּרַטַּשְׁנָה וּפְרִי־בֶטֶן לֹא יְרַחֵמוּ¹ עַל־בָּנִים לֹא־תָחוּס עֵינָם׃	13:18
...	
כִּי יְרַחֵם¹ יְהוָה אֶת־יַעֲקֹב וּבָחַר עוֹד בְּיִשְׂרָאֵל וְהִנִּיחָם² עַל־אַדְמָתָם	14:1
...	
וְהָיָה בְּיוֹם הָנִיחַ² יְהוָה לְךָ מֵעָצְבְּךָ וּמֵרָגְזֶךָ וּמִן־הָעֲבֹדָה הַקָּשָׁה אֲשֶׁר עֻבַּד־בָּךְ׃	14:3

¹ רחם connects the regathering of Israel to the Medes destruction

² נוח connects the regathering of Israel to the *mashal*

While the verbs in Isaiah 14:1 bind the *massaʾ* together, 14:3a ties into the *timeframe* (cataclysmic destruction, devastation of Babylon, Median slaughter, Israelite regathering) of 13:22b and 14:1a by referencing the *day* (13:6a, 9a, 13d, 22d) when the *Lord* (14:1a,) gives Israel *rest* (14:1c) (see Table 3.6).[75] Fry also agrees with this conclusion, "Line 3a picks up the theme of vv 1–2, the coming compassion of Yahweh for Jacob/Israel in a reversal of fortunes between Israel and its oppressors 'on a day' now not only of Yahweh's burning anger (as in Isa 13:9b) but also of his giving rest to Israel (הניח, Isa 14:3a) as he sets (הניחם) them on their own soil (Isa 14:1c)."[76]

---

75. Blenkinsopp recognizes the connection between 14:1 and 14:3, "The link is by catchword—Yahveh gives Israel rest on its land (*hinnîḥām* 14:1); Yahveh gives you respite from your troubles (*hānîaḥ* 14:3)" (Blenkinsopp, *Isaiah 1–39*, 286). Blenkinsopp fails to note the corresponding "day."

76. Fry, "'Oracle Concerning Babylon,'" 94. See also Tucker, "Book of Isaiah 1–39," 158.

The Massa' against Babylon—Isaiah 13:2—14:2

Table 3.6. Timeframe of the Mashal (Proverb)

וְהָיָה¹ כִּצְבִי מֻדָּח	13:14
...	
וְעָנָה אִיִּים בְּאַלְמְנוֹתָיו וְתַנִּים בְּהֵיכְלֵי עֹנֶג²	13:22
וְקָרוֹב לָבוֹא עִתָּהּ וְיָמֶיהָ² לֹא יִמָּשֵׁכוּ:	
כִּי יְרַחֵם יְהוָה אֶת־יַעֲקֹב וּבָחַר עוֹד בְּיִשְׂרָאֵל וְהִנִּיחָם³ עַל־אַדְמָתָם	14:1
וְנִלְוָה הַגֵּר עֲלֵיהֶם וְנִסְפְּחוּ עַל־בֵּית יַעֲקֹב:	
...	
וְהָיָה¹ בְּיוֹם² הָנִיחַ³ יְהוָה לְךָ מֵעָצְבְּךָ וּמֵרָגְזֶךָ וּמִן־הָעֲבֹדָה הַקָּשָׁה אֲשֶׁר עֻבַּד־בָּךְ:	14:3
וְנָשָׂאתָ הַמָּשָׁל⁴ הַזֶּה עַל־מֶלֶךְ בָּבֶל	14:4

¹ והיה introduces a new section in 13:14 and 14:3

² The temporal ביום connects to the timeframe of chapter 13

³ The temporal ביום also connects to the regathering of Israel in 14:1–2

⁴ Isaiah 14:3–4a introduces the *mashal* (proverb)

The implications of this structural analysis for understanding the identity of the king of Babylon cannot be understated. *When* Babylon is destroyed *and* Israel is restored, *then* Israel will lift up the *mashal* against the king of Babylon. The *mashal* against the king of Babylon is tied directly to the events in Isaiah 13:2—14:2.

Discontinuity between Isaiah 14:2 and 14:3

There are four reasons why there is a major section break after Isaiah 14:2. The first reason is והיה ("And it will be ...") in Isaiah 14:3.[77] The second is the Masoretic s^{e}ṯûmā' after Isaiah 14:2 (p^{e}ṯûḥā' in 1QIsa^a).[78] The third is the temporal dependent clause, "in the day when the Lord gives you rest," which hearkens back to the day of the Lord and regathering of Israel. The

---

77. Roos, "Babylon in the Book of Isaiah," 27–28.

78. Wildberger agrees, "The *parashiyyot* (paragraph) divisions in the MT make clear that a new body of material begins with v. 3. This cannot be a completely decisive factor for modern scholarship; however, observations dealing with both form and content also show that a new section begins with v. 3" (Wildberger, *Isaiah 13–27*, 47).

fourth is the transition to the second-person singular in Isaiah 14:3–4.[79] Others have also recognized this division. Sweeney states, "The prophetic instruction to utter a taunt song against the king of Babylon in 14:3–23 is clearly marked by its narrative introduction in verses 3–4a."[80] These four reasons substantiate the division between Isaiah 14:2–3.

The *Massa'* Concludes—The Structure of Isaiah 14:3–27

The third division focuses on the *mashal* (proverb) in Isaiah 14:4b–21. Isaiah 14:3–4a is a prose introduction to the *mashal*; 14:4b–21 is the *mashal*; 14:22–23 concludes the section that directly pertains to Babylon and its king. Finally, Isaiah 14:24–27 describes the Lord's determination to accomplish his will and includes a short-term sign (Assyrian destruction, 14:25) which validates the long-term prophecy against Babylon (13:2—14:23).

This section focuses on the conclusion of the *massa'* (oracle). First, the conclusion to the *mashal* is argued to be in Isaiah 14:21; second, the Babylonian *massa'* ends in Isaiah 14:23; finally, the entire *massa'* ends in Isaiah 14:27.

Conclusion of the Mashal

The conclusion to the *mashal* is not a strong division which is why some authors believe it continues to Isaiah 14:23.[81] There are four indicators, however, that the *mashal* ends in Isaiah 14:21, and 14:22–23 concludes the section against Babylon. The first reason is the change in speaker.[82] Isaiah 14:22 asserts, "I will

---

79. Sweeney agrees with this point and states, "It is distinguished by its 2nd-person singular address form, apparently directed to Israel" (Sweeney, *Isaiah 1–39*, 225).

80. Sweeney, *Isaiah 1–39*, 224–25. Contra, Fry, "Oracle Concerning Babylon," 94.

81. Childs, *Isaiah*, 127; Smith, *Isaiah 1–39*, 319; Clements, *Isaiah 1–39*, 145; Brueggemann, *Isaiah*, 133; Goldingay, *Isaiah*, 103.

82. Van Wyk lists five reasons why the *mashal* concludes after Isa 14:21, "(a) A switch to the 1st pers. sing. from the 3rd pl.; (b) from vv. 22–23 God is the subject of the verb which was nowhere the case in the poem itself; (c) in connection with (b) the occurrence of the oracular formulae נאם יהוה צבאות thrice in this short pericope; (d) in vv. 22–23 we have four verses (distichs) which, if added would cause an imbalance in the length of the last strophe as compared to the other four. Adding two of them would have had as a result five strophes of equal length, but according to no linguistic criteria can we sever vv. 22 and 23 or add vs. 22 to vs. 21; (e) the addition of vv. 22–23 (or the insertion of 4b–21 before it) can best be explained by the use of קום in 21 and 22 (though with different subjects, mere Stichwortprinciple); by the specific mentioning of Babel in 22 (actualization) and by the resemblance between the thought of vv. 20c–21b, the declaration of Yahweh Himself that He would leave

rise up against them, declares the Lord of hosts." Isaiah 14:4 said the people of Israel would take up this *mashal* against the king of Babylon. Thus, the speaker has changed and the *mashal* must have concluded before Isaiah 14:22.

The second reason the *mashal* has ended corresponds to the first, the change in pronouns.[83] There are no first-person forms in the *mashal* except the five assertions of the Babylonian king (vv. 13–14). The first-person perfect verbs in Isaiah 14:22–23 hearken back to the first-person perfect verbs in Isaiah 13:11, adding continuity to the entire *massa'*.

The third and strongest reason the *mashal* has ended is the recurring phrase in Isaiah 14:22–27 "declares the Lord of hosts."[84] This refrain does two things; it binds Isaiah 14:22–27 together, but the slight variations also create discontinuity. The complete refrain "declares the Lord of hosts" occurs in Isaiah 14:22b and 23d, marking it off as a unit. The abbreviated refrain "declares the Lord" separates the human destruction in Isaiah 14:22cd from the city's destruction in 14:23abc. The refrain is modified slightly again in Isaiah 14:24 to "the Lord of hosts," which creates continuity with 24–27 but also discontinuity. Thus, the refrain "declares the Lord of hosts" functions as an inclusio binding Isaiah 14:22–23 together and points forward to the inclusio in 14:24–27 (see Table 3.7).

Table 3.7. Concluding Inclusios

וְקַמְתִּי עֲלֵיהֶם נְאֻם יְהוָה צְבָאוֹת[1]	22
וְהִכְרַתִּי לְבָבֶל שֵׁם וּשְׁאָר וְנִין וָנֶכֶד נְאֻם־יְהוָה:	
וְשַׂמְתִּיהָ לְמוֹרַשׁ קִפֹּד וְאַגְמֵי־מָיִם	23
וְטֵאטֵאתִיהָ בְּמַטְאֲטֵא הַשְׁמֵד נְאֻם יְהוָה צְבָאוֹת[1] ׃ פ	
נִשְׁבַּע יְהוָה צְבָאוֹת[2] לֵאמֹר אִם־לֹא	24
...	
כִּי־יְהוָה צְבָאוֹת[2] יָעָץ וּמִי יָפֵר וְיָדוֹ הַנְּטוּיָה וּמִי יְשִׁיבֶנָּה: פ	27

[1] The refrain "declares the Lord of hosts" binds 22–23 together

[2] The refrain "the Lord of hosts" binds 24–27 together

Note: The similarity of these refrains argues that 24–27 is part of the Babylon *massa'*.

---

no remnant of Babel, nor child or offspring" (Van Wyk, "Isaiah 14:4b–21," 242).

83. Van Wyk, "Isaiah 14:4b–21," 242.

84. Van Wyk, "Isaiah 14:4b–21," 242.

Israel's Eschatological Enemy

The fourth reason the *mashal* has ended is the reference to Babylon and the destruction of the city. Watts correctly claims Isaiah 14:22–27 "balance[s] the words in 13:17–22."[85] The themes of complete destruction, utter abandonment, and the city becoming a habitation of animals are revisited in Isaiah 14:22–23, thus concluding the section of the *massa'* against Babylon.

While four reasons were presented why the *mashal* (proverb) has ended in Isaiah 14:21, there are also four reasons why the *massa'* (oracle) continues. First, the repetition of "arise" (קום) in Isaiah 14:22 ["Lest they arise" (14:21c) cf. "And I will arise" (14:22a)].[86] Blenkinsopp correctly explains that "arise" (קום) is functioning as a catchword to conclude the *mashal*.[87] The *mashal* began using a catchword, "rest" (נוח) in 14:1–3, and now concludes using a catchword, "arise" (קום) in 14:21–22. The use of "inheritance" (ירש — מורש) also argues for continuity ["lest they inherit" (14:21c) cf. "And I will make it [Babylon] an *inheritance* for the hedgehog" (14:23a)]. Third, the text has historically been divided after v. 23.[88] Fourth, the *mashal* ends thematically with an imperative to "prepare his sons for slaughter" and the annihilation of the king's children. While some claim these points of comparison create continuity with the *mashal*, the points of discontinuity, particularly the refrain "says the Lord of hosts," outweigh the points of continuity.

Conclusion of the Massa'

Views concerning the conclusion of the *massa'* abound. Smith claims Isaiah 14:24–27 is "an appendix about Assyria at the end of the Babylon oracle."[89]

---

85. Watts, *Isaiah 1–33*, 214. Smith believes the *mashal* extends to Isaiah 14:23 but still acknowledges the parallels between 14:22–23 and 13:17–22 (Smith, *Isaiah 1–39*, 318).

86. Van Wyk considers the use of קום as a concluding sign: "The addition of vv. 22–23 (or the insertion of 4b–21 before it) can best be explained by the use of קום in 21 and 22 (though with different subjects, mere *Stichwort*-principle); by the specific mentioning of Babel in 22 (actualization and by the resemblance between the thought of vv. 20c–21b expressing the desire that the tyrant should have no offspring and v. 22b, the declaration of Yahweh Himself that He would leave no remnant of Babel, nor child or offspring" (Van Wyk, "Isaiah 14:4b–21," 242). The use of קום creates continuity and discontinuity. Van Wyk emphasizes the discontinuity and Blenkinsopp the continuity.

87. Blenkinsopp explains, "The sons are not to rise up (*yaqûmû*) to take possession of the earth; Yahveh will rise up (*wĕqamti*) against them" (Blenkinsopp, *Isaiah 1–39*, 286). See also Van Wyk, "Isaiah 14:4b–21," 242.

88. The MT includes a *pᵉṭûḥā'* after verse 23. 1QIsa^a does not note this division.

89. Smith, *Isaiah 1–39*, 319. See also Mackay, *Study Commentary on Isaiah*, 360.

The Massa' against Babylon—Isaiah 13:2—14:2

Brueggemann believes it is a completely different *massa'*.⁹⁰ Roberts claims Isaiah 14:24–27 was placed here by a later editor who "was fully aware that the preceding taunt song . . . was really about an Assyrian tyrant."⁹¹ Oswalt rejects Roberts's redaction theory but concludes similarly that "the prophet has been using 'Babylon' in a representative way," and that representative use is made known in Isaiah 14:24–27.⁹² Sweeney extends the *massa'* against Babylon to the end of the chapter, including Isaiah 14:28–32 (the *massa'* against the Philistines) as an appendix.⁹³ Hassler takes an eschatological interpretation claiming, "The end-time Assyrian army defeats the end-time Babylonian army and temporarily kills the Babylonian king in Israel when he defends Israel because of their covenant (cf. Dan 9:27)."⁹⁴ This section first explains why the *massa'* concludes with Isaiah 14:27 and then argues for a "sign" function of Isaiah 14:24–27.

There are eight reasons why the *massa'* ends after Isaiah 14:27. First, Isaiah 14:28 begins with a temporal reference, "In the year King Ahaz died, this oracle (משא) came." Hassler notes that "all the other dated oracles in the book begin sections (1:1; 6:1; 7:1; 20:1; 36:1),"⁹⁵ thus it would be irregular for Isaiah 14:28 to not begin a new section. Second, Isaiah 14:28 introduces a new *massa'*.⁹⁶ Third the refrain, "Lord of hosts" concludes in

---

90. "This oracle constitutes yet another oracle against a nation, this time Assyria" (Brueggemann, *Isaiah*, 134).

91. Roberts, *First Isaiah*, 217.

92. Oswalt, *Book of Isaiah*, 326–27.

93. Sweeney, *Isaiah 1–39*, 221, 238. See also Childs, *Isaiah*, 127–28. Sweeney claims 14:28–32 is included with the *massa'* against Babylon because the "prophetic pronouncement . . . does not correspond to the standard form of the title in chs. 13–23" (Sweeney, *Isaiah 1–39*, 221). He claims the *massa'* to Philistia, "was included as an appendix to the pronouncement of Babylon to demonstrate the assertion that YHWH's intention to punish Assyria is applied to all the nations (14:26) and to demonstrate that YHWH alone will protect Zion (14:32; cf. 14:25). Consequently, the present unit comprises 13:1–14:32" (Sweeney, *Isaiah 1–39*, 221–22). Sweeney, however, admits there is "no overt connection to the preceding material" (Sweeney, *Isaiah 1–39*, 230). It seems more logical to identify 14:28–32 as its own section and group it with neighboring nations in whom Israel may be tempted to trust.

94. Hassler, "Isaiah 13:1—14:27," 108.

95. Hassler, "Isaiah 13:1—14:27," 105.

96. Hassler, "Isaiah 13:1—14:27," 105–6. Bailey agrees with Hassler and gives two additional reasons why Isaiah 14:24–27 is a self-contained unit: "(1) The transition from the previous prose to poetry; (2) The switch from Babylon (13:1—14:23) to Assyria as the subject; (3) The shift in speaker: Judeans, voicing a sarcastic lament, are now replaced by the deity who takes an oath; and (4) The formal introduction of a new 'oracle' at the end

Isaiah 14:27. Concerning this refrain, Brueggemann, believes the Babylonian *massa'* ends with Isaiah 14:23 and 14:24–27 is its own *massa'* because of the refrain, "Lord of hosts." He explains, "We notice the awesome title 'Lord of hosts' at beginning and end, a framing device for the entire oracle (vv. 24, 27)."[97] Brueggemann correctly notes the inclusio but fails to notice other structural clues which bind Isaiah 14:24–27 to the preceding context. For example, it has already been noted that "Lord of hosts" (יהוה צבאות) also corresponds to Isaiah 14:22–23.[98]

Fourth, the "hand" that is "stretched out" in Isaiah 14:26–27 is functioning as an inclusio with 13:2.[99] Fifth, there is a *pᵉṭûḥāʾ* after Isaiah 14:27. The sixth reason comes from Hassler, "The combination of 'stretched-out hand' and 'turn back' (14:27) conclude sections as refrains elsewhere in the book (9:12, 17, 21; 10:4)."[100]

Seventh, there are several catchwords which link Isaiah 14:24–27 to the *massa'* against Babylon. It has already been noted that Blenkinsopp identified the catchword קום, linking Isaiah 14:21–22 together, but Blenkinsopp failed to extend that catchword to 14:24. There are three uses of קום ("to arise") in the space of four verses, and they bind Isaiah 14:24–27 to both the *mashal* and 14:22–23.[101]

דמה ("to feel inclined [to do something], to be like") also occurs as a catchword. Isaiah 14:24–27 focuses on the way God's plan will be fulfilled. This focus is clear from the repeated use of the verb יעץ ("to plan, purpose;" three times [14:24, 26, 27]) and the noun (one time [14:26]). The accomplishing of God's plan, however, is introduced with the first-person perfect of דמה ("to like"). The parallelism between דמה ("to feel inclined, to be like") and יעץ ("to plan, purpose") is clear, but the allusion back to the king of Babylon's assertion to be like (דמה) the Most High is veiled. דמה ("to feel inclined, to be like") functions as catchword connecting verses 24–27 to the *massa'* and creating a contrast between the king of Babylon and the Lord. The pun in Hebrew even corresponds to English: while the king of

---

(v. 28)" (Bailey, "Expository Articles," 171).

97. Brueggemann, *Isaiah*, 134.

98. Hassler, "Isaiah 13:1—14:27," 105.

99. Motyer agrees, "The outstretched hand of verse 27 forms an inclusio with 13:2." Motyer, *Prophecy of Isaiah*, 146. See also Hassler, "Isaiah 13:1—14:27," 105.

100. Hassler, "Isaiah 13:1—14:27," 105.

101. The use of a three-word catchword is not without precedent. Watson references a three-word catchword in Isaiah 30:13–14 and 30:26 (Watson, *Classical Hebrew Poetry*, 288).

Babylon seeks to be "like" (דמה—"to be like") the Most High (14:14), the Most High does whatever he "likes" (דמה—"to feel inclined") (14:24). Thus, the first colon of the Lord's oath in Isaiah 14:24 hearkens back to 14:14 using דמה ("to feel inclined, to be like"); parallelism extends the second colon with יעץ ("to plan, purpose") and the text proceeds using יעץ as the key word to bind 24–27 together.

An additional catchword, occurring in Isaiah 14:19 and 25, is בוס ("to trample"). The king of Babylon is described as a trampled (בוס) corpse, and the Lord claims he is going to trample (בוס) the Assyrians on his mountain.[102] Roberts concludes, "Thus, the vocabulary of v. 25 links it both to the taunt song and to other passages in First Isaiah."[103]

---

102. Roberts, *First Isaiah*, 218.
103. Roberts, *First Isaiah*, 218.

Israel's Eschatological Enemy

Table 3.8. Isaiah 14:24–27's Structural Connection to the Massa' against Babylon

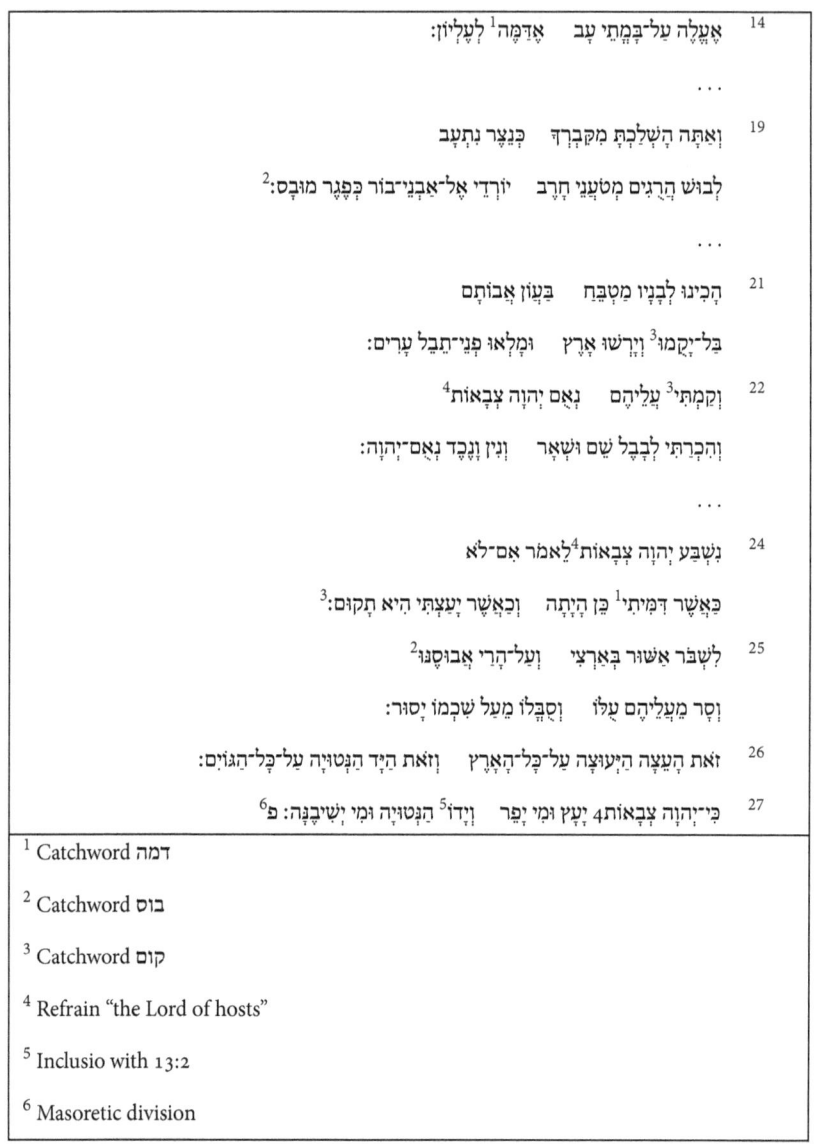

14	אֶעֱלֶה עַל־בָּמֳתֵי עָב אֶדַּמֶּה[1] לְעֶלְיוֹן׃
	...
19	וְאַתָּה הָשְׁלַכְתָּ מִקִּבְרְךָ כְּנֵצֶר נִתְעָב
	לְבֻשׁ הֲרֻגִים מְטֹעֲנֵי חָרֶב יוֹרְדֵי אֶל־אַבְנֵי־בוֹר כְּפֶגֶר מוּבָס׃[2]
	...
21	הָכִינוּ לְבָנָיו מַטְבֵּחַ בַּעֲוֺן אֲבוֹתָם
	בַּל־יָקֻמוּ[3] וְיָרְשׁוּ אָרֶץ וּמָלְאוּ פְנֵי־תֵבֵל עָרִים׃
22	וְקַמְתִּי עֲלֵיהֶם נְאֻם יְהוָה צְבָאוֹת[4]
	וְהִכְרַתִּי לְבָבֶל שֵׁם וּשְׁאָר וְנִין וָנֶכֶד נְאֻם־יְהוָה׃
	...
24	נִשְׁבַּע יְהוָה צְבָאוֹת[4] לֵאמֹר אִם־לֹא
	כַּאֲשֶׁר דִּמִּיתִי[1] כֵּן הָיָתָה וְכַאֲשֶׁר יָעַצְתִּי הִיא תָקוּם׃[3]
25	לִשְׁבֹּר אַשּׁוּר בְּאַרְצִי וְעַל־הָרַי אֲבוּסֶנּוּ[2]
	וְסָר מֵעֲלֵיהֶם עֻלּוֹ וְסֻבֳּלוֹ מֵעַל שִׁכְמוֹ יָסוּר׃
26	זֹאת הָעֵצָה הַיְּעוּצָה עַל־כָּל־הָאָרֶץ וְזֹאת הַיָּד הַנְּטוּיָה עַל־כָּל־הַגּוֹיִם׃
27	כִּי־יְהוָה צְבָאוֹת[4] יָעָץ וּמִי יָפֵר וְיָדוֹ[5] הַנְּטוּיָה וּמִי יְשִׁיבֶנָּה׃ פ[6]

[1] Catchword דמה

[2] Catchword בוס

[3] Catchword קום

[4] Refrain "the Lord of hosts"

[5] Inclusio with 13:2

[6] Masoretic division

The eighth reason Isaiah 14:24–27 is part of the *massa'* is the presence of common words consistent with the vocabulary of Isaiah 13:2—14:23. ארץ ("earth, land") occurs thirteen times (two times in 14:24–27). גוי ("nation") occurs six times (one time in 14:24–27). The phrase "all the earth (ארץ)" appears three times (13:5; 14:7, 26), and universal language is found throughout the *massa'*. The language of Isaiah 14:24–27 matches the language of 13:2—14:23.

While any one of these reasons may not be the strongest by itself, collectively they make a strong case that Isaiah 14:24–27 should be included with the *massa'* against Babylon. The question now turns to its function.

Function and Fulfillment of Isaiah 14:24–27

Isaiah 14:24–27 focuses on the Lord's intention to fulfill the Isaiah 13–14 *massa'*. First, the Lord swears an oath (נשבע), then the oath is transcribed, "Just as I like (דמה), thus it will be; and just as I purposed (יעץ), thus it will stand" (v. 24). The oath ends with two rhetorical questions which emphasize the certitude of fulfillment, "For the Lord of hosts has purposed (יעץ), and who will annul it? The *hand* is stretched out, and who will bring it back?" Between these assertions is the reference to Assyria.

The function of Isaiah 14:24–27 is a mystery to some. Wildberger simply states, "One cannot say for sure why this section was appended to the conclusion of 14:23."[104] Smith believes Isaiah 14:24–27 was fulfilled in Hezekiah's day: "Although the prophet gives no insight as to when or how this would eventually happen, the miraculous killing of 185,000 Assyrian troops in 701 BC at Jerusalem (37:36–37) seems to fulfill this prediction."[105] Motyer agrees with Smith's fulfillment but claims it is a short-term sign which validates the eschatological judgment: "The historical act which they see [the Lord's destruction of Assyria] will be replicated in the eschatological judgment on the whole world and now acts as a guarantee of it."[106] Hassler rejects both this fulfillment and function, and argues for an eschatological fulfillment:

> For the purpose of this study, Isaiah 10:5–34 will serve as the primary text of comparison. Isaiah 14:25 repeats 10:27 almost identically, establishing a tie of some kind:
> - "[Assyria's] burden will be removed from your [Israel's] shoulders and his yoke from your neck" (10:27).
> - "[Assyria's] yoke will be removed from them [Israel] and his burden removed from their shoulder" (14:25).[107]

---

104. Wildberger, *Isaiah 13–27*, 79.
105. Smith, *Isaiah 1–39*, 321.
106. Motyer, *Prophecy of Isaiah*, 146.
107. Hassler, "Isaiah 13:1—14:27," 107.

Hassler's position is based almost completely on the connection to Isaiah 10:27. He exegetes Isaiah 10, demonstrates it is eschatological, and concludes, "To summarize, the ancient fulfillment of Assyria's demise (the killing of Sennacherib's 185,000 troops) has much appeal, but a futuristic fulfillment prevails primarily because of the oracle's end-time context, and because of the link with Isaiah 10:27, an end-time text."[108] Thus, his argument is twofold: (1) the eschatological context of Isaiah 13–14; and (2) the intertextual connection with Isaiah 10:27.

According to Hassler, the function of Isaiah 14:24–27 is to describe how the king of Babylon dies the first time. He states, "The end-time Assyrian army defeats the end-time Babylonian army and temporarily kills the Babylonian king in Israel when he defends Israel because of their covenant (cf. Dan 9:27)."[109] Hassler's interpretation of Isaiah 14:24–27 is based upon a tenuous connection with Isaiah 10:27 which must be rejected. Even if one agrees with Hassler's theology, the function of Isaiah 14:24–27 fails to correspond with the immediate context. Isaiah 14:22–23, even according to Hassler, describes the comprehensive destruction of the Babylonians by the Lord.[110] It does not make sense that Isaiah would then include a description of the Lord's annihilation of Assyria three years earlier.

It seems better to see the reference to Assyria's destruction functioning as a short-term sign to validate the long-term prophecy. Other scholars, while disagreeing with the timeframe, agree with this function. Blenkinsopp states, "The reader is also being told once again that the prophetic message about Assyria provides the key for interpreting the course of events during the rise and fall of the Babylonian Empire."[111] Childs believes the Assyrian conquest was historical to the redactor but still agrees with its function: "Just as God's plan against Assyria has unfolded and Assyria has been destroyed, so also the promise to include equally arrogant Babylon is part of the selfsame promise."[112] Sweeney, again, agrees with the function:

> Isaiah 14:24–27 presents the fall of Babylon and the Babylonian ruling dynasty as the fulfillment of YHWH's promise to destroy

---

108. Hassler, "Isaiah 13:1—14:27," 110.
109. Hassler, "Isaiah 13:1—14:27," 108.
110. Hassler, "Isaiah 13:1—14:27," 48.
111. Blenkinsopp, *Isaiah 1–39*, 289.
112. Childs, *Isaiah*, 127. Elsewhere Childs explains, "The function of vv. 26–27 is both to summarize the oracle: *this* is the purpose, and to evaluate it: it will succeed because it is from Yahweh" (Childs, *Isaiah and the Assyrian Crisis*, 129).

Assyria. Although these verses say nothing about Babylon, they point to YHWH's oath as a decision made concerning the entire world and all nations. Babylon, as the head of the nations in the mid-6th century, would provide a natural target for such an oath in this period and an analogy for the world-dominating Assyrian empire of the late 8th century.[113]

Sweeney is correct; it is an oath, but 14:24–27 is not a redacted comparison with sixth-century Babylon. Instead, this passage serves to validate the long-term prophecy of Babylon's destruction at the hand of the Lord. How does the reader know that God will destroy Babylon? Because he will, very shortly, destroy the Assyrian army.

Thus, the historical setting of the *massa'* is likely around the days of Isaiah 36–39. Perhaps the city was surrounded by Assyria at the time of its proclamation. What better way for the Lord to validate a long-term prophecy than by wiping out an army that seems on the brink of victory. The sickness of Hezekiah and coming of the Babylonian envoy probably preceded the invasion of Sennacherib.[114] Thus Hezekiah is healed, the Babylonian envoy comes, Isaiah utters this *massa'* against Babylon, and the Lord validates the long-term prophecy against Babylon by annihilating Assyria. Perhaps the *massa'* was even given in the days of Isaiah 36:1 when all the fortified cities had fallen. The fall of Jerusalem looked certain, but the Lord demonstrated that he is king over all the nations.

ESCHATOLOGY IN ISAIAH 13:2—14:2

Having discussed preliminary issues and analyzed the structure of Isaiah 13:1—14:27, this section now argues that Isaiah 13:2—14:2 is eschatological. Some scholars believe Isaiah 13 is historical. Young, for example, believes all of Isaiah 13 describes the fall of Babylon at the hand of the Medes.[115] Others believe part of Isaiah 13 is eschatological and part of it is historical. Oswalt, for example, claims Isaiah 13:2-13 is eschatological, but 13:14-22

---

113. Sweeney, *Isaiah 1–39*, 236.

114. Smith states, "Chaps. 38–39 are in chronological order, but they both took place before chaps. 36–37" (Smith, *Isaiah 1–39*, 654).

115. Young recognizes the Medes did not fulfill all that is described in 13:19-22 and claims Babylon gradually came to a state of desolation (Young, *Book of Isaiah*, 1:427).

Israel's Eschatological Enemy

is historical.[116] Based on exegesis, Isaiah 13:2–22 describes two battles, and they are both eschatological.

Two Battles

Young correctly claims the prophecy in Isaiah 13 is one unified prophecy concerning one time period, but he incorrectly asserts the text concerns historic Babylon. Young reads Isaiah 13:14–22 back into 13:2–13 which cannot be supported exegetically. This first section argues for two battles in Isaiah 13. Having established that there are two battles, this section then contends that the former battle is eschatological.

The Armies

There are three armies (perhaps four) in Isaiah 13 fighting two different battles. There is an angelic army fighting against a united nations force, presumably under the control of the king of Babylon (13:2–13), and a Median army slaughtering the inhabitants of Babylon and destroying the city (13:14–22).

God's Army in Isaiah 13:2–13

The first reason why the battle described in Isaiah 13 concerns eschatological Babylon is the description of God's army. Roberts believes the army being summoned is a human army, "The motif of raising a signal flag for Yahweh to summon humans is common in Isaiah of Jerusalem (5:26; 11:10, 12; 18:3; 30:17; 31:9)."[117] Roberts believes Yahweh is commanding his generals in verse 2 to raise a banner and bring the men together for battle. Two observations, however, support an angelic interpretation: the description of the army (13:3) and the origin of the army (13:5).

The description of the army in Isaiah 13:3 requires an angelic interpretation.

This angelic army is engaged in a holy war.

---

116. Oswalt, *Isaiah*, 200.
117. Roberts, *First Isaiah*, 197.

3a. I have commanded,	אֲנִי צִוֵּיתִי 3a
3b. My sanctified ones.	לִמְקֻדָּשָׁי 3b
3c. Indeed, I have called my warriors for my anger,	גַּם קָרָאתִי גִבּוֹרַי לְאַפִּי 3c
3d. Those who rejoice in my eminence	עַלִּיזֵי גַאֲוָתִי: 3d

    Isaiah describes God's army in Isaiah 13 with three "abstract from concrete" metaphors.[118] Holiness is abstract, but God's warriors are concrete. By describing the army as "holy," Isaiah contrasts them with the sinners who are destined for destruction in verse 11. Similarly, God's army is described as "ones who exult in God's eminence" (עַלִּיזֵי גַאֲוָתִי), and this description contrasts with the "arrogance of the proud" (גְּאוֹן זֵדִים) and "eminence of tyrants" (גַּאֲוַת עָרִיצִים) in verse 11. Two of the three metaphors highlight not the military might of the warriors, but their relationship with the Lord. The one description that emphasizes their military strength is augmented to describe their purpose, "to mete out God's anger." Concerning this description of God's army, Smith explains, "It makes more sense to interpret these warriors as God's holy troops in his heavenly army who have dedicated themselves for holy war (cf. Josh 3:5; Deut 23:9–14)."[119]

    Motyer disagrees and claims God's army in Isaiah 13 is a human army, specifically, a wicked army.[120] He explains that the "holy ones," "refers not to sanctity of character but to status, as set apart for a divine service, the 'holy war' (Dt. 20; 23:9<10>; 1 Sa. 21:5)."[121] Motyer is correct that the general meaning of קדש is "to separate,"[122] but the purpose of the separation in a military context would be holiness. God's "holy ones" were set apart for "holy war," and they were supposed to be holy. Deuteronomy 23:9 [H: 10], which Motyer references, states, "When you go out as an army against your enemies, then you will keep yourself from every wicked thing (דְּבַר רָע)."[123] God's army is separated from wickedness because God is with them (Deut 23:14).

---

    118. Watson, *Classical Hebrew Poetry*, 314.

    119. Smith, *Isaiah 1-39*, 299.

    120. Motyer appears to be building off Young's exegesis (Young, *Book of Isaiah*, 1:417). See also Knoblet, "Investigation of Isaiah Thirteen," 45; Alexander, *Prophecies of Isaiah*, 270.

    121. Motyer, *Prophecy of Isaiah*, 137.

    122. Kornfeld, "קדש," *TDOT* 12:523.

    123. Deuteronomy 20 and 1 Samuel 21 also speak of the purity/holiness of the armies.

Israel's Eschatological Enemy

That God is with this army is also evident through the use of first-person pronouns (Isa 13:2). Miller agrees, "The use of the first-person suffix might suggest that these warriors are indeed Yahweh's assembly. Most important is the use of the term *mᵉquddāš*, sanctified, consecrated," which belongs to the practice of holy war, in which the soldiers were purified and set under certain taboos before battle."[124] Miller also draws a parallel example in Joel 3:9 [H: 4:9] where holy war is being declared and Yahweh's army is being assembled for battle.[125] The contextual and intertextual evidence favors a sanctified host.

Concerning "those who rejoice in my eminence" (עֲלִיזֵי גַאֲוָתִי), Motyer translates the phrase, "who rejoice in my triumph." He calls his own translation "dubious," then claims the literal translation of the phrase is "my exulting ones of arrogance." He then explains, "The Lord calls them *my* not because he approves their arrogance but because, in all their arrogance, he owns them and directs the overflowings of their arrogance to his own ends."[126] Motyer's interpretation is unlikely. Motyer correctly recognizes that God is speaking and the first-person pronoun refers to God. He incorrectly believes, however, the pronoun refers to the entire construct chain rather than the absolute noun, גאוה (eminence, arrogance). It is true that, according to Waltke and O'Connor, "In an attributive genitive, a pronominal suffix is attached to the genitive but usually modifies the whole chain."[127] Weingreen, however, qualifies this rule. He explains there are three exceptions: possessive genitives, subjective genitives, and objective genitives. He then states, "Our interest here is restricted to such cases where the noun in the genitive (with a suffix attached to it) expresses the idea of a *quality* which it gives to the noun immediately preceding it in the construct state."[128] Weingreen later explains this "qualifying effect [is] similar to that of an adjective upon the noun with which it is associated."[129] If Isaiah 13:3 is an attributive genitive as Motyer suggests, one would translate it "my arrogant exulting ones."

There are four reasons to reject Motyer's translation. The first argument comes from the context. The previous two first-person suffixes (my holy ones, my anger) are possessive suffixes, so one would expect גאותי

---

124. Miller, "Divine Council," 102.
125. Miller, "Divine Council," 103–4.
126. Motyer, *Prophecy of Isaiah*, 137 (emphasis original).
127. Waltke and O'Connor, *Introduction to Biblical Hebrew Syntax*, 150.
128. Weingreen, "Construct-Genitive Relation in Hebrew Syntax," 50.
129. Weingreen, "Construct-Genitive Relation in Hebrew Syntax," 50–51.

(my eminence/arrogance) to be possessive as well and to be translated similarly. Concerning the attributive genitive, Weingreen states, "We are not concerned here with cases where the dependence of the noun in the construct state upon the noun immediately following it (in the genitive) conveys the idea of possession, נְשֵׁי־בָנָיו 'the wives of his sons', i.e., his sons' wives.'"[130] Since Isaiah 13:3 is possessive, it is unlikely an attributive genitive.

Second, translating עליזי גאותי "my arrogant exulting ones" creates even more ambiguity in the text which is unexpected at this point. What are these individuals exulting in? Motyer's "dubious" translation, "who rejoice in my triumph" resolves this tension, but his translation is stepping outside the text ("in my triumph" is not in the text).

Third, there seems to be an inclusio between 13:3 and 13:11.[131] The contrast between God's eminence and the rulers' arrogance is destroyed with Motyer's interpretation.

Finally, it seems better to take עליזי גאותי (ones who rejoice in my eminence) as an adverbial genitive where גאותי is a "genitive of a mediated object." Waltke and O'Connor explain, "The relationship of the genitive and implicit verb may be of the sort usually mediated by a preposition; the *genitive of a mediated object* involves the relation C does to/by/with G."[132] Thus:

> [construct noun] does "in" [genitive noun]
> [those who rejoice] "in" [my exultation]
> those who rejoice in my exultation

Motyer's dubious translation, "who rejoice in my triumph," even follows the "genitive of a mediated object" formula, though he has to supply the object. It seems better to understand the army in Isaiah 13:3 as a righteous, holy army of God.

---

130. Weingreen, "Construct-Genitive Relation in Hebrew Syntax," 50. While Weingreen claims exemption for possessive genitives, his illustrations of the attributive genitive in the succeeding pages use possessive genitives. Simply stating it is possessive and thus it cannot be an attributive genitive does not work.

131. Note the use of first-person pronouns and similar vocabulary mentioned above.

132. Waltke and O'Connor, *Introduction to Biblical Hebrew Syntax*, 146 (emphasis theirs).

Israel's Eschatological Enemy

The origin of the army in Isaiah 13:3 also requires an angelic interpretation.

Concerning the origin of this army, Kaiser writes, "Verse 5 once again emphasizes the weirdness of what is taking place: the attackers are not familiar neighbouring nation [sic] but hosts who come from the uttermost ends of the earth, from the unknown distance, in order to carry out the anger of Yahweh."[133] Kaiser is correct; the language is "weird" because God's army originates in heaven.

5a. Coming from a distant land,	בָּאִים מֵאֶרֶץ מֶרְחָק	5a
5b. From the ends of the heavens.	מִקְצֵה הַשָּׁמָיִם	5b
5c. The Lord and his instruments of indignation;	יְהוָה וּכְלֵי זַעְמוֹ	5c
5d. To destroy all the earth.	לְחַבֵּל כָּל־הָאָרֶץ׃	5d

The key phrase concerning the origin of God's army is מקצה השמים (from the ends of the heavens). The more common phrase is מקצה הארץ (from the ends of the earth) as found in Deuteronomy 28:49; Psalm 135:7; Isaiah 5:26; 42:10; 43:6; and Jeremiah 10:13; 12:12; 51:16. "From the ends of the earth" occurs nine times (Deut 13:7; 28:49, 64; Isa 5:26; 42:10; 43:6; Jer 25:33; Psa 61:2; 135:7) and always references a place where man is able to walk. "From the end of the heavens," however, occurs three times (Deut 4:32; Isa 13:5; Psa 19:6) and always references a place beyond which man is able to walk.[134] Geyer explains, "Some of [Yahweh's forces] may indeed have been terrestrial but which are of significance only so far as they join forces with the heavenly host."[135] Wildberger takes a similar position: "To be sure, *end of the heavens* in 13:5 means the same thing as *end of the earth*, but the way it is formulated is shaped by the notion that Yahweh was able to summon the heavenly hosts to fight in his battles."[136] Smith correctly explains:

> The impression is that people from the far ends of the earth will be willing to serve as instruments of God's wrath in order to bring

---

133. Kaiser, *Isaiah: 13–39*, 15.

134. Deuteronomy 4:32 is a rhetorical question, for just as the Israelites cannot travel back in time and question Adam, neither can they travel to the end of the heavens.

135. Geyer, "Twisting Tiamat's Tail," 167. Geyer does then say that "ends of the heavens" is only a superlative of "ends of the earth," and claims the army is an earthly army. Geyer's "superlative" explanation fails to convince considering other uses of this phrase in Scripture.

136. Wildberger, *Isaiah 13–27*, 21 (emphasis original).

destruction on his enemies. The group also comprises those who are coming "from the ends of the heavens," an idea that suggests that these may be the same warriors seen by Elisha, the heavenly hosts who fight for God (2 Kgs 6:16–17), not just human troops.[137]

While it is possible to claim there is a merism in Isaiah 13:5 and the armies of God are coming from everywhere, it is more likely God's warriors are coming literally from heaven to reinforce, assist, or more likely deliver the remaining beleaguered remnant on earth. While recognizing ambiguity elsewhere, Miller is confident of this conclusion, "Whatever the case may be on these various points where certainty seems impossible, there can be no equivocation over the fact that the prophet announces a day of destruction, in which the divine army of Yahweh and possibly other armies will carry on a great holy war of judgement."[138]

United Nations Enemy

While Isaiah 13:3 describes God's army as holy ones who exult in his eminence, Isaiah 13:4 describes an army that is gathering for war. Several commentators claim this is an additional description of God's army. For example, Hayes and Irvine believe Isaiah 13:4 is God's Assyrian army coming to destroy Babylon.[139] Clements argues it is God's Babylonian army, coming to judge wicked Judah.[140] Young states it is God's Persian army which is led by Cyrus.[141] Geyer takes a mythological view.[142] Smith contends Isaiah 13 is eschatological and the army in 4ab is God's army: "Verse 4 merely describes the great noise created by many people who are gathering together as God's army."[143] All five believe the army in 4ab is God's army even though they differ concerning the historical setting and timing.

Rather, Isaiah 13:4a–d arguably describes God's enemy which is being marshalled together to do a battle royale with God Almighty.

---

137. Smith, *Isaiah 1–39*, 299–300. See also Brueggemann, *Isaiah*, 116.
138. Miller, "Divine Council," 13.
139. Hayes and Irvine, *Isaiah*, 224–25.
140. Clements, *Isaiah 1–39*, 134.
141. Young, *Book of Isaiah*, 1:418. See also Mackay, *Study Commentary on Isaiah*, 323–24.
142. Geyer, "Twisting Tiamat's Tail."
143. Smith, *Isaiah 1–39*, 299.

Israel's Eschatological Enemy

4a. A sound of a multitude in the hills;	קוֹל הָמוֹן בֶּהָרִים	4a
4b. A likeness of many people	דְּמוּת עַם־רָב	4b
4c. A roaring sound of kingdoms,	קוֹל שְׁאוֹן מַמְלָכוֹת	4c
4d. Of nations gathering together.	גּוֹיִם נֶאֱסָפִים	4d

Two reasons are proffered; both build off the use of "kingdoms." First, an army of "kingdoms" must refer to a united nations force. Clements disagrees:

> The references to kingdoms and nations should not be taken as an indication that the prophet was envisaging a world-wide eschatological battle between the nations of the world. Rather, the terms reflect the different ethnic elements which made up the armies of the ancient imperial powers, and the large scale of the conquests which Babylon achieved.[144]

Clements notes the army consists of "different ethnic elements." This assessment could come from the word "nations," but not "kingdoms." Furthermore, the parallel presence of kingdoms reveals "nations" likely does not refer to ethnic diversity either. Clements, in a different publication, presents "three major aspects of race, government, and territory" to the meaning of "nation" (גּוֹי). He then states:

> The aspect of government is also important, as is indicated by the frequent use of *goy* in parallelism with *mamlakhah*, "kingdom." In such cases, we are to think of each *goy* as constituting a separate kingdom, each ruled by its own separate *melekh* ("king"), even though the measure of independence enjoyed by such kingdoms naturally varied from case to case. It was clearly considered normal in ancient Israel for each *goy* to be ruled by its own particular *melekh*, who stood at its head (Isa. 14:6, 18; 41:2; Jer. 25:14).[145]

Thus, the parallelism with "kingdom" (ממלכות) reveals "nation" (גּוֹי) in Isaiah 13:4d must refer to governmental nations. Geyer correctly explains, "It is true that *gôyim* in v. 4 may refer to the different ethnic elements in an army, but surely not *mamlekôt* which in historical terms would imply a united nations' force under the supreme command of Babylon, for which there is no evidence."[146] Finding a fulfillment in the Assyrians, Babylonians,

---

144. Clements, *Isaiah 1–39*, 134.

145. Clements, "גּוֹי," *TDOT* 2:428. It is also noteworthy that Clements identifies Isaiah 14:6, 18 as referring to kingdoms.

146. Geyer, "Twisting Tiamat's Tail," 167.

or Medes and Persians could potentially account for the gathering "peoples" (גוים) but certainly not "kingdoms" (ממלכות). Geyer comes close to the right conclusion but rejects it for theological and historical reasons.[147]

"Kingdoms" and "nations" should also be understood as actual kingdoms because they are consistently used this way in the oracle against Babylon. "Kingdoms" occurs three times, and each time it refers to the kingdoms of the earth (13:4, 19; 14:16). In Isaiah 13:19, Babylon is described appositively as the "glory of kingdoms." More forceful is the description of the king of Babylon in Isaiah 14:19 as one who made "kingdoms quake." Thus, the kingdoms in 13:4 are also earthly kingdoms and not likely a description of the Lord's army.

"Nations" (גוים) occurs six times in Isaiah 13–14, five of which are in chapter 14. The king of Babylon is described as one who "ruled the nations" (14:4) and "defeated the nations" (14:12). Thus, the king of Babylon is the ruler of the kingdoms, and, by implication, the ruler and commander of these kingdoms of nations in 13:4.[148]

The final use of "nations" comes at the very end where the Lord's hand is "stretched out over all the nations." This "stretching out" of the hand is not in governance but in a demonstration of power and subjugation. The Lord, in Isaiah 14:24–27, is described as the "Lord of hosts" which corresponds to Isaiah 13:4c ("The Lord of hosts musters the army for battle"). Just as the Lord of hosts demonstrates his subjugation over the nations in Isaiah 14:24–27, so also does the Lord of hosts demonstrate his dominion over the nations in 13:4 by wiping them out in 13:6–8. Thus, the kingdoms and nations in Isaiah 13–14 always refer to the earthly kingdoms and nations who oppose God. They gather in 13:4 to do battle against the Lord, not for the Lord.

Armies of Isaiah 13:14–22

The "battle" of Isaiah 13:14–22 is between two peoples, the Babylonians and the Medes. While 13:2–13 uses ambiguity and metaphors to describe the army, 13:14–22 clearly reveals the peoples involved. While 13:2–13 describes one army composed of angels and the other army composed of

---

147. Geyer requires a historical event. Since he cannot find a historical event, he concludes it is mythological.

148. The other two uses of "nations" in the *mashal* refer to the "kings of the nations." For a discussion of these two references see chapter 4.

kingdoms of nations, neither description fits the Babylonians or the Medes described in 13:14–22.

Conclusion

Taking Isaiah 13:3 by itself, one could conclude that God's army is the nation of Israel or, more unlikely, some righteous gentile army. When one puts all the details together, however, it is unlikely that God's army consists solely of physical men who are holy, who are warriors, who exult in God's eminence, and who originate from all over the place to follow the Lord into battle. Rather, Isaiah 13:2–5 presents an eschatological battle between the Lord and the kingdoms of the earth.

Isaiah 13:14–22, however, describes a different scene. Rather than "kingdoms of nations," only two kingdoms are involved, the Medes and Babylonians. Instead of being described as holy warriors, rejoicing in God's eminence, the warriors are doing rather ungodly deeds.

The Place of Battle

The place of battle in Isaiah 13:2–13 is not explicitly stated but could suggest Jerusalem. The place of battle in Isaiah 13:14–22, however, is clearly the area in and around Babylon (Isa 13:14–19). Isaiah 13:2–13 starts on the "hills" (4a, הר) and extends to all the earth (5b). While a strong exegetical argument cannot be made, the description in Isaiah 13:4 *allows* for a siege of Jerusalem from which the Lord delivers Israel. The siege of Jerusalem is a regular theme in the Old Testament. Motyer takes a historical view of Isaiah 13, but concerning 13:4 he states, "Isaiah is drawing on traditional terminology depicting Zion as beset on all sides by enemies (Cf. Pss. 46:3<4>, 6<7>; 65:7<8>; 83:2–3)."[149] Even if one rejects the Jerusalem siege in Isaiah 13:2–13, the place of battle in 13:2–13 eventually encompasses all the earth; whereas, the place of battle in 13:14–22 concerns only the region of Babylon.

The Leaders of the Armies

The Lord is clearly the leader in Isaiah 13:2–13, but the leader in Isaiah 13:14–22 is unstated. The Lord "stirs up" the Medes, but he does not lead

---

149. Motyer, *Prophecy of Isaiah*, 137.

them. Those who see a historic view of Isaiah 13 claim the Lord is emphasizing his sovereignty over the situation and meting out justice through an earthly ruler. There are three reasons to reject this proposal and recognize that the Lord himself is leading the armies in Isaiah 13:2–13. The first reason, referenced above in the description of God's army, is the use of first-person pronouns in Isaiah 13:3. Miller explains, "The use of the first-person suffix might suggest that these warriors are indeed Yahweh's assembly."[150] The use of first-person pronouns also illustrates God's nearness to these troops (cf. Isa 40:26) which is why the troops must be holy.

The second reason is because the Lord is described as "mustering an army" in Isaiah 13:4c. The one who commands in Isaiah 13:2 and speaks in the first-person in 13:3 is finally introduced at the end of 13:4.

| 4c. The Lord of hosts is mustering, | יְהוָה צְבָאוֹת מְפַקֵּד | 4c |
| 4d. An army for battle. | צְבָא מִלְחָמָה | 4d |

Wildberger explains,

> Ancient Israel thus reckoned with the possibility that cosmic or heavenly powers could intervene to assist Israel's warriors, or, more specifically yet: human and heavenly powers were able to work in consort when in battle. Thus it is most fitting to presume that, according to v. 4b, Yahweh himself is the one who musters the troops who are going to war.[151]

The Lord himself is the one going to war.

The third reason is because the Lord is the destroyer in Isaiah 13:6.

| 6a. Wail! For the day of the Lord is near, | הֵילִילוּ כִּי קָרוֹב יוֹם יְהוָה | 6a |
| 6b. Like destruction from Destroyer it will come | כְּשֹׁד מִשַּׁדַּי יָבוֹא׃ | 6b |

Watts explains, "*The Destroyer* is the Divine name, *Shaddai*, which is common as אל שדי 'El Shaddai' in the patriarchal section of Genesis and in Job."[152] The poet uses a simile and compares the day of the Lord to a day of El Shaddai's destruction. The poet also creates a play on words between destruction (שד) and El Shaddai (שדי). By calling God שדי, he also emphasizes God's destructive capabilities. Thus, the day of the Lord has come, and the Destroyer has come to destroy.

150. Miller, "Divine Council," 102.
151. Wildberger, *Isaiah 13–27*, 21.
152. Watts, *Isaiah 1–33*, 197 (emphasis original).

Israel's Eschatological Enemy

While the leader of the army in Isaiah 13:2–13 is the Lord himself, the leader of the army in 13:14–22 is only stirred up by the Lord.

17a Behold, I am stirring up against them the Medes	הִנְנִי מֵעִיר עֲלֵיהֶם אֶת־מָדָי 17a

Smith explains:

> The reference to the Medes as the nation that God will use to defeat the Babylonians is parallel to God's use of Assyria as his rod of punishment in 10:5 or God's sending Nebuchadnezzar to defeat Judah in Jer 25:1,9. In each case God was the one directing the course of history through the use of strong armies.[153]

The Lord is not leading the Medes the way that he is leading the army in Isaiah 13:2–13; rather, he awakens them for battle. The way God uses the Medes is similar to the way he has used other nations in history to accomplish his will. Therefore, the leader of the army in 13:14–22 is not the Lord.

The Results of the Battles

Finally, the results of these battles are different. The first battle results in a cosmic destruction. The entire earth is laid waste (13:5–6), and nearly all mankind is killed (13:12). The second battle contains uncompassionate destruction which focuses on a city and its inhabitants.

The Worldwide Comprehensive Battle—Isaiah 13:2–13

Isaiah 13:5 declares the cosmic comprehensiveness of the Lord's destruction; it is revisited in 13:9–11 and summarized in 13:13. Isaiah 13:5 claims God's army is going to "destroy the whole land." Clements makes a lexical argument that חבל does not connote a worldwide destruction, "The translation destroy (Heb. *ḥabbēl*) is probably rather strong for a verb meaning fundamentally 'to bind, twist' (*BDB ḥbl*, I; a second stem, *ḥbl*, II, meaning 'to ruin, destroy', is also listed)."[154] Geyer also claims חבל I is the foundational meaning to חבל. He contends there is a mythological background to the text and suggests the translation "he will twist the world."[155] Contextually,

---

153. Smith, *Isaiah 1–39*, 303.
154. Clements, *Isaiah 1–39*, 134 (emphasis his).
155. Geyer, "Twisting Tiamat's Tail," 172. Geyer claims the idea is still destruction,

The Massa' against Babylon—Isaiah 13:2—14:2

Isaiah 13:5 concerns a battle and destruction; thus, it seems best to translate חבל as "to destroy."[156]

The extent of the destruction is emphasized with the adjective "all." Miller correctly explains, "If indeed *kol-ha'areṣ* is to be interpreted as the whole earth, as seems to be the case, the picture is one of final destruction in the Day of Yahweh—a destruction wrought by Yahweh and his heavenly army (vs. 5a)."[157] Isaiah 13:5 narrates a cosmic destruction, not a localized one.

Young believes this prophecy was fulfilled in the days of Cyrus, "Great was the Babylonian empire; indeed, in all world history it was the first of empires, and in its destruction all the earth had been involved."[158] Young applies the adjective "all" to Babylon's influence. Wolf recognizes the cataclysmic language but refuses to let go of the 539 BC fulfillment: "In its ultimate fulfillment this day looks ahead to the judgment on the world during the Great Tribulation and the second coming of Christ. The near fulfillment has in view the campaign against Babylon in 539 B.C."[159] History, however, does not support a 539 BC fulfillment.[160]

The manner of man's annihilation is described in verse 8: "Each man will look with terror at his friend; faces of flames will be their faces." The poet does not seem content to describe their pain in a collective sense. Here he uses a dramatic effect of zooming in and looking at God's enemies' destruction from an individual perspective.

The poet describes what each man sees as he looks at his friend: "faces of flames." The NET ("their faces are flushed red") incorrectly interprets the flames as a metaphor describing the color of their faces. The emotion in Isaiah 13:8 is not anger or embarrassment (emotions that cause one to blush), but fear. Fear leads to a pale face (Nah 2:10). In what way should faces of flames be understood? Perhaps this is not a poetic device and their faces are literally on fire.

Continued support for a comprehensive destruction comes from the succeeding context. Isaiah 13:11 references the "world" again (תבל this

---

but the way destruction is communicated is through a mythological allusion.

156. Smith agrees, "This obscure connection is not preferred, for the usual translation 'destroy' makes perfectly good sense" (Smith, *Isaiah 1–39*, 300n50).

157. Miller, "Divine Council," 103.

158. Young, *Book of Isaiah*, 1:418.

159. Wolf, *Interpreting Isaiah*, 110.

160. See "Extent of the Destruction" below.

time). Isaiah 13:13 states that the earth (ארץ) will shake (רעש) from its place (ממקומה). Watts explains, "הארץ 'the earth' may point to the world or to a particular land. The setting seems to lean toward a universal meaning."[161] The use of "world" (תבל) also argues for a universal meaning.[162] Thus, the cosmic destruction is revealed not only in Isaiah 13:5 but also in 13:11.

The extent of the human destruction is most clearly illustrated in Isaiah 13:12.

| 12a. I will make mankind scarcer than refined gold, | אוֹקִיר אֱנוֹשׁ מִפָּז | 12a |
| 12b. And humanity scarcer than the gold of Ophir. | וְאָדָם מִכֶּתֶם אוֹפִיר | 12b |

Motyer explains, "This verse is a fearful image of extermination: people with the same scarcity value as the most precious metal. *Ophir*, which is of uncertain location, was famous for fine gold (*cf.* 1 Ki. 9:28; Jb. 28:16)."[163] First-person verbs continue in this final line as the poet describes the extent of the punishment which God will mete out. The verb is ellipsed in the second line allowing the poet to insert אוֹפִיר (Ophir) and thus create two literary devices. First, the verb אוֹקִיר (I will make) creates assonance and alliteration with אוֹפִיר (Ophir) making a clear bicolon. Second, he intensifies the first line by elaborating on the gold in the second line. As if mankind becoming as scarce as gold were not enough, the poet heightens the scarcity by claiming they will be sparser than this specific kind of gold, the gold of Ophir.

Finally, Isaiah 13:13 concludes with a description of the heavens and earth shaking.

| 13a. Therefore, I will shake the heavens | עַל־כֵּן שָׁמַיִם אַרְגִּיז | 13a |
| 13b. and the earth will shake from its place | וְתִרְעַשׁ הָאָרֶץ מִמְּקוֹמָהּ | 13b |

The Lord himself is, again, the one who shakes the heavens and earth. "Heaven" and "earth" form a merism depicting universal upheaval. Smith explains, "The heavens and earth itself will totter and shake (13:13; 24:19–20). These descriptions portray the enormous power of God and the hopelessness of surviving his onslaught."[164] Thus 13:2–13 depicts a universal upheaval which affects the heavens and earth.

---

161. Watts, *Isaiah 1–33*, 198.
162. See chapter four, "Makes the World a Wilderness."
163. Motyer, *Prophecy of Isaiah*, 139 (emphasis original).
164. Smith, *Isaiah 1–39*, 302.

The Massa' against Babylon—Isaiah 13:2—14:2

Isaiah 13:14–22, however, describes a local confrontation between the Medes and the Babylonians which results in a "this-worldly" destruction—fleeing (14), execution (15), dashing of children (16a), plundering of houses (16b), and raping of women (16c). Smith explains,

> No one will be left alive; every man, woman, and child will die. Even the small innocent children will be mercilessly and savagely killed while their parents helplessly watch. Their wives will be raped; anarchy and inhumanity will reign. There will be no safe place where one can hide, not even in a person's own home (13:16). These verses picture the horrors of war and the inhuman suffering of those who are defeated in battle.[165]

Thus, the individual horrors of an earthly war are pictured in Isaiah 13:14–16; a very different destruction than the one described in 13:2–13.

Motyer recognizes the theological difficulty of having the "day of the Lord" army rape women and dash children, but he maintains that Isaiah 13 describes one battle. Concerning Isaiah 13:14–16, he states,

> No protection (14), no escape (15) and now, no mercy [16]. Should any reach home it will be only to see all they held dear destroyed: the children they begat, the homes they built, the wives they loved. How is all this to be understood as the day *of the LORD* (6)? In a word, the answer is that this is what people are like to each other (*cf.* verse 18).[166]

Motyer has stepped outside the text and created a third group of "attackers," other civilians. It is more plausible to identify the attackers as the Medes who are referenced in the next verse.

The destruction continues through the rest of the chapter, transitioning from the people of Babylon to the city itself. The destruction of the city is complete, leaving no inhabitants and becoming a place of habitation for unclean animals. The description of Babylon's judgment could correspond to the judgment in Isaiah 13:2–13 (on a metropolitan scale). Motyer states, "This verse [vs 20] describes the local, historical equivalent of what will be universal on the day of the Lord (9, 13–16)."[167] Thus the different results concern primarily Isaiah 13:14–16.

---

165. Smith, *Isaiah 1–39*, 302.
166. Motyer, *Prophecy of Isaiah*, 139.
167. Motyer, *Prophecy of Isaiah*, 141.

Conclusion

The first battle arguably takes place on the hills of Israel between the Lord's angelic army and the king of Babylon's united nations force resulting in worldwide destruction. The second battle is between the Medes and the inhabitants of Babylon resulting in a "this-worldly" destruction (see Table 3.9). Both of these battles transpire around the same time, allowing for the regathering of Israel to their homeland and the establishment of the Messiah's kingdom on the earth.

Table 3.9. Two Battles in Isaiah 13:2–22

	Isaiah 13:2–13	Isaiah 13:14–22
Armies	Angelic Army vs. United Nations Force	Median Army vs. Inhabitants of Babylon
Place of Battle	Suggests Jerusalem	In and Around Babylon
Leaders	The Lord	Indirectly the Lord
Results	Worldwide Cataclysmic Destruction	"This-Worldly" Destruction

Eschatological Battle in Isaiah 13:2–13

There are four reasons why the battle in Isaiah 13:2–13 is eschatological. First, the Lord himself is leading the armies into battle (13:4); second, the armies are angelic (13:3, 5); third, the battle ultimately encompasses the entire earth (13:5). Wildberger explains:

> The judgment against Babylon, which the author announces at the outset, is now expanded and shaped so as to proclaim a far-reaching judgment over the whole earth. This viewpoint is not a new one. Isaiah himself had already announced a "day of Yahweh" against all human arrogance (2:12; see also 14:26). According to Zeph. 1:17, that day is to be all-inclusive, against all human beings; and, according to v. 18 (certainly a secondary passage), it will thus encompass the entire earth.[168]

Wildberger also lists Ezekiel 30:3 and Obadiah 15 as texts which speak of a worldwide judgment.[169] Watts agrees, "Whether this refers to a limited

---

168. Wildberger, *Isaiah 13–27*, 25.
169. Wildberger, *Isaiah 13–27*, 25.

The Massa' against Babylon—Isaiah 13:2—14:2

geographical area (Palestine in 10:23; the lower Euphrates in 13:5) or to the whole world must remain open. Perhaps the ambiguity is deliberate? All the descriptions of the 'Day of Yahweh' in Isaiah imply a universal application as well as a specific target area."[170]

Fourth, cosmological signs accompany the day of the Lord. Isaiah 13:13 was analyzed above.[171] Isaiah 13:10 also describes cosmological signs.

10a. For the stars of the heavens and their constellations,	כִּי־כוֹכְבֵי הַשָּׁמַיִם וּכְסִילֵיהֶם	10a
10b. Their light will not shine,	לֹא יָהֵלּוּ אוֹרָם	10b
10c. The sun will darken when it rises,	חָשַׁךְ הַשֶּׁמֶשׁ בְּצֵאתוֹ	10c
10d. And the moon will not shine its light.	וְיָרֵחַ לֹא־יַגִּיהַ אוֹרוֹ׃	10d

Concerning the cosmological signs, Young explains, "We are not to understand these upheavals in the realm of nature as necessarily demanding a literal fulfillment. But through figures of speech such as these, Isaiah is permitting us to perceive how great is the judgment which God will bring."[172] Motyer also understands the light and darkness in Isaiah 13:10 to be symbolic:

> Many ideas combine in this verse: the denial to sinners of all the beneficent influences of creation, symbolized by *light;* the visitation of wrath on a whole creation corrupted by sin (*cf.* 2:12ff.; 5:5–6, 10); the withdrawal of light, an apt symbol of the oncoming darkness of divine judgment (*cf.* 5:30); the thought of darkness as a drawing near of the God of absolute holiness (Ex. 19:16; Dt. 4:11).[173]

Concerning the shaking of the heavens and earth, Brueggemann explains, "The scholarly term for such rhetoric is *apocalyptic,* and here the Isaiah tradition moves in a distinctively apocalyptic direction. We must, however, not permit such an interpretive category to slot the terms, as though to explain and domesticate them and fit a scheme."[174]

---

170. Watts, *Isaiah 1–33,* 197.

171. See above "Worldwide Comprehensive Battle."

172. Young, *Book of Isaiah,* 1:424–25.

173. Motyer, *Prophecy of Isaiah,* 138 (emphasis original). Brueggemann also agrees, "The poet must engage in 'limit expressions'—that is, exaggerated, picturesque imagery—in order to communicate 'limit experiences' of public life being dismantled by Yahweh's holiness" (Brueggemann, *Isaiah,* 118).

174. Brueggemann, *Isaiah,* 119 (emphasis original).

Interpreting the darkening of the luminaries symbolically is possible, assuming certain presuppositions, but the natural reading of the text describes darkening luminaries. Smith agrees, "The cosmic significance of this catastrophe (13:10) will shut out the light from the sun, moon, and stars (cf. Amos 5:19,20; Jer 4:23; Joel 2:10). This phenomenon is not explained in detail, but the imagery is identical to the eschatological imagery of complete destruction on the final day of the Lord (cf. 24:1–23)."[175] Hassler explains the cosmic proportions are found through the entire *massa'*:

> Some statements in the poem are global, cosmic, or cataclysmic.... For instance, the Day of Yahweh statements (13:10–13) depict celestial blackout, worldwide punishment (תֵּבֵל, "world"), the cessation of pride, the near-extinction of humanity, an earthquake and heavenly trembling. The world's "peoples" and "nations" suffer persecution (14:6). The "whole earth" rests when the global dictator perishes (v. 7). The dictator instills fear in the world's kingdoms (v. 16). He ruins the whole "world" (תֵּבֵל) and its/his cities (v. 17). Indeed, Yahweh's plans in this oracle encompass the "whole earth" and "all the nations" (v. 26).[176]

This language is not specific to Isaiah either. Wildberger explains, "The coming of the Day of Yahweh is accompanied by cosmic phenomena: sun, moon, and stars all lose their customary brightness. This concept is not new either; cf. Amos 5:18, 20; 8:9f.; Jer. 4:23; Zeph [sic] 1:15; Ezek. 32:7; Joel 2:10; 3:4."[177] The darkening of the luminaries is associated with the final day of God's judgment upon the earth.

Historically Unfulfilled Battle and Regathering in Isaiah 13:14—14:2

While Isaiah 13:2–13 more clearly refers to an eschatological judgment, Isaiah 13:14—14:2 could refer, theoretically, to a historic destruction of Babylon and regathering of Israel. For example, Oswalt claims Isaiah 13:2–13 is eschatological, but then claims 13:14–22 is historical because "there is a turn toward more this-worldly imagery with a special emphasis upon

---

175. Smith, *Isaiah 1–39*, 301. Oswalt writes, "One of the features of the day of the Lord will be darkness. The heavenly bodies will cease to shine and the world will be plunged into a terrible darkness" (Oswalt, *Book of Isaiah*, 306).

176. Hassler, "Isaiah 13:1—14:27," 52.

177. Wildberger, *Isaiah 13–27*, 25.

the savagery with which the proud city will be thrust down."[178] This section argues that no historic fulfillment can be found. Furthermore, the previous section on structure demonstrated that Isaiah 13:19—14:2 is a single unit which introduces the king of Babylon in Isaiah 14:4. Thus, Oswalt would have to find four fulfillments: (1) Median slaughter; (2) eternal devastation of Babylon; (3) Israelite regathering; and (4) the identity of the king of Babylon. This section argues that he cannot do the first three. First, this section dismisses the 689 BC fulfillment view. Then it rejects the 539 BC view because the extent of Babylon's destruction and the extent of Israel's regathering cannot be reconciled with Isaiah 13–14.

689 BC Fulfillment

Heater believes Sennacherib's destruction of Babylon in 689 BC fulfilled Isaiah 13. There are several problems with this view. First, there was no regathering in 689 BC. Concerning this point, Heater states:

> The prophecy of the fall of Babylon leads to a beautiful statement about the return from the exile in chap. 14. Just as the promise of judgment of the exile in Isaiah 39 is followed by beautiful promises of deliverance in Isaiah 40–66, so the promise of judgment upon Babylon in Isaiah 13 is followed by promises of the blessings of return from exile in Isaiah 14:1–3.[179]

Heater creates a false analogy with Isaiah 39–40. As the structure section has already delineated, one cannot consider only a fall of Babylon as a potential fulfillment. One must also consider the regathering of Israel in 14:1–2. Chisholm prefers a 539 BC fulfillment and presents an additional reason why this prophecy could not be fulfilled in 689 BC:

> Some argue that the prophecy was fulfilled in 689 B.C. when the Assyrians under Sennacherib sacked and desecrated the city, an event mentioned in 23:13. However, the demise of Babylon in 689

---

178. Oswalt, *Book of Isaiah*, 307. Concerning 13:14–22 he states, "Isaiah now takes up a somewhat more historical note" (Oswalt, *Isaiah*, 200). Smith takes a similar view claiming, "Having described the horrors of God's judgment on the Day of the Lord, the prophet now turns to apply the principle that God will destroy proud sinners on the Day of the Lord (13:6–16) to the present situation in the nation of Babylon (13:7–22)" (Smith, *Isaiah 1–39*, 303).

179. Heater, "Do the Prophets Teach?," 29. Heater's view on the regathering is explained and rebutted further in the "Sterotypical Language View" section below.

B.C. did not lead to the restoration of Israel, as 14:1–3 suggests would happen. Furthermore, this view has a hard time explaining the reference to the Medes in 13:17, for they participated in Cyrus's conquest of Babylon in 539 B.C. (see Jer. 51:11, 28).[180]

The reference to the Medes makes the 689 BC view unlikely.[181]

Finally, even though Babylon was completely destroyed in 689 BC, it was rebuilt. Heater then has to appeal to stereotypical language to explain why Babylon was rebuilt. Thus, these three reasons (no regathering, no Median army, and Babylon was rebuilt) render the 689 BC fulfillment highly unlikely.

Extent of the Destruction

Isaiah 13:14–18 describes a destruction that is implacable (17) and compassionless (18). The scene painted is apocalyptic, leaving few alive. The description of the city's destruction is comprehensive, rendering the city abandoned. Yet the destruction described in the Cyrus Cylinder reveals a very different destruction:

> And he (Cyrus) did always endeavor to treat according to justice the black-headed whom he (Marduk) has made him conquer. Marduk, the great lord, a protector of his people/worshipers, beheld with pleasure his (i.e., Cyrus') good deeds and his upright mind (lit.: heart) (and therefore) ordered him to march against his city Babylon (K á . d i n g i r . r a^{ki}). He made him set out on the road to Babylon (DIN.TIR^{ki}) going at his side like a real friend. His widespread troops—their number, like that of the water of a river, could not be established—strolled along, their weapons packed away. Without any battle, he made him enter his town Babylon (Š u . a n . n a), sparing Babylon (K á . d i n g i r . r a^{ki}) any calamity. He delivered into his (i.e., Cyrus') hands Nabonidus, the king who did not worship him (i.e., Marduk). All the inhabitants of Babylon (DIN.TIR^{ki}) as well as of the entire country of Sumer and Akkad, princes and governors (included), bowed to him (Cyrus) and kissed his feet, jubilant that he (had received) the kingship, and with shining faces. Happily they greeted him as a master through whose help

---

180. Chisholm, *Handbook on the Prophets*, 52.

181. Heater's explanation that the Medes were mercenaries in the Assyrian army is unsatisfactory (Heater, "Do the Prophets Teach?," 28).

they had come (again) to life from death (and) had all been spared damage and disaster, and they worshiped his (very) name.[182]

The destruction of Babylon in 539 BC simply cannot be reconciled with the destruction described in Isaiah 13:14–22. There are five possible responses to this disparity.

Isaiah's Prophecy Failed

According to Wildberger, if Isaiah was attempting to describe the destruction in 539 BC, then he failed: "Just as is true for the authors of Jeremiah 50–51 and Deutero-Isaiah (chap. 47), the author of Isaiah 13 anticipates that there will be a complete destruction of the city. In this, he was to be disappointed."[183] Wildberger's position is exegetically plausible but discredits Isaiah as a prophet of the Lord. Isaiah 42:9 claims, "Behold, the first things have come to pass, now new things I declare; before they sprout, I make you hear them." Furthermore, if one believes, as Wildberger does, that Isaiah 13–14 has been redacted, then why would a redactor not fix a prophecy that failed?

Gradually Fulfilled Prophecy

Several scholars claim Isaiah 13 was gradually fulfilled. Young extends the destruction to the days of Strabo,

> Cyrus left the walls and the city of Babylon itself still standing. Later, in 518 B.C., the walls were destroyed. Then Xerxes ruined the temple of Belus. As Seleucia rose, so Babylon declined, and in Strabo's time Babylon was a desert of which he says, "a great desert is the great city." Here then is a complete destruction (cf. Isa. 47:1; Rev. 18:7). Babylon must be wiped off the face of the earth. She will not sit as an inhabited city, not even a solitary city like Jerusalem,

---

182. Pritchard, *ANET* 315–16.

183. Wildberger, *Isaiah 13–27*, 29. Clements similarly states, "The completeness of God's judgment upon Babylon will be shown by the fact that no reconstruction of the ruins will be undertaken. In fact the capture of Babylon by the Medo-Persian armies in 538 BC took place without any significant destruction to the city, further strengthening the conclusion that this prophecy was made before that event took place" (Clements, *Isaiah 1–39*, 137).

after the banishment. Neither will she be inhabited from generation to generation. How truly this prophecy has been fulfilled!¹⁸⁴

Mackay claims it continued until AD 200, "Subsequently, however, a long process of economic decline set in, followed by diminished religious significance for the site, until by A.D. 200 it was utterly deserted."¹⁸⁵ Alexander admits that the presence of a park or hunting ground in the days of Jerome which means it had not been fulfilled at that time.¹⁸⁶ Wolf pushes the complete destruction ahead to the Muslim conquest, "Babylon gradually fell into decay, and the prophecy of Isaiah was fulfilled. Babylon became completely depopulated by the time of the Muslim conquest in the seventh century A.D., and to this day it lies deserted."¹⁸⁷ Koldewey finds inhabitants until AD 1200.¹⁸⁸ Alexander cannot find a historic fulfillment but knows it has been destroyed in his day and claims, "So fully has this prophecy been verified that the Bedouins, according to the latest travelers, are even superstitiously afraid of passing a single night upon the site of Babylon."¹⁸⁹ Interestingly, Lang reports the exact opposite:

> It is highly doubtful if the site has ever been wholly uninhabited, as is required by Jer. 50:39, 40, and Isa. 13:20. The last passage says

---

184. Young, *Book of Isaiah*, 427. See also, Delitzsch, *Biblical Commentary on the Prophecies of Isaiah*, 304.

185. Mackay, *Study Commentary on Isaiah*, 335.

186. Alexander, *Prophecies of Isaiah*, 281.

187. Wolf, *Interpreting Isaiah*, 111.

188. Koldewey, *Excavations at Babylon*, 314. Koldewey describes inhabitants at least in the area of Babylon even when he began his excavations (Koldewey, *Excavations at Babylon*, 20). Dyer believes Koldewey is describing inhabitants in Babylon, not just in its environs (Dyer, *Future Babylon*, 23).

189. Alexander, *Prophecies of Isaiah*, 281. Alexander explains, "It is certain, however, that the destruction of the city was by slow degrees, successively promoted by the conquests of Cyrus, Darius Hystaspes, Alexander the Great, Antigonus, Demetrius, the Parthians, and the founding of the cities of Seleucia and Ctesiphon. Strabo calls Babylon μεγάλην ἐρημίαν. Pausanias says that in his day οὐδὲν ἔτι ἦν εἰ μὴ τεῖχος. In Jerome's time this wall only served as the enclosure of a park or hunting ground. From this apparent disagreement of the prophecy with history, Cocceius seems disposed to infer that it relates not to the literal but spiritual Babylon. The true conclusion is that drawn by Calvin, that the prophecy does not relate to any one invasion or attack exclusively, but to the whole process of subjection and decay, so completely carried out through a course of ages, that the very site of ancient Babylon is now disputed. This hypothesis accounts for many traits in the description which appear inconsistent only in consequence of being all applied to one point of time, and one catastrophe exclusively" (Alexander, *Prophecies of Isaiah*, 281).

that the Arabian shall never pitch his tent there after the destruction. Now in a diary of Dr. W. E. Blackstone, the author of *Jesus is Coming*, which I read in Egypt many years ago, just after he had toured Babylonia, he stated distinctly that he had tested the point with his Arab guides and they made no objection at all to pitching in the midst of the ruins.[190]

Newton similarly writes in the nineteenth century, "Even on the very site of Babylon itself, there stand in the midst of its ruins, a city, several villages, and numberless gardens and date groves, whose fertility is proverbial. The Arabian also still pitches his tent there. Indeed, it is anything rather than '*as when God overthrew Sodom and Gomorrah.*'"[191] Thus, this view still fails to find a desolation consistent with Isaiah 13:20–22.

Hassler has demonstrated that there has been continuous activity in Babylon up to the present day.[192] Saddam Hussein began rebuilding Babylon, and his palace still functions as a tourist attraction.[193] Hassler concludes, "In summary, people perpetually forsake Babylon after her demise (Isa 13:19–20). At no time in ancient, Medieval, or modern history has that occurred. This suggests that the fulfillment still looms."[194] Thus, the greatest problem for the gradual destruction view is finding an actual terminus that corresponds with the destruction in Isaiah 13.

The Medes present a second problem for the gradual fulfillment view. The attacking army in 539 BC was the Persians, not the Medes. Motyer acknowledges this discrepancy and explains:

> The reference to *the Medes* as the destroyers of Babylon is at first sight surprising since we are accustomed to ascribe the conquest to Cyrus the Persian. However, phrases which give the Medes priority over the Persians (*e.g.*, "the law of the Medes and Persians," Dn. 6:8, 12, 15; *cf.* Est. 10:2) and the mysterious description of Babylon's conqueror as "Darius the Mede" (Dn. 5:30) at least indicate that the Medes were by no means mere shadowy adjuncts to a Persian victory. Isaiah doubtless had his own contemporary reasons for singling them out.[195]

---

190. Lang, *Histories and Prophecies of Daniel*, 33.
191. Newton, *Aids to Prophetic Enquiry*, 26–27.
192. Hassler, "Isaiah 13:1–14:27," 46.
193. Damon, "Bringing Babylon Back from the Dead."
194. Hassler, "Isaiah 13:1–14:27," 48.
195. Motyer, *Prophecy of Isaiah*, 140 (emphasis his).

Motyer's conclusion is unacceptable. Erlandsson explains, "[Cyrus] left Babylon completely intact. Nor has it been noticed how unlikely it is that the Medes should stand as synonyms for the Persians."[196] The specific reference to the Medes as the Lord's agent of destruction necessitates a specific battle in which the Medes not only destroy Babylon but slaughter its inhabitants as well.

Stereotypical Language

Others seem to recognize the difficulties with the gradually fulfilled prophecy view and resort to a stereotypical destruction. Blenkinsopp even combines the two views. He describes several conquests of Babylon, the worst being in 482 BC, and concludes, "But the language of the poem is too stereotypical and lacking in specificity to allow for any definite conclusion along these lines."[197] Heater appeals to ancient Near Eastern suzerainty treaties as evidence of stereotypical language and appeals to a 689 BC fulfillment:

> Included in many of these treaties is stereotypical language calling for judgment upon those who violate the terms of the treaty. The judgment from the gods upon the vassal will result in desolation and destruction of the worst sort.
>
> Isaiah 13:19-22; 14:22-23; 23:13 have been linked with the language of the treaty curses. . . . For want of a better term we might call it destruction genre. This is not to suggest that the promise of destruction is not real. It is indeed, and, as we have seen, it did happen to Babylon in the seventh century. . . . When Yahweh speaks, the destruction will take place. But the language was stereotypical, and no one expected to see the implementation of the precise details.[198]

Chisholm also appeals to stereotypical language but argues for a 539 BC fulfillment:

> How then does one explain the prophecy's description of the city's violent fall? It is possible that the fall of Babylon in 689 B.C. has contributed to the imagery of the oracle. However, it is more likely that the language is stylized and exaggerated. For dramatic effect,

---

196. Erlandsson, *Burden of Babylon*, 164.
197. Blenkinsopp, *Isaiah 1-39*, 277.
198. Heater, "Do the Prophets Teach?," 32.

the prophets sometimes used such stereotypical language to describe the divine judgment of a city or nation.[199]

These three authors all appeal to stereotypical language, but they all find different fulfillment dates. There are four problems with the stereotypical interpretation view. Hassler summarizes the first problem:

> Although the use of stereotypical language in Isaiah 13 is possible, this approach does not allow for the prediction to unfold according to the details, as is customary of biblical prophecy. Just because extrabiblical curses use stereotypical language does not mean that biblical curses do as well. Unlike mere mortal suzerains, God can fulfill curses in ways that mortal suzerains cannot.[200]

The second problem is the Medes. The Medes never conquered Babylon. Roberts agrees, "If one takes 'Medes' here literally, there was *no* Median conquest of Babylon(ia) at all. If 'Medes' here means the Median-Persian ruler Cyrus II, there was a conquest, but not, it appears, with the destruction described here in Isaiah."[201] Thus there never was a real Median conquest of Babylon. The conquest in 539 BC was not a real destruction, much less a slaughter of the inhabitants. All later destructions of Babylon were performed by other nations. Thus, the reference to the Medes makes the stereotypical language view unlikely.

The third problem is the regathering of Israel. There was no regathering of Israel in either 482 BC or 689 BC. To get around this issue, Heater explains:

> To some extent the message of Isaiah 14 and chaps. 40–55 must refer to the return from Babylonian exile since this entire section refers to the Chaldeans, Babylonians and Cyrus. But the return of the Jews under Zerubbabel was rather pathetic in comparison to Isaiah's description. Only a relatively small number of Jews returned. They were living among the ruins of Jerusalem, and their

---

199. Chisholm, *Handbook on the Prophets*, 53.

200. Hassler, "Isaiah 13:1—14:27," 45.

201. Roberts, *First Isaiah*, 198 (emphasis his). Roberts continues to say, "Despite the power of the Medes that contributed to the fall of Assyria between 615 and 609 BCE, and the Medes' potential threat to Babylon, their former ally, which became particularly acute in the early years of Nabonidus (556–539 BCE), the last Neo-Babylonian ruler, the Medes never took Babylon. It was not until the rise of the Persians that Babylonia fell to Cyrus II (539 BCE), and the city of Babylon, far from being destroyed in battle, opened its gates to Cyrus as a deliverer from what the priests of Marduk regarded as the misrule of Nabonidus" (Roberts, *First Isaiah*, 198).

> efforts to rebuild the temple were met with staunch resistance by the Gentiles (whereas 14:2 says the Gentiles will be servants). *The language of the passage forces the interpreter who is trying to take the language seriously to see a future for Israel that far exceeds what happened when Cyrus permitted the Jews to return to Jerusalem (as in 11:11ff.).* The same is true of chaps. 40–55. The language of the second part of Isaiah is so universal and comprehensive and is so often applied to NT situations that *the ultimate fulfillment of these promises must be eschatological.*[202]

Heater's position is perplexing. He appeals to stereotypical language in Isaiah 13 but appeals to the eschaton in Isaiah 14:1–2. Heater fails to recognize the structural catchwords through Isaiah 13:22—14:3 which hold the destruction, regathering, and king of Babylon together. Exegetically, the regathering must connect to the destruction of Babylon.

Even if one applied stereotypical language to the regathering in Isaiah 14:1–2, the 482 BC and 689 BC fulfillments simply do not work. Those Babylonian destructions contain no regathering consequent enough to fulfill even a stereotypical interpretation of Isaiah 14:1–2.

Further issues with the stereotypical language view concern the king of Babylon and the surrounding eschatological context of Isaiah 13:2–13 and 14:1–2. Heater fails to see the structural connection between Isaiah 13:22 and 14:1–4 when he states, "The identity of the king of Babylonia is not important to the argument of the unit. Whether it refers to an Assyrian king ruling in Babylon or a Chaldean like Merodach-Baladan or to his sixth-century counterpart Nebuchadnezzar, the point is that Babylon will fall."[203] Heater's stereotypical language view fails to produce a reasonable exegetical explanation.

Chisholm's 539 BC destruction does have a corresponding regathering of Israel, but neither of these events correspond to Isaiah 13–14. First, as already described by Heater, Isaiah 14:1–2 was not fulfilled in 539 BC even in a stereotypical way. Second, the destruction in 539 BC was not a destruction, much less a destruction worthy of even a stereotypical destruction reminiscent of Isaiah 13.

Even if one appeals to stereotypical language and gaps between the destructions and regatherings, these views simply do not work. The structural

---

202. Heater, "Do the Prophets Teach?," 29–30 (emphasis mine).
203. Heater, "Do the Prophets Teach?," 30.

The Massa' against Babylon—Isaiah 13:2—14:2

analysis already presented renders the stereotypical interpretation highly unlikely.

Falsified Cyrus Cylinder

The Cyrus Cylinder has potentially overstated the conquest of Babylon and exaggerated the generosity of the conqueror. Blenkinsopp acknowledges this possibility:

> The Cyrus Cylinder talks about the Persian army strolling into the city with their weapons tucked away. . . . But the extent to which autocratic rulers were (and are) prepared to dissimulate in the interests of self-aggrandizement can be illustrated by comparing this propagandistic statement with Herodotus's description of the siege and eventual capture of the city by the Persians after lowering the level of the Euphrates (1.188–191).[204]

If one believes that the language used in Isaiah 13 is stereotypical and the Cyrus Cylinder has falsified Cyrus's generosity, then, presumably, there was a fiercer destruction which could fit the stereotypical language of Isaiah 13.

Biblically and archaeologically, however, this view is unlikely. Biblically, the fall of Babylon described in Daniel seems to be a rather peaceful transition with Daniel obtaining a high position in the Persian government. Archaeologically, latter destructions were worse than the destruction in 539 BC arguing for the accuracy of the Cyrus Cylinder. Blenkinsopp even acknowledges the more severe destructions of Babylon:

> Darius I also besieged and captured the city, destroyed the walls and gates, and executed several thousand of its inhabitants after putting down the revolt of the Babylonian pretender Arakha in 521. The city was treated even more harshly by Xerxes after suppressing the revolt of Shamash-eriba in 482, the worst blow of all being the carrying off and melting down of the great gold statue of Marduk.[205]

Thus, even according to Blenkinsopp, the destructions in 521 BC and 482 BC were more severe than the destruction in 539 BC. Blenkinsopp even recognizes the improbability of this view and eventually appeals to

---

204. Blenkinsopp, *Isaiah 1–39*, 277.
205. Blenkinsopp, *Isaiah 1–39*, 277.

stereotypical language: "But the language of the poem is too stereotypical and lacking in specificity to allow for any definite conclusion along these lines."[206]

Spiritually/Figuratively Fulfilled

Perhaps the destruction of Babylon symbolizes the judgment of God against human pride. Presumably, support for this position, ironically, comes from the inability to find a literal fulfillment. Oswalt explains, "The chief function of Babylon is figurative at this point. This understanding is supported by the fact that neither in 689 . . . nor in Cyrus's much more peaceful takeover in 539 B.C. was Babylon abandoned."[207] There are two problems with this position.

The first problem with the spiritual fulfillment view is the presence of "the Medes." Oswalt explains the presence of "the Medes" when he states:

> Because it was the Medes and Persians who overthrew Babylon in 539, many scholars believe that this reference is to that event and must therefore have been written about that time. However, it is equally significant to note that Isaiah makes no mention of the Persians, who were the main factor in the defeat in 539. It seems unaccountable that anyone writing in the sixth century could have made such a glaring omission. On the other hand, it is quite possible that Isaiah of Jerusalem, writing in the late 700s, knew something of the Medes' fearsome reputation and used them as a figure of the pitiless destruction characterizing the day of the Lord, without intending any specific prediction.[208]

Oswalt's explanation, however, is unsatisfactory. The nation known for its ruthless, uncompassionate nature, who crushed Judah and their neighbors, was not the Medes but the Assyrians. If eighth-century Isaiah wanted a nation with a "fearsome reputation" known for "pitiless destruction," he could have found a more relevant option.

Furthermore, if eighth-century Isaiah was, according to Oswalt, figuratively creating a "powerful contrast between the temporary results of human pride and the ultimate results,"[209] then why would he select Babylon as his illustration of pride? Assyria was the eighth-century superpower

---

206. Blenkinsopp, *Isaiah 1–39*, 277.
207. Oswalt, *Book of Isaiah*, 309.
208. Oswalt, *Book of Isaiah*, 308.
209. Oswalt, *Book of Isaiah*, 308.

whose arrogance was in full array from the walls of Jerusalem in Isaiah 36–37. Oswalt's explanation that Babylon was the "cultural and economic superior to the Assyrian cities in the north and was bidding for political sovereignty as well"[210] is lacking. If Isaiah was only teaching a spiritual lesson, one would expect Assyria to be involved as either the conqueror or the conquered. These two problems render the spiritual interpretation view unlikely.

Conclusion

The eschatological context of 13:2–13 and 14:1–2 favors an eschatological reading of Isaiah 13:14–22. An eschatological interpretation presents the best exegetically and historically logical interpretation of Isaiah 13:14–22.

Extent of the Regathering

The third reason why the prophecy in Isaiah 13:14—14:2 was not fulfilled concerns the extent of the regathering. The regathering described in Isaiah 14:1–2 does not correspond to the regathering after 539 BC. This section identifies three details concerning the regathering of Israel and argues that none of these details were fulfilled in 539 BC.

Israel at Rest

Isaiah 14:1 describes God's relationship toward Israel and begins with an introductory tricolon.

1a. But the Lord will have compassion on Jacob;	כִּי יְרַחֵם יְהוָה אֶת־יַעֲקֹב	14:1a
1b. And choose again Israel;	וּבָחַר עוֹד בְּיִשְׂרָאֵל	1b
1c. And make them rest on their ground	וְהִנִּיחָם עַל־אַדְמָתָם	1c

As noted in the structure section above, there are three verbs in Isaiah 14:1a–c; the first and third are functioning as catchwords and the middle one functions as the center of an inclusio. The middle verb, בחר ("to choose"), highlights God's choosing of Israel. Oswalt notes, "As God chose

---

210. Oswalt, *Book of Isaiah*, 308.

Israel's Eschatological Enemy

Israel once before in Egypt, he will chose [sic] her again in Mesopotamia (Deut. 4:37; 7:6, 7; Ps. 135:4)."[211]

The first two cola contain general descriptions of the Lord's new dealings with Israel; the third colon, however, is physical. Gray believes the third colon is only referring to resettlement. He translates the third colon והניחם על־אדמתם, "and he will settle them on their ground" and states, "הִנִּיחַ is generally used to place a person in a particular place after his removal from another; cf. 46⁷, Gn 19¹⁶, Jos 6²³, Lv 24¹², Nu 15³⁴."[212] Wildberger, however, counters:

> When considering the expression וְהִנִּיחָם עַל־אַדְמָתָם (and he will transplant them into their homeland), one might question whether וַהֲנִיחָם (cause to rest) (see Deut. 3:20) should be read instead, which would bring into the picture the concept that the land that had been given as an inheritance was a מנוחה (resting place) (see Deut. 12:9), though one does find הניח על־א׳ (leave on its own land) in Jer. 27:11 and Ezek. 37:14 as well.[213]

Wildberger nonsensically amends the Masoretes vowel pointing. Both forms are *hifil*, thus, "to make rest" (הניח) could refer to a regathering or an anticipated theological "rest." The basic meaning of נוח is to "rest." Preuss explains, "There are 30 occurrences of the qal of *nûaḥ*, meaning 'settle down (to rest), become quiet and (consequently) rest.'"[214] The meaning in the *hifil* is "to cause to rest," and it can be applied to objects and people whom one is "to place somewhere, set, lay."[215] Preuss recognizes this nontheological use of "rest" (נוח).[216] Yet it is more likely that "rest" (נוח) is being used in a theological/Deuteronomistic sense in Isaiah 14:1, and 14:3. Preuss explains the theological use of "rest" (נוח):

> It is Yahweh who gives his people or their king rest from their enemies: Dt. 12:10; 25:19; Josh. 21:44; 23:1; cf. also 1 Macc. 14:4; 16:2; etc.; also 2 S. 7:1; analogously in 2 S. 7:11, but as a renewed promise; 1 K. 5:18(Eng. v. 4) (v. 17[3] contradicts 2 S. 7:1,11!); 1 Ch. 22:9,18; 23:25; 2 Ch. 14:5f.(6f.); 15:15; 20:30.

---

211. Oswalt, *Book of Isaiah*, 312.
212. Gray, *Isaiah I–XXXIX*, 244.
213. Wildberger, *Isaiah 13–27*, 35.
214. Preuss, "נוּחַ," *TDOT* 9:278.
215. HALOT, "נוח I," 2:679.
216. Preuss, "נוּחַ," *TDOT* 9:282.

The Massaʾ against Babylon—Isaiah 13:2—14:2

Even a brief survey of these texts makes three things clear: (a) for the most part they are associated with Deuteronomistic thought and its influence; (b) they mean rest as relief from enemies and war (sometimes "on all sides" instead of "from the enemy"); (c) this relief from enemies is often expanded to peace and prosperity in the land (cf. šālôm explicitly in 2 Cf. 20:30). Deuteronomist influence is clear in Dt. 3:20; 12:10; 25:19; Josh. 1:13,15; 21:44; 22:4; 23:1; 2 S. 7:1,11 (both verses belonging to the Deuteronomistic recension of the chapter); 1 K. 5:18. Here rest is living at peace in the land—a Deuteronomistic benefit of hope and the fruit of (Deuteronomistic) obedience, as well as the substance of God's promise.[217]

Thus, when Isaiah 14:1 states, "God will make you rest," this rest implies relief from war, peace in the land, and the fulfillment of divine Deuteronomic blessing. Smith agrees, "NIV translates וְהִנִּיחָם as 'and will settle them,' but the essence of this root is God's gift of rest and peace, not just the ability to settle in a certain place. 'Rest' (נוּחַ) is a broader concept that has theological implications of divine blessing without war, not just putting down roots."[218]

Nations Escort Israel Home

Second, the nations escort Israel back to their land.

1d. And the sojourner will join them;	וְנִלְוָה הַגֵּר עֲלֵיהֶם	1d
1e. And they will attach themselves to the house of Jacob;	וְנִסְפְּחוּ עַל־בֵּית יַעֲקֹב׃	1e
2a. And peoples will take them;	וּלְקָחוּם עַמִּים	2a
2b. And bring them to their place.	וֶהֱבִיאוּם אֶל־מְקוֹמָם	2b

This tetracolon describes the manner in which Israel will return to their land. The relationship between Israel and the nations is completely reversed. Israel was previously the "sojourner," but now the nations are sojourners. Colon 14:1e emphasizes colon 14:1d by describing the sojourners as not only joining Israel but attaching themselves to Israel.

Isaiah 14:2ab continues to add emphasis to the tetracolon. These last two cola describe the peoples as not only joining and attaching themselves

---

217. Preuss, "נוּחַ," *TDOT*, 9:280.
218. Smith, *Isaiah 1-39*, 306n74.

Israel's Eschatological Enemy

to Israel, but actually taking Israel and bringing them back to "their place." Roberts correctly notes the role reversal here, "According to v. 2, it will be these foreign peoples who take Israel and bring them back to their own place."[219] Mackay also correctly states, "They will have their return facilitated by the action of 'peoples' of other nationalities."[220] Thus, the peoples will escort Israel back to their land.

The Rab-shakeh promises in Isaiah 36:17 that he would come (בֹּא) and take (לקח) Israel to a land like their own land. The people of Israel were familiar with being "taken" and "brought" somewhere. Isaiah uses this language but reverses it. Instead of being taken away from their land, they are being taken to their land.

Israel Possesses the Nations

Finally, the ones who were captive are now the captors.

2c. And the house of Israel will possess them,	וְהִתְנַחֲלוּם בֵּית־יִשְׂרָאֵל	2c
2d. Upon the ground of the Lord,	עַל אַדְמַת יְהוָה	2d
2e. Male slaves and female slaves.	לַעֲבָדִים וְלִשְׁפָחוֹת	2e
2f. And they will take captive their captors,	וְהָיוּ שֹׁבִים לְשֹׁבֵיהֶם	2f
2g. And they will rule over their oppressors.	וְרָדוּ בְּנֹגְשֵׂיהֶם: ס	2g

The text builds and becomes more emphatic. The very nations that subjected Israel to bondage are now subjected by Israel. Roberts explains, "These foreigners will be Israel's male and female slaves, so that Israel will end up as captors of their former captors, and they will now rule over their former oppressors."[221] Smith notes that three peoples are involved in Israel's escort back to their land. He states:

> It appears that three groups of foreigners will have close social relationships with the Israelites at that time. First, the "alien residents" (gēr in 14:1b) will join themselves with God's people.... Second, some unidentified nations [עַמִּים in 14:2a] will assist the

---

219. Roberts, *First Isaiah*, 202.

220. Mackay, *Study Commentary on Isaiah*, 339.

221. Roberts, *First Isaiah*, 202. Roberts also acknowledges this intertextual theme, "This motif of the foreign nations bringing God's people back to their own land and serving them there is found in Second Isaiah (49:22–26) and in Third Isaiah (60:9–16; 61:5)" (Roberts, *First Isaiah*, 202).

Israelites in the process of returning.... Third, there is a final group [שֹׁבִים in 14:2b] of unidentified foreigners who previously took the Israelites captive (possibly some Egyptians, Assyrians, or Babylonians; cf. 19:19–25).[222]

While Smith's interpretation is possible, it is more likely the tricolon builds in emphasis as the line progresses. The sojourner would have been a free man, but not a citizen. The final group consists of slaves. Thus, Israel will bring slaves back to Israel when they are regathered.

Fulfillment of Isaiah 14:1–2

At what time in Israel's history have they truly been at "rest?" The regathering in 539 BC was accompanied by political turmoil and threats on all sides.[223] Mackay correctly explains, "[Rest] points to the fulfilment of the covenant pledge that in the promised land Yahweh would give them rest from their enemies round about (cf. 63:14; Exod. 33:14; Deut. 25:19; Josh. 1:13; 2 Sam. 7:1; 1 Kgs. 8:56). This rest after the Exodus and after the exile anticipates that of the messianic era (cf. 11:10)."[224] The lack of "rest" after 539 BC argues that Isaiah 14:1 was not fulfilled and thus awaits a future fulfillment.

Furthermore, at what time did the nations escort Israel home? When did Israel enslave the nations who enslaved them? There is wide agreement that Isaiah 14:1–2 was *not* literally fulfilled after 539 BC. Young believes Isaiah 14:1 was fulfilled after 539 BC. Concerning 14:2, however, he resorts to a figurative interpretation of Israel,[225] and applies it to the church:

> They had led her captive, but now Israel will act toward them as a captor. Once they had oppressed Israel, but now she will rule over her former oppressors. Through Christ the heathen are being spiritually subdued; that is to say, through Christ working by means of His ministers and missionaries, they are being subdued.[226]

---

222. Smith, *Isaiah 1–39*, 307.

223. See ch. 4: Nabonidus.

224. Mackay, *Study Commentary on Isaiah*, 338.

225. Young states, "The promise was not fulfilled in the return to the Jews from Babylonian bondage, but is being fulfilled when the Gentiles who oppose God are conquered through the house of Israel, the Israel of God, the church, and are subdued by the Holy Spirit and made heirs of the promises" (Young, *Book of Isaiah*, 1:434).

226. Young, *Book of Isaiah*, 1:434

Heater believes Isaiah 13 refers to Babylon, but concerning Isaiah 14 he admits, "The language of the passage forces the interpreter who is trying to take the language seriously to see a future for Israel that far exceeds what happened when Cyrus permitted the Jews to return to Jerusalem (as in 11:11ff)."[227] Chisholm sees a double fulfillment, "The prophecy anticipates Israel's release from exile following Cyrus's conquest of Babylon, but the language also transcends that event and envisions a time when Israel will become the dominant nation on earth (see 11:14)."[228] Oswalt spiritualizes the passage, "This language can be taken as a figurative expression of the prophet's inspired conviction that the present relationship between Israel and the nations would not always obtain. The nations' pride was passing, but the glory of Israel's God was unending, and the day would come when the temporal would bow to the eternal."[229] Smith correctly explains, "Although it may be tempting to interpret these promises as a description of the Israelites' return from Babylonian captivity with the aid of the Persian king Cyrus, a reading of Haggai, Zechariah, Ezra, and Nehemiah demonstrates that this prophecy in Isaiah is talking about something far more wonderful than what happened in the post-exilic era."[230]

CONCLUSION

This chapter focused on the structure and content of Isaiah 13:2—14:2. It began by discussing some preliminary issues: genre, historical setting, and the broader context. Isaiah 13:1 explicitly declares Isaianic authorship and labels the prophecy a *massa'*. The *massa'* is a broad genre label which works well in eschatological texts. It also employs more specific genres like the *mashal* in Isaiah 14. The function of Isaiah 14:24–27 argues that this

---

227. Heater, "Do the Prophets Teach?," 30.

228. Chisholm, *Handbook on the Prophets*, 49. Webb sees a partial fulfillment, "A partial fulfillment came when Cyrus of Persia and his successors not only allowed Judean exiles to return, but gave them material assistance and forced others to serve them in the same way. But the complete fulfillment awaits the day anticipated in the New Testament when the meek will inherit the earth and share in Jesus' rule over the nations" (Webb, *Message of Isaiah*, 82).

229. Oswalt, *Book of Isaiah*, 313. Leupold claims verse 2 is "somewhat more idealized coloring bordering on hyperbole." He later explains, "What we have is an emphatic and colorful way of expressing how deeply Gentiles will appreciate how much they owe to God's chosen nation, Israel" (Leupold, *Exposition of Isaiah*, 253).

230. Smith, *Isaiah 1–39*, 307.

oracle was proclaimed before the Assyrian destruction described in Isaiah 37. Thus, a latter eighth-century composition of Isaiah 13–14 is convincing (704–1 BC). Concerning the broad context, Isaiah 13:1 begins a new major section in the book. An eschatological interpretation of Isaiah 13–14 fits within this broader context as the Lord is asserted as the ruler of the kingdoms.

Having discussed the preliminary issues, this chapter then analyzed the structure of Isaiah 13:2—14:27. It was argued that the *oracle* was one unit, divided into three sections by והיה ("And it will be . . .") with a validating sign at the end (14:24–27). Most important for an eschatological interpretation of the *mashal*, it was argued that Isaiah 14:3a "And it will be, in the day when the Lord gives you rest" contains three catchwords which allude back to the Israelite regathering, eternal devastation of Babylon, Median slaughter, and cataclysmic destruction of the Lord. Thus, Isaiah 14:3 places the *mashal* in the *timeframe* of the events in Isaiah 13:2—14:2. It was then purported that Isaiah 14:24–27 is part of the *massa'* against Babylon and is functioning as a short-term sign to validate the long-term prophecy against Babylon.

Finally, this chapter analyzed Isaiah 13:2—14:2 and argued three things: (1) there are two battles in Isaiah 13; (2) Isaiah 13:2–13 is an eschatological battle; and (3) Isaiah 13:14—14:2 is unfulfilled and, therefore, eschatological as well. An analysis of the armies, places of battle, leaders, and results argued for two different battles in Isaiah 13. Four reasons were proffered why the battle in Isaiah 13:2–13 is eschatological: (1) the Lord himself leads the army; (2) the armies are angelic; (3) the battle encompasses the entire earth; and (4) cosmological signs accompany the destruction. Isaiah 13:14—14:2 could theoretically have been fulfilled historically. A historical study of Babylon, however, reveals that it has never been eternally destroyed as Isaiah 13 describes. Furthermore, the Medes have never conquered and slaughtered the Babylonians as Isaiah 13 states. Finally, Israel has never been regathered as Isaiah 14:1–2 explains. Thus, Isaiah 13:2—14:2 remains unfulfilled today.

Chapter 4

The King of Babylon

SCHOLARS ARE OFTEN SELECTIVE in either their criteria, or their evaluation of the evidence when arguing for a prospective king of Babylon. For example, Cobb presents four criteria concerning the king of Babylon. He was: (1) an oppressive tyrant; (2) a world-ruler; (3) famous for pomp and pride; and (4) brought to an inglorious end.[1] Some kings are brought to an "inglorious end," but few have their bodies exposed. Smith, on the other hand, offers incomplete evidence. He proffers two reasons why Merodach-baladan is the king of Babylon: (1) historical setting—Smith "places all of chaps. 13–14 in the context of the political events in 39:1–8;"[2] and (2) destruction of Babylon—Smith states, "Merodach-baladan's reign ended and the city of Babylon was decimated in 689 BC."[3] Smith concludes, "Certainly it would be wiser to trust in God's plans (14:24–27) than the scheming plots of this proud Babylonian king."[4] The *mashal*[5] alludes to eleven criteria of the king of Babylon, some of which are very specific (like an exposed corpse), and to which Smith does not allude or reconcile. The two "proofs" presented by

---

1. Cobb, "Ode in Isaiah XIV," 25. van Keulen makes the same mistake. He lists a few general criteria and then states, "This description fits more than one king of the Neo-Assyrian and Neo-Babylonian empires" (Van van Keulen, "On the Identity of the Anonymous Ruler," 109).

2. Smith, *Isaiah 1–39*, 310.

3. Smith, *Isaiah 1–39*, 311.

4. Smith, *Isaiah 1–39*, 311.

5. See chapter 2 for a discussion of the *mashal*. *Mashal* means "proverb" and includes Isaiah 14:4b–21.

Smith are not even taken from the *mashal* but are assumptions from the surrounding context.

There are four contextual criteria by which one may determine the identity of the king of Babylon: (1) cataclysmic destruction (13:5–13); (2) eternal devastation of Babylon (13:19–22); (3) Median slaughter (13:17); and (4) Israelite regathering (14:1–2). In addition to these contextual criteria, the *mashal* reveals five attributes and six activities of the king of Babylon. These eleven criteria in the *mashal* and the four contextual criteria create a list of fifteen criteria by which one can identify the king of Babylon.[6] This chapter first analyzes the eleven criteria, then each historic king is evaluated in light of the fifteen criteria.

QUESTIONABLE CRITERIA

There are three questionable criteria which will not be used in the analysis of the king of Babylon: (1) collected tribute (14:4b); (2) name forgotten (14:20); and (3) progeny killed (14:21).

Brangeberg states, "[The king of Babylon] exacted tribute from the nations (v. 4)."[7] This attribute is based on a questionable reading of Isaiah 14:4b.

4a. How has the oppressor ceased	אֵיךְ שָׁבַת נֹגֵשׂ 4a
4b. (?) has ceased	שָׁבְתָה מַדְהֵבָה 4b

The question concerns what has ceased in line 4b. The KJV and NKJV follow the MT and translate מדהבה "the golden city." The NET (hostility), ESV (insolent fury), CSB (the raging), NASB (fury), and NIV (his fury) support some kind of emendation. Hassler provides an analysis of the issues, prefers the MT, and concludes, "The issue determines what

---

6. Brangenberg creates a list of eleven "historical allusions" by which he attempts to identify the king of Babylon. He states, "There are a large number of historical allusions made in the taunt-song which may be used to identify the intended subject: he was known as the King of Babylon (v. 4); he exacted tribute from the nations (v. 4); he smote the nations with fury (v. 6); his ambitious building projects resulted in mass harvesting of the cedars and cypresses of Lebanon (v. 8); he aspired to world dominion (vv. 12–15); he ruled in anger with unhindered persecution (v. 16); he shook kingdoms and leveled cities, transforming the land into a wilderness and deporting their populations (v. 17); he died in battle and was left unburied (vv. 19–20); his exploits ruined his own land (v. 20); his dynasty came to an end shortly after his death and all memory of him was suppressed (vv. 21–22); and Babylon soon thereafter would be laid waste and flooded (v. 23)" (Brangenberg III, "Re-Examination," 87).

7. Brangenberg III, "Re-Examination," 87.

Israel's Eschatological Enemy

ceases—onslaught (1QIsaᵃ), a person (LXX, Targum Jonathan, Peshitta), hunger (Aquila), taxes (Theodotion, Symmachus, Vulgate), or something else."[8] Even if one retains the MT's reading, מדהבה is a hapax and of questionable meaning.[9] Because of these uncertainties, this criterion cannot be used to determine the identity of the king of Babylon.

Some claim the king of Babylon's progeny are killed and his name forgotten based on Isaiah 14:20–21. Sweeney, for example, claims Nebuchadnezzar cannot be the king of Babylon "because his son Amel-Merodach succeeded him to the throne after his death in 562."[10] But later when he argues that Sargon II is the king of Babylon, he states, "That Sargon's son Sennacherib maintained the throne after his death does not undermine this interpretation. The taunt song does not report the death of the king's sons as an established fact, but anticipates such an outcome."[11] Sweeney excludes Nebuchadnezzar because his progeny endured, but then excludes this criterion when it potentially invalidated Sargon II.

20d. Let him not be mentioned forever,	לֹא־יִקָּרֵא לְעוֹלָם	20d
20e. Offspring of evildoers	זֶרַע מְרֵעִים׃	20e
21a. Prepare his sons for slaughter	הָכִינוּ לְבָנָיו מַטְבֵּחַ	21a
22b. Because of the iniquity of their fathers	בַּעֲוֺן אֲבוֹתָם	22b
22c. They must not arise and possess the earth	בַּל־יָקֻמוּ וְיָרְשׁוּ אָרֶץ	22c
22d. Nor fill the face of the world with cities	וּמָלְאוּ פְנֵי־תֵבֵל עָרִים	22d

The *mashal* ends with curses that the king of Babylon be forgotten and his progeny killed.[12] While the verb יקרא could be an imperfect and be making a statement of fact ("he will not be mentioned"), it is more likely expressing a desire ("Let him not be mentioned"). These are curses and not necessarily a statement of fact; therefore, these statements cannot invalidate a possible king of Babylon. Even though the eschatological interpretation

---

8. Hassler, "Isaiah 13:1—14:27," 18.

9. HALOT, "מַדְהֵבָה," 2:548. Hassler retains the MT but does not translate it (Hassler, "Isaiah 13:1—14:27," 14–18).

10. Sweeney, *Isaiah 1–39*, 232.

11. Sweeney, *Isaiah 1–39*, 233.

12. Fry agrees, "The taunt against the King of Babylon ends with curses and an oath. The curses are leveled at the king's memory and his sons' lives (lines 20d–21e)" (Fry, "'Oracle Concerning Babylon,'" 127).

proffered in this dissertation surmises that these curses will be fulfilled, they cannot be used to exclude a potential king.

ATTRIBUTES OF THE KING OF BABYLON

The *mashal* reveals five attributes of this individual: king of *Babylon* (14:4); brutal ruler (14:6); ruler of vast kingdom (14:6); king of kings (14:6, 9–14, 16); and exposed corpse (14:18–20).

King of Babylon

The first attribute of the king of Babylon is that he is the king of *Babylon*.

| 4. And you will lift up this proverb against the king of Babylon, and you will say: | וְנָשָׂאתָ הַמָּשָׁל הַזֶּה עַל־מֶלֶךְ בָּבֶל וְאָמָרְתָּ 4 |

Many kings proffered as the king of Babylon were never kings of *Babylon*. For example, Wildberger states, "Questions about dating revolve around the difficulties of explaining what is meant by 'Babylon.'" He then explains, "Therefore the name 'Babylon' must function as a symbolic name used to identify the 'world power' for this redactor, who initially had the Persian Empire in mind."[13] This section, however, provides three reasons why Babylon must refer to literal Babylon: (1) Isaianic context; (2) reference to the Chaldeans in Isaiah 13:19; and (3) destruction of "Babylon" in Isaiah 13:20–22.

First, there are no clear symbolic uses of Babylon in the Old Testament. Roos explains:

> The Hebrew and Aramaic proper noun בָּבֶל has 287 occurrences in the Hebrew Bible, distributed as follows: twice in the Pentateuch, 237 times in the Prophets, and forty-eight occasions in the Writings. The thirteen instances in Isaiah (13:1, 19; 14:4, 22; 21:9; 39:1, 3, 6, 7; 43:14; 47:1; 48:14, 20) represent 4.53% of the occurrences in the Hebrew Bible and 6.34% of those in the prophetic books. The word בָּבֶל refers to the city of Babylon, to the country of Babylonia, to the people of Babylonia, and to the Neo-Babylonian

---

13. Wildberger, *Isaiah 13–27*, 49. Nielsen agrees with Wildberger, "The text is nevertheless reused, but now to the effect that 'the king of Babylon' is seen as a code-name for the world power. The apparent closing of the text by means of a geo-political decision is cancelled by turning the name into a cipher, or, if one prefers, by understanding it figuratively" (Nielsen, *There is Hope for a Tree*, 160).

empire. It is translated "Babylon" (when referring to the major city in central Mesopotamia) and "Babylonia" (when referring either to the country or to the land and its people).[14]

Thus, when Babylon is referenced in the Old Testament, and specifically in Isaiah, it refers to the city or area of Babylon. Scholars who claim Babylon in Isaiah 13–14 is symbolic are reading a possible New Testament use of Babylon into the Old Testament.[15]

Second and most important is the reference to the Chaldeans in Isaiah 13:19. Roos explains:

> The Hebrew proper noun כַּשְׂדִּים appears eighty times in the Hebrew Bible, distributed as follows: three times in the Pentateuch, seventy occurrences in the Prophets, and seven occasions in the Writings. The seven entries of כַּשְׂדִּים in Isaiah (13:19; 23:13; 43:14; 47:1, 5; 48:14, 20) represent 8.75% of the occurrences in the Hebrew Bible and 11.3% of those in the prophetic books. The word כַּשְׂדִּים has three basic meanings in the Hebrew Bible: name of a people ("Chaldeans" or "Babylonians"), name of a territory ("Chaldea"), *terminus technicus* in the book of Daniel ("Chaldeans" as a learned class skilled in interpretations, "astrologers," "sages").[16]

Again, with the exception of the technical term employed in Daniel, the reference to Chaldeans (כשדים) argues in favor of a literal Babylon. That Babel and Chaldeans are used in the same place makes an even stronger argument.

Third, the immediate context describes the destruction of an actual city named Babylon.[17] These three reasons demonstrate that a symbolic interpretation of Babylon in Isaiah 14:4 is unlikely.

Brutal Ruler

The king of Babylon is a brutal ruler:

---

14. Roos, "Babylon in the Book of Isaiah," 350. Analyzing every use of Babylon in the Old Testament falls outside the scope of this dissertation. Ringgren does not identify a symbolic use of Babel in the Old Testament (Ringgren, "בָּבֶל," *TDOT* 1:466–69). Neither does Margueron (Margueron, *ABD* 1:563–64).

15. Watson identifies arguable symbolic uses of Babylon in the New Testament (Watson, *ABD* 1:565–66).

16. Roos, "Babylon in the Book of Isaiah," 350–51.

17. See ch. 3.

6a. The one who struck peoples with wrath,	מַכֶּה עַמִּים בְּעֶבְרָה	6a
6b. Blows without ceasing;	מַכַּת בִּלְתִּי סָרָה	6b
6c. The one who ruled with anger the nations;	רֹדֶה בָאַף גּוֹיִם	6c
6d. Persecution without ceasing	מֻרְדָּף בְּלִי חָשָׂךְ׃	6d

The parallelism in this tetracolon is clear: "Peoples" and "nations" are parallel, as are "with wrath" and "with anger." The participle "one who struck" (מכה) is parallel with the participle "one who ruled" (רדה) revealing the manner of his rule.[18] He *struck* the peoples "with wrath" and *ruled* the nations "with anger." Oswalt illustrates his brutality using Assyrian domination:

> The picture here of unceasing and relentless oppression accords very well with the claims of the Assyrian kings. In their annals, they report at great length the violence and the unwavering nature of their assaults upon their neighbors.... The blows which would come upon anyone who dared to dissent from Assyrian domination were so massive and so total that nation after nation was cowed into submission. The thought of being delivered from such terror must have been almost too delightful to speak of.[19]

The problem with Oswalt's illustration is that Isaiah 14:5 is not talking about how the king of Babylon conquered, but how he *ruled*. Motyer explains better, "The king is accused of malevolence, violence, a reign of terror (*unceasing blows*), and *relentless aggression/ 'persecution.'* In sum, the toleration of only one opinion and ideology and the suppression of all others."[20] Stalin is an example of a brutal ruler who delivered "blows without ceasing" and "persecution without ceasing." Khlevniuk describes Stalin's brutality:

> Furthermore, in addition to the 26 million who were shot, imprisoned, or subjected to internal exile, tens of millions were forced to labor on difficult and dangerous projects, arrested, subjected to lengthy imprisonment without charges, or fired from their jobs and evicted from their homes for being relatives of "enemies of the people." Overall, the Stalinist dictatorship subjected at least

---

18. Fry explains, "The lines of verse 6 form a quatrain with line a parallel to c and line b parallel to line d" (Fry, "'Oracle Concerning Babylon,'" 103).

19. Oswalt, *Book of Isaiah*, 316–17.

20. Motyer, *Prophecy of Isaiah*, 143 (emphasis original).

60 million people to some sort of "hard" or "soft" repression and discrimination.

To this figure we must add the victims of periodic famines or starvation, which during 1932–33 alone took the lives of between 5 and 7 million people. The Stalinist famine was largely the result of political decisions. In its campaign to break peasant opposition to collectivization, the Stalinist government used famine as a means of "punishing" the countryside. All opportunities to relieve the situation—such as purchasing grain abroad—were rejected. Starving villages had their last stores of food expropriated.

> We can conclude from this horrific summation that a significant proportion of Soviet citizens suffered some form of repression or discrimination during the Stalin period.[21]

The king of Babylon may be a brutal conqueror, but Isaiah 14:6 portrays him as a brutal ruler.

Ruler of Vast Kingdom

Also from Isaiah 14:6, the king of Babylon strikes "peoples" and "nations" (both words are plurals), indicating a vast domain. "Peoples" likely refers to a multi-nation group. This is the third use of "people(s)" in the oracle against Babylon. First, "many people" (עַם־רָב) assemble for battle in 13:4, then "peoples" (עַמִּים) bring Israel back to their land (Isa 14:2), and "peoples" (עַמִּים) are abused by the king of Babylon (Isa 14:6). In Isaiah 13:4, "people" is singular but the adjective "many" modifies it. The singular is likely used to illustrate their unity in opposition to God. In Isaiah 14:2 and 6, "people" is plural which likely means multiple nations are involved. Lipiński notes that there are seven collective uses of עַם: (1) assembly of Israelites; (2) people of the land of Judah; (3) postexilic assembly; (4) people as a whole; (5) warriors; (6) people of God; and (7) foreign peoples.[22] Under the "foreign peoples" section, he states:

---

21. Khlevniuk, *Stalin*, 38. Radzinsky explains, "No one knows how many people famine carried off. Estimates vary between five and eight million. Stalin fought famine with his usual weapon—Terror" (Radzinsky, *Stalin*, 258). Khlevniuk also writes, "Between 1930 and 1952, some 20 million people were sentenced to incarceration in labor camps, penal colonies, or prisons" (Khlevniuk, *Stalin*, 38).

22. Lipiński, "עַם," *TDOT* 11:174–77.

Finally, *'am* can refer to a foreign nation like Cush (Isa. 18:2) or Egypt (30:5); in the plural (*'ammîm*), it can mean the foreign nations in contrast to Israel (2:3; 8:9; 12:4; etc.), a meaning found also in the expressions *'ammê hāāreṣ* (Est. 8:17) and *'ammê hāᵃrāṣot* (Neh. 9:30). This usage appears frequently in the Essene literature, where *'ammê hāᵃrāṣot* (1QM 10:9; 1QH 4:26), *kōl hā 'ammîm* (1QpHabakkuk 3:6,11,13; 6:7; 8:5), and *(hā)'ammîm* (CD 8:10; etc.) refer to the gentile nations.[23]

Thus, the king of Babylon is a ruler of a vast domain because it includes "peoples."

The use of "nations" with "peoples" makes an even stronger case that the king of Babylon rules a vast domain.[24] It was already argued that the forces that oppose God are composed of kingdoms and governmental nations.[25] It was argued that the governmental meaning of "nation" (גוי) was implied because "nation" (גוי) and "kingdom" (ממלכה) were parallel. The governmental nuance of "nation" (גוי) is also likely here because Isaiah 14:9, 18 reference "all the kings of the nations (גוים)." Furthermore, Isaiah 14:12 describes the king of Babylon as one who defeats (חלש) the nations (גוים).[26] While the content in these three passages is different, the governmental use of "nation" (גוי) is still being used. Since "nation" (גוי) is being used in its governmental sense in Isaiah 13:4, 14:9, 12, 18, and there are no textual clues indicating a nongovernmental use in Isaiah 14:6, the likelihood of the governmental use in Isaiah 14:6 is quite high. Clements agrees with this point: "It was clearly considered normal in ancient Israel for each *goy* to be ruled by its own separate *melekh* ('king'), who stood at its head (Isa. 14:6, 18; 41:2; Jer. 25:14)."[27]

The king of Babylon's vast domain is also displayed by the use of comprehensive terminology in the *mashal*. At his death, *all* the earth is still, and

---

23. Lipiński, "עַם," *TDOT* 11:177.

24. Clements explains, "Since the OT does not contain any ordered or consistent doctrine of nationhood, we find that there is no precise definition of what constitutes a *goy*. Instead, we find that the three major aspects of race, government, and territory all contribute features of their own toward a comprehensive picture" (Clements, "גוי," *TDOT* 2:428).

25. See ch. 3, Two Battles: United Nations Enemy.

26. See "Perceived Divinity and Conqueror of Nations" below.

27. Clements, "גוי," *TDOT* 2:428. Clements omitted the Isaiah 14:9 reference perhaps because it is the same use in 14:18.

then breaks out into singing (14:7). He shakes the earth and kingdoms.[28] He has influence over the entire world (14:17).[29] The king of Babylon was not some minor ruler, but the king of mortal kings.

King of Kings

There are four reasons why the king of Babylon is the king of mortal kings. This is evident by the vastness of his kingdom (14:6),[30] the activities in Sheol (14:9–11), the brightest star (14:12–14), and the trembling of the earth and kingdoms (14:16). Each of these descriptions compositely demonstrates that the king of Babylon is the "greatest of all time" king.

The King of Mortal Kings

In Isaiah 14:9–10, the king of Babylon's greatness is revealed through his interactions with other deceased notable beings.[31]

9a. Sheol from below trembles for you,	שְׁאוֹל מִתַּחַת רָגְזָה לְךָ	9a
9b. To meet your coming.	לִקְרַאת בּוֹאֶךָ	9b
9c. It awakens for you the Rephaim,	עוֹרֵר לְךָ רְפָאִים	9c
9d. All the leaders of the earth.	כָּל־עַתּוּדֵי אָרֶץ	9d
9e. It causes them to arise from their thrones,	הֵקִים מִכִּסְאוֹתָם	9e
9f. All the kings of the earth.	כֹּל מַלְכֵי גוֹיִם:	9f
10a. All of them answer,	כֻּלָּם יַעֲנוּ	10a
10b. And they say to you,	וְיֹאמְרוּ אֵלֶיךָ	10b
10c. "You also have become weak like us,	גַּם־אַתָּה חֻלֵּיתָ כָמוֹנוּ	10c
10d. You have become equal to us."	אֵלֵינוּ נִמְשָׁלְתָּ:	10d

---

28. See "Made Kingdoms Tremble" below.

29. See "Put Israel and Judah to Forced Labor" below.

30. See "Vast Kingdom" above.

31. Hassler notes several arguable comparisons between the king of Babylon and Jesus the Messiah though he seems to miss that they are both "King of Kings" (Hassler, "Isaiah 13:1—14:27," 142). Isaiah 14:9–11 is one strophe, but only Isaiah 14:9–10 is relevant to this point.

The King of Babylon

Sheol is personified and performs three actions in Isaiah 14:9–11.[32] First, Sheol trembles (רגז) at his coming. Mackay notes, "'Stirred up' [רגז] pictures the arrival of the King of Babylon as causing unaccustomed agitation and excitement in a realm generally characterized as being inactive and still."[33] "Trembles" (רגז) is a catchword in the oracle against Babylon. The Lord makes the heavens tremble (13:13); the Lord gives Israel rest from their trembling (14:3); and the earth trembles before the king of Babylon (14:16).[34] Just as God is a trembler of the earth (13:13), so also is the king of Babylon (14:16), and this trembling follows him into Sheol (14:9).[35]

The second verb describes Sheol awakening the Rephaim.[36] The first verb, "trembles" (רגזה), is 3fs, but the second and third verbs, "stirs up" (עורר) and "raises up" (הקים), are 3ms. The LXX resolves the change in gender by making the Rephaim and the kings of the nations the subjects of "stirs up" and "raises up." This modification is unlikely. While "all the kings of the nations" may be viewed collectively, Rephaim consistently takes a plural verb (Deut 2:20; Job 26:5; Ps 88:10; Job 26:5; Prov 2:18; Isa 26:14). König suggests Sheol (שאול) is a noun that can take both genders.[37] Fry suggests, "The shift in gender may, however, be understood as an indication that the subject is no longer sxpecifically שאול [Sheol], but the situation in general, that is, the trembling of Sheol at the oppressor's arrival."[38] Fry's view is not much different from the LXX. Neither König nor Fry explains *why* Isaiah changed the verbs' gender. It is very possible that this is a case of inverted gender-matching which can be done, according to Watson, "to

---

32. Wildberger agrees, "שאול (Sheol) . . . is nothing more than a poetic personification of the place where the dead reside" (Wildberger, *Isaiah 13–27*, 60). This point is discussed further in the "Exposed Corpse" section below.
  Sheol is defined as the realm of the dead. It can include the grave and/or the place of departed souls. See "Exposed Corpse" below.

33. Mackay, *Study Commentary on Isaiah*, 348.

34. See "The Earth and Kingdoms Tremble" below for more information concerning this point.

35. Fry agrees with this connection, "The stirring up of Sheol at the oppressor's coming recalls Yahweh's shaking (ארגיז) of the heavens at his coming (13:13a) inviting comparison between Yahweh and the oppressor. Yahweh's presence causes shaking because of his powerful activity; the oppressor's presence causes shaking because of his fall from power and his impotence in death" (Fry, "'Oracle Concerning Babylon,'" 108–9).

36. Fry, "'Oracle Concerning Babylon,'" 109–10.

37. König, *Historisch-comparative Syntax der hebräischen Sprache*, 161. Erlandsson follows König (Erlandsson, *Burden of Babylon*, 33).

38. Fry, "'Oracle Concerning Babylon,'" 108–9.

emphasise an unusual event."[39] Watson applies inverted gender-matching only to nouns, but there is no reason why it cannot be applied to verbs. Thus, the king of Babylon's entry is a very unusual event, and Isaiah uses inverted gender-matching to emphasize it.

Mystery surrounds the identity of the Rephaim. The parallelism with "kings of the earth" denotes they were individuals of some exalted status, perhaps even god-like.[40] Rouillard presents several theories concerning the Rephaim, most claiming some leadership characteristic, but then references Isaiah 14:9 specifically: "A key text in the books of the prophets is Isaiah 14:9. Here the Rephaim are mentioned in parallelism with 'all the leaders (literally: goats) of the earth' (*kol-'attûdê 'āreṣ*) and 'all the kings of the nations' (*kōl malkê gôyim*). Their royal character is evident."[41] Thus, even if Rephaim could pertain to some insignificant person, the parallelism in Isaiah 14:9 infers that the Rephaim are kings, demi-gods, or gods.

---

39. Watson, *Classical Hebrew Poetry*, 127.

40. The Rephaim are some exalted individuals (kings, heroes), demigods, or gods. L'Heureux claims the Rephaim were gods. He explains the Ugaritic *rp'* is applied to El and the guests at El's feast are *rp'm*. Thus, the supreme deity, El, is a *rp'*, and the minor deities are *rp'm*. L'Heureux ("Ugaritic and Biblical Rephaim," 266–68). Pope claims they are the "deified dead" (Pope, *EL in the Ugaritic Texts*, 192). Suriano claims they are gods or heroes, "[Ugaritic] epic literature typically portrays the Rephaim in an active manner relative to the contemporary (living) characters of the storyline, be they gods or heroes" (Suriano, *Politics of Dead Kings*, 152). These authors agree the Rephaim are some exalted individuals.

Gray, however, claims the Rephaim could be less important people, "Our conclusion is that the *rp'um* of the texts we have examined were human agents, cultic functionaries, probably the king and his immediate associates, who were termed *'elnym* "divine beings" in virtue of their function" (Gray, "Rephaim," 138). But Gray's argument is not persuasive. Even in his statement above, the word to describe the Rephaim is *'elnym* which Gray acknowledges means, "divine beings" (Gray, "Rephaim," 136). Suriano explains that in KTU 1.6 VI: 45-47, "the *rapi'ūma* are paralleled with 'gods' (*'ilā nīyima*) and associated with the 'divine ones' (*'ilūma*) and the 'dead' (*mituma*)" (Suriano, *Politics of Dead Kings*, 152). Similarly, the parallelism in Isaiah 14:9 argues that the Rephaim are deceased leaders, kings, or some similar position, not a mere cultic attendant.

Hassler presents four factors why the Rephaim are "a peculiar race that resulted from angels ('sons of God') generating human male bodies and impregnating human females ('daughters of men,' Gen 6:4)" (Hassler, "Isaiah 13:1—14:27," 116). Hassler's four factors are: (1) the description "sons of God" is an early name for angels (Gen 6:2, 4; Job 1:6; 2:1; 38:7); (2) the Nephilim reflect a "suprahuman nature"; (3) the "sons of God" could only sire males; and (4) the New Testament confirms this position (1 Pet 3:18–20; 2 Pet 4:4–10) (Hassler, "Isaiah 13:1—14:27," 116–18). The Rephaim were god-like individuals, and the king of Babylon is so noteworthy that he draws their attention.

41. Rouillard-Bonraisin, "Rephaim," 695.

Hassler comments, "The fact that the Rephaim even acknowledge the king when he descends to Sheol reinforces the king's portrait as a supremely significant totalitarian. A lesser stature would not command such attention."[42] That Sheol stirs up these leaders to greet the king of Babylon infers that he is a very important person.

The third verb describes Sheol making all the kings of the earth rise from their thrones to meet the king of Babylon. Sitting on one's throne is a symbol of power. For Sheol to raise the kings from their thrones likely means a greater king has arrived.

Fabry demonstrates that ancient Near Eastern cultures understood that the throne and sitting on the throne were symbols of power. Concerning Mesopotamian use of the throne, he states:

> The king received the acclamation of his subjects while seated on his throne. Sennacherib had his throne set up before Lachish to review the spoils taken from the city. Sargon's throne, likewise, was set up before the city gate so that he could witness the battle; seated on his golden throne, he is described as being "like a god." . . . *The throne and above all sitting upon it were thus symbols of power.*[43]

In Ugaritic, he explains, "The throne is the ruler's center of power; here he pronounces his threats against rivals. To 'occupy' (*ywḫd ks*) this throne, 'ascend' (*yrd*) it, or 'sit upon' it (*yṯb*) is synonymous with 'being king.'"[44] Concerning Egypt, Fabry writes, "the throne of the ruler and the throne of the gods are identical. The throne of Pharoah is there called 'throne of Horus,' 'throne of Re,' 'throne of Amon,' etc., but especially 'throne of his father Aten.'"[45] He later states, "The complexity of this throne theology is also illustrated by the fact that the pharaoh likewise represents all the divine kings sitting on the thrones of Geb and exercising the office of the Atum like Re."[46] Thus Mesopotamian, Ugaritic, and Egyptian literature employed "sitting on the throne" as a symbol of power.

---

42. Hassler, "Isaiah 13:1—14:27," 115.

43. Fabry, "כִּסֵּא," *TDOT* 7:235 (emphasis mine). Fabry also says, "'Place someone on the throne' (*wašābu Š*) means 'give power to'; 'ascend the throne' (*elû, erēbu ṣabātu*), 'possess the throne' (*kullu* II), and 'sit upon the throne' (*wašābu*; Assyr. also *kammu*) mean 'have power'" (Fabry, "כִּסֵּא," *TDOT*, 7:235).

44. Fabry, "כִּסֵּא," *TDOT*, 7:237.

45. Fabry, "כִּסֵּא," *TDOT*, 7:240.

46. Fabry, "כִּסֵּא," *TDOT*, 7:240.

Israel's Eschatological Enemy

The Old Testament does not deviate from this pattern. In Deuteronomy 17:18, "sitting on the throne" refers to a king's coronation.[47] When Esther came before the king, he was "sitting upon the throne of his kingdom" (Esth 5:1). Isaiah 6:1 describes the Lord "sitting on a throne." Concerning this vision Wildberger explains, "When Yahweh is depicted sitting upon such a throne, he is presented as king; cf. 40:22; in v. 5, he is actually called מלך (king), Yahweh of hosts."[48] Fabry concludes, "*Sitting upon the throne is taken as a sign of uncontested sovereignty* (Ps. 9:5[4]; 132:12; Jer. 33:21; Zec. 6:13)."[49]

If "sitting on the throne" means uncontested sovereignty, then the meaning of Sheol raising these kings from their thrones must be determined. Fabry explains, "The violent end of a reign is described by 'being toppled from the throne' (Hag. 2:22; Ps. 89:45[44]; Dnl. 5:20) or 'falling from the throne' (1 S. 4:18; Isa. 14:12 [with mythological hyperbole])."[50] In Isaiah 14:9, Sheol does not cast the kings from their thrones, but "raises" (הקים) them up to greet the king of Babylon. Concerning enthronement and deposition, Fabry also explains:

> The semantic field of enthronement includes "placing someone on the throne" (*hôšîḇ lᵉ*) [Job 36:7], *hôšîḇ 'al* [1 K. 2:24; 2 Ch. 23:20], *nāṯan 'al* [1 K. 5:19(5); 10:9; 2 Ch. 9:8], *śîm 'al* [2 K. 10:3], and *šîṯ lᵉ* Ps. 132:11]); the opposite is *hēqîm mikkissē'*, "raise from the throne" (Isa. 14:9) or *nḥt*, "be deposed" (Dnl. 5:20). Related is "sit upon the throne" (*yāšaḇ lᵉ* [Ps. 9:5(4); 132:12], *yāšaḇ 'al* [Ex. 11:5; 12:29; 1 K. 1:13, 17,20,24,27,30,35; 22:10; Est. 1:2; 2 Ch. 18:9], *hāyâ* [Zec. 6:13(?)], *māšal* [Zec. 6:13], and *mālaḵ* [Jer. 33:21]), with the antonyms "fall" or "rise" from the throne (*nāp̄al* [1 S. 4:18], *yāraḏ* [Ezk. 26:16], *qûm* [Jgs. 3:20; Jon. 3:6]) and "sit in the dust without a throne" (*'ĕn-kissē'* [Isaiah 47:11]).[51]

Fabry mentions Isaiah 14:9 as the "opposite" of enthronement. While it may be tempting to claim Sheol dethrones the kings of the nations, this position is unlikely. There are three times in the Bible when kings rise from their thrones. First, Eglon rises from his throne to hear Ehud's pointed

---

47. McIntosh, *Deuteronomy*, 214; Lundbom, *Deuteronomy*, 541; Tigay, *Deuteronomy*, 168.
48. Wildberger, *Isaiah 1-12*, 261.
49. Fabry, "כִּסֵּא," *TDOT* 7:257 (emphasis mine).
50. Fabry, "כִּסֵּא," *TDOT* 7:257.
51. Fabry, "כִּסֵּא," *TDOT* 7:244.

message from God (Judg 3:20). Second, the king of Nineveh rises from his throne, sets aside his royal garments, and puts on sackcloth.[52] In both of these cases, the act of rising from the throne is not dethroning. They are merely standing up for some purpose.

Most revealing is Solomon's arising from his throne at Bathsheba's approaching in 1 Kings 2:19. When Bathsheba came before David (1 Kgs 1:17), she paid homage to him (חוה); but when she came before Solomon, he rose (קום) from his throne and paid homage to her (חוה).[53] Just as Solomon rose (קום) to meet (קרא) Bathsheba and pay homage (חוה) to her, so also does Sheol raise up (קום) the kings of the earth from their thrones to meet (קרא) the king of Babylon. The kings of the nations should pay homage to the greater king. Instead of paying him homage, however, they speak and say, "Indeed, you have become weak like us; you are like us."[54] The king of Babylon, though greater than they in the land of the living, is just like them in Sheol. Oswalt correctly explains, "When the mighty king appears they rise as though to do homage, which one might expect if this were a normal lament. But instead they mock him by reminding him that in the sight of death all human distinctions are meaningless."[55] In the land of the living, the king of Babylon was the king of mortal kings, but in Sheol, he is another dead king.[56]

---

52. "In response to the news of Jonah's proclamation and the growing response among his subjects, the king of Nineveh humbled himself in four steps. . . . First he rose from the throne, relinquishing the trappings of his royal authority. Next he removed his robe, signifying his wealth and prestige, and replaced it with sackcloth. Finally, he joined the rest of Nineveh in the dust, adding his pleas for mercy to theirs" (Youngblood, *Jonah*, 137).

53. There is a textual issue in 1 Kings 2:19. The Septuagint reads καὶ κατεφίλησεν αὐτὴν (and he kissed her). This was likely done because the Septuagint translators acknowledged the difficulty of having the queen mother bow before the king.

54. Oswalt acknowledges, "When the mighty king appears they rise as though to do homage, which one might expect if this were a normal lament" (Oswalt, *Book of Isaiah*, 318).

55. Oswalt, *Book of Isaiah*, 318.

56. A potential objection concerns Bathsheba's obeisance to Solomon, the higher authority. Could, potentially, the kings of the nations simply pay homage to the king of Babylon in like manner? Preuss writes, "Very often we find *hishtach^{a}vāh* in the sense of 'homage to the king.' Many of the occurrences belonging here make it clear that we are dealing with a gesture of submission or surrender (1 S. 24:9[8]; 2 S. 1:2; 9:6; 14:4,22; 15:5; 16:4; 18:28; 24:20 [cf. 1 Ch. 21:21]; 1 K. 1:23,53; 2 Ch. 24:17). Even Bathsheba bows to David (1 K. 1:16, 31; cf. Ps. 45:12[11], the royal bride to the king). Solomon, on the other hand, bows to Bathsheba, since she is the mother of the king (1 K. 2:19)" (Preuss,

Second, the speech of the kings of the nations proves that the king of Babylon is the king of mortal kings. First, "Even you ..." (גַּם־אַתָּה) reveals their astonishment. Clements explains, "Here, the shades... of the dead rulers of earth are pictured as getting up from their thrones in astonishment to greet this great world-ruler who has come to share their fate."[57] According to HALOT, גַּם is a "particle of association and emphasis."[58] It communicates emphasis because it begins the line and functions with the pronoun "you" (אַתָּה).[59] The use of the pronoun and "even" (גַּם) reveal the astonishment of the inhabitants of Sheol at the arrival of the king of Babylon. Smith believes the king of Babylon is Merodach-baladan, a very ignominious king, but he still acknowledges, "The dead kings immediately respond that 'even you,' the great Babylonian king, are now weak and no different from the other kings who have died."[60] Oswalt also recognizes the contrast, "Although his glory had made him seem almost immortal, he too must bow to corruption and decay."[61] Thus, the astonishment of the kings of the nations also argues that the king of Babylon is the king of mortal kings.

The Brightest Star and Conqueror of Nations

The king of Babylon is the brightest star and conquers nations.

"חוה," *TDOT* 4:251–52). Bowing before a king was an act of submission and surrender. Preuss does not resolve the tension in 1 Kings 2:19 and seems content leaving Bathsheba in a more powerful position than Solomon. Cushman argues for a very powerful Bathsheba, stating: "Again Bat-Sheba enters the throne room unheralded. She neither bows nor kneels before Solomon. Rather, when she enters Solomon stands up from his throne, the symbol of his royal power, and bows to his mother in an act of homage. Solomon provides her with a throne at his right side" (Cushman, "Politics of the Royal Harem," 339–40). First Kings 2:19 is the exception, not the norm, and a full explanation is beyond the scope of this dissertation.

57. Clements, *Isaiah 1–39*, 142.

58. HALOT, "גַּם," 1:195.

59. Fry agrees, "The use of the independent pronoun (אַתָּה) is emphatic. It underscores the surprise of the disturbed shades" (Fry, "'Oracle Concerning Babylon,'" 211). The particle and independent subject pronoun work together to illustrate the astonishment of the deceased.

60. Smith, *Isaiah 1–39*, 314.

61. Oswalt, *Book of Isaiah*, 318. Wildberger says, "He seemed to be stronger than anyone else; now he is also just as 'weak' as all the other Rephaim" (Wildberger, *Isaiah 13–27*, 62).

The King of Babylon

12a. How you have fallen from heaven,	אֵיךְ נָפַלְתָּ מִשָּׁמַיִם	12a
12b. Shining one, son of the dawn.	הֵילֵל בֶּן־שָׁחַר	12b
12c. You have been hewn down to the earth,	נִגְדַּעְתָּ לָאָרֶץ	12c
12d. One who defeated the nations.	חוֹלֵשׁ עַל־גּוֹיִם:	12d
13a. And you said in your heart,	וְאַתָּה אָמַרְתָּ בִלְבָבְךָ	13a
13b. "I will ascend to the heavens.	הַשָּׁמַיִם אֶעֱלֶה	13b
13c. Above the stars of God,	מִמַּעַל לְכוֹכְבֵי־אֵל	13c
13d. I will exalt my throne.	אָרִים כִּסְאִי	13d
13e. And I will sit in the mount of the assembly,	וְאֵשֵׁב בְּהַר־מוֹעֵד	13e
13f. In the far reaches of the north.	בְּיַרְכְּתֵי צָפוֹן:	13f
14a. I will ascend above the heights of the clouds,	אֶעֱלֶה עַל־בָּמֳתֵי עָב	14a
14b. I will be like the Most High."	אֶדַּמֶּה לְעֶלְיוֹן:	14b

Isaiah 14:12–14 is one of the most controversial sections of Isaiah 13–14. First, this section unpacks the criterion that the king of Babylon is a "conqueror of the nations." Then, through an analysis of the structure and identity of הילל בן־שחר (shining one [Lucifer], son of dawn), this section argues that the king of Babylon is personified as a star which thinks arrogant thoughts.

Conqueror of Nations

"Defeat" (חלש) is a rare root occurring only four times (Exod 17:14; Job 14:10; Isa 14:12; Joel 4:10). Burns analyzes all four uses of "defeat" (חלש) and claims it should be translated "warrior over the nations." He explains that even in the nonmilitary use in Job 14, "[חלש] cannot be totally divorced from the idea of cutting down. The man, like the tree, is cut down by death and remains fallen."[62] Exodus 17:13 states, "And Joshua defeated (חלש) Amalek and his people with the blade of the sword." Just as Joshua defeated a nation (Amalek), so also the king of Babylon defeats nations.[63]

---

62. Burns, "'ḥôlēš ʿal' in Isaiah 14:12," 200.

63. Burns recognizes the militaristic connotation of חלש though he argues for the translation "warrior," Burns, "Does Helel 'go to Hell?'"

Israel's Eschatological Enemy

One king who has been identified as one of the greatest conquerors of all time is Alexander the Great. Concerning his generalship, Cartledge writes, "[Alexander the Great's] ancient greatness and his present claim to remembrance alike rest primarily and ultimately on his generalship, his leadership of men in war. It has been said of him that a list of his field successes reads like the logbook of a military Midas—everything that that legendary king of Phrygia touched turned to gold."[64] Cartledge also puts Alexander the Great's achievements in perspective: "When Julius [Caesar] was on an early tour of imperial duty in Spain, Plutarch relates, he is said to have gazed at a statue of Alexander. . . . And he wept because, whereas Alexander had died at thirty-two, king of so many people, he himself at that same age had not yet achieved any brilliant success."[65] The king of Babylon is a conqueror like Alexander the Great.

Discontinuity with Isaiah 14:11

Alden claims the deceased kings of the nations (14:11) are still the ones speaking in Isaiah 14:12.[66] There are three reasons, however, why the dead kings' speech ended in 14:11. First, just as the *mashal* began with the interrogative "How" (איך), so also "How" (איך) occurs again, marking the second section of the *mashal*.[67] Second, there is a scene change. "Shining one" (הילל) has fallen from heaven to *the earth*, not Sheol.[68] Third, "shining one" (הילל) is described at the end of Isaiah 14:12 as "one who destroyed nations." This is the activity of the king of Babylon during his days of living

---

64. Cartledge, *Alexander the Great*, 157.

65. Cartledge, *Alexander the Great*, 39.

66. Alden states, "The ghosts of those already there express surprise at the newcomer. 'You too!' they say (v. 10). Verse 12 is a quotation of the fellow shades in Sheol. 'How are you fallen from heaven, O Day Star, son of Dawn!' They continue, reminding the king of his boasts of equality and even superiority to God, but conclude noting that his death was more ignominious than most having been 'cast out, away from your supulchre'" (Alden, "Lucifer, Who or What?," 37–38).

67. Fry agrees, "The איך of line 12a, like that of 4d, emphasizes the remarkable nature in the reversal of fortune for the oppressor and signals the beginning of a new strophe (vv 12–15) in the taunt which is to be recited by the Israelites when Yahweh gives them rest" (Fry, "'Oracle Concerning Babylon,'" 114–15).

68. Burns explains, "'ereṣ is used exclusively as the place of the king's this-worldly activities and šĕʼōl as the locus of his other-worldly fate" (Burns, "Does Helel 'go to Hell?,'" 90). For an explanation of the figures of speech used here, see the "Shining One, Son of the Dawn (הילל בן שחר)" section below.

on earth, not an activity in Sheol. While the scene will transition back to Sheol in Isaiah 14:15, first the king of Babylon's hubris is described through his exalted status *on earth*.

SHINING ONE, SON OF THE DAWN (הילל בן שחר)

Traditionally, "shining one [Lucifer], son of the dawn" (הילל בן שחר) has been identified as Satan.[69] Some claim Isaiah is alluding to some myth.[70] Others believe "shining one" is simply the king of Babylon.[71] This section analyzes these three views and argues that the king of Babylon is personified as a star.

Three arguments have been proffered that favor the Satan view. First, Hassler claims:

> In pressing the identity of הֵילֵל בֶּן־שָׁחַר a bit further, one can attempt to determine which end-time ruler is in view. He might be the king of Babylon spoken of throughout the taunt song, since he experiences a fall (Isa 14:4, 12), weakens the nations (vv. 4–6, 12, 16–17), and exhibits pride (vv. 11, 13–14). But verses 13–14 do not seem to convey the thoughts of a mere human being.
>
> For that reason, the current writer believes that verses 12–14 refer to the *angelic ruler, Satan*.[72]

While Hassler seems open to "shining one" (הילל) being the king of Babylon, he ultimately claims he is Satan because the language does not "convey the thoughts of a mere human being." Bertoluci similarly writes, "Vss. 12–15 are that point in the poem where the prophet, in a clearer way, gives the impression that the implications of the poem transcend mere historical figures in the human earthly realm. Those verses seem to pertain to

---

69. See ch. 1, "History of Interpretation."

70. See below. Authors who claim a mythological allusion include: Childs, *Myth and Reality*, 70–72; Hayes and Irvine, *Isaiah*, 232; Roberts, *First Isaiah*, 210; Sweeney, *Isaiah 1–39*, 237–38; Kaiser, *Isaiah: 13–39*, 40–41; Chisholm, *Handbook on the Prophets*, 50; Blenkinsopp, *Isaiah 1–39*, 288; Brueggemann, *Isaiah*, 129; Goldingay, *Isaiah*, 103; Motyer, *Prophecy of Isaiah*, 144–45; Clements, *Isaiah 1–39*, 142–43; Watts, *Isaiah 1–33*, 209–11; Gowan, *When Man Becomes God*; Pope, *EL in the Ugaritic Texts*, 161–63; Craigie, "Helel Athtar and Phaethon," 223–25; Smith, *Isaiah 1–39*, 314–15.

71. Young, *Book of Isaiah*, 1:441–42; Oswalt, *Book of Isaiah*, 321–22.

72. Hassler, "Isaiah 13:1—14:27," 124–25 (emphasis mine).

the heavenly realm of the sphere of the heavenly beings."[73] Hassler and Bertoluci seem to limit the extent of human pride and arrogance to the mortal.

It was common practice among rulers to consider themselves gods.[74] Some have even contested that the Old Testament viewed rulers and judges as gods.[75] Thus, it would be likely that the king of mortal kings would think of himself as a god, and, in his arrogance, seek to be the highest god.

Consider the arrogance of Alexander the Great. Cartledge explains, "Alexander was one of the first Greeks—though not quite the very first—to be worshipped as a god in his lifetime."[76] Alexander claimed to be the son of Zeus.[77] Arrian recounted an incident where some were desiring to perform obeisance before Alexander:

> As to Callisthenes' opposition to Alexander regarding obeisance, the following story is also prevalent. It had been agreed between Alexander and the Sophists and the most illustrious of the Persians and Medes at his court that mention of this topic should be introduced at a wine-party. Anaxarchus began the subject, saying that it would be far more just to reckon Alexander a god than Dionysus and Heracles . . . in any case there was no doubt that when Alexander had departed from men [died] they would honour him

---

73. Bertoluci, "Son of the Morning," 192.

74. Redford, *ABD* 5:289; Steinkeller, *ABD* 4:724–32. Smith explains that in the ancient Near Eastern world, divine figures could include "not only major deities but also a wide variety of other phenomena: monstrous cosmic enemies; demons; some living kings; dead kings or the dead more generally; deities' images and standards as well as standing stones; and other cultic items and places" (Smith, *Origins of Biblical Monotheism*, 6).

75. In Exodus 4:16 and 7:1 Moses is the mouthpiece of God. In Deuteronomy 1:17, the judge's judgment is God's. Even in the Bible there is a relationship between God and humans who are in positions of authority. Psalm 82, while extremely controversial, appears to build on this idea. While there are several interpretations of Psalm 82, in some way "gods" die and, therefore, must be human (cf. John 10:34). Ross explains, "The most plausible explanation is that the psalmist used the word 'gods' to refer to both human judges and the supernatural powers behind them. The announcement of doom on the one would necessarily include the other (see also Ps. 97 and Isaiah 27:1)" (Ross, *Commentary on the Psalms*, 719). Goldingay claims the Bible uses words for "god" just like the ancient Near Eastern world does, and it can refer to many things including kings (Goldingay, *Psalms 42–89*, 561).

76. Cartledge, *Alexander the Great*, 237.

77. Dodge, *Alexander*, 497. Cartledge explains, "Philotas may also have been known to disapprove of Alexander's claim—as articulated and broadcast after his visit to Ammon's oracle in the Siwah oasis—to be the son of Zeus (or/and Ammon)" (Cartledge, *Alexander the Great*, 98).

as a god; how much more just, then, that they should give him his due in life rather than when he was dead and the honour would profit him nothing.⁷⁸

Callisthenes refused to perform obeisance before Alexander, and, according to Arrian, was rebuked for it.⁷⁹ Cartledge correctly notes concerning this incident:

> Strictly speaking, however, this does not prove that Alexander ordered his own deification, only that these Greeks were prepared to grant it. Nor, by any means, were they the only ones. Almost certainly, the Greeks of Asia—those whom Alexander had claimed to have come to liberate from Persian despotism—were also worshipping him as a god in his lifetime, and probably had been for several years already.⁸⁰

While Alexander may not have ordered his own deification, he certainly accepted it. Historians today sometimes even speak as if he were divine.⁸¹

In Isaiah 14:13–14, the *thoughts* of the king of Babylon are described. A great king like Alexander the Great would very likely think such great and arrogant thoughts as contained in Isaiah 14:12–14. Hassler and Bertoluci's claim that Isaiah 14:12–14 does not "convey the thoughts of a mere human" fails to account for the seemingly endless limit of human pride.

Hassler provides a second reason why Isaiah 14:13–14 refers to Satan:

> In developing my approach more, the disjunctive clause in Isaiah 14:13–14 expresses parenthetical background information, explaining why Satan falls from heaven to earth—because of his sinful thoughts in antiquity. In other words, these statements in verses 13–14 offer "flashbacks to his original intentions" as "parenthetical matter."⁸²

Thus, the disjunctive clause (ואתה), according to Hassler, introduces the "parenthetical background information." This interpretation is unlikely

---

78. Arrian, *Arrian*, 373–75.

79. Arrian, *Arrian*, 381.

80. Cartledge, *Alexander the Great*, 247.

81. Dodge writes, "[Alexander's] indefatigable pursuit was due to his own unrestrained, relentless will. It was almost superhuman in its energy" (Dodge, *Alexander*, 425).

82. Hassler, "Isaiah 13:1—14:27," 126. See also Dickason, *Angels*, 64, 140; McCune, *Systematic Theology of Biblical Christianity*, 377–79.

Israel's Eschatological Enemy

for two reasons. First, one cannot separate Isaiah 14:13-14 from verse 15. One of the characteristics of the dirge is the contrast motif.[83] The king of Babylon sought not only the heights, but also the highest of the heights (14:13, far reaches of the North). Instead, he received not just the depths, but the depths of the depths (14:15, far reaches of the pit). Reality (14:15) contrasts with hubris (14:13-14). The being in Isaiah 14:13-14 is the same being in 14:15.[84] Second, Isaiah 14:19 employs the same clause (ואתה), but Hassler does not argue for "parenthetical background information" there.

The strongest argument for the Satan view comes from Isaiah 14:12—"shining one" is cast out of heaven to *the earth*, not Sheol. This intermediate state which "shining one" occupies is a mystery. According to the Satan view, this is Satan's fall from heaven when he sinned. As a mortal, the king of Babylon could never actually exist *in* heaven, so this begs the question who is in heaven and cast to the earth? Bertoluci writes, "Those verses seem to pertain to the heavenly realm or the sphere of the heavenly beings."[85] More likely, no one is cast from heaven just as no kings are actually rising from their thrones in Sheol. Isaiah has just personified Sheol and dead kings; now he personifies the stars. The king of Babylon, the brightest "star," has lost his dominion and is thus "cast to the earth."

Isaiah creates a comparison among the stars. He calls the king of Babylon הילל בן שחר because he is the brightest star, the greatest ruler. הילל is literally "shining one," and בן שחר is literally "son of dawn."[86] Both are references to the planet Venus. Isaiah 14:12 may be an instance of polyonymia

---

83. See ch. 2.

84. Fry agrees, "But with the naming of God in 14b, there is a climactic invocation of the divine reality which is at work demonstrating in the downfall of the oppressor that his thoughts are merely a haughty delusion. The interjection אך at the beginning of line 15a divides the preceding line 14b, the climax of the oppressor's delusion, from lines 15a and b, the summary of the real fate of the oppressor" (Fry, "'Oracle Concerning Babylon,'" 118).

85. Bertoluci, "Son of the Morning," 192.

86. Bertoluci summarizes several views concerning הילל בן שחר (Bertoluci, "Son of the Morning," 193-99). Concerning the vocalization of הילל, Grelot explains that the historic interpretation is preferred and concludes, "De ce fait, les traductions d'*Is.* XIV 12 dans les LXX (ἑωσφόρος) et la Vulgate *(Lucifer)* song excellentes, et la paraphrase du Targum est bien dans la ligne du texte original" (Grelot, "Isaïe 14:12-15 et Son Arrière-Plan Mythologique," 30). Watts resolutely claims, "שחר 'Shachar' is known as a god's name. In the OT Ps 139:9 speaks of his 'wings'; Job 3:9; 41:18 'his eyelashes' or 'rays.' Other references (Cant 6:19; Pss 57:9; 108:3; 110:3) show personalized poetic views of the dawn that may reflect such an idea" (Watts, *Isaiah 1-33*, 210). Each of these uses, however, can be understood as figures of speech.

as well.[87] The king of Babylon attains a new name, הילל בן שחר.[88] According to Rose, "The 'name' is a 'distinguishing mark.'"[89] This name reveals that the king of Babylon is the greatest ruler (brightest star) of all the rulers (stars). Hassler agrees:

> Given that the taunt song describes rulers symbolically ("rulers," lit., "male goats," v. 9; "stars," i.e., rulers, v. 13), Bible interpreters can consider the possibility that the "morning star" also symbolizes a *ruler*. As a ruler he possesses authority ("my throne . . . I will sit," v. 13). As a ruler ("morning star," v. 12) he seeks to exalt himself over other rulers ("stars of God," v. 13).[90]

Each star is a "ruler," and rulers have dominion. Hassler explains:

> Throughout Scripture stars can symbolize rulers in contexts of dominion—whether those rulers are human (Rev 1:20) or the Son of God (Num 24:17). More specifically, the "morning star" symbolizes rulers such as Jesus (2 Pet 1:19; Rev 22:16) or holy angels (Job 38:7). Whenever the Son of God is called a star, it is always in a context of His rulership. . . . In 2 Peter 1:19 Jesus appears as the morning star in a context of His rulership, the end-times day of the Lord. John calls Jesus the "Bright Morning Star" in a context of rulership, namely, the mention of King David and Jesus' Parousia (Rev 22:16).[91]

---

87. Bullinger explains polyonymia, "It is not uncommon for persons or places to be known by different names" (Bullinger, *Figures of Speech*, 775). Interestingly, Bullinger uses Isaiah 14:4 as an illustration and explains, "The Antichrist is called 'the King of Babylon,' because he is the end and final outcome of Babel" (Bullinger, *Figures of Speech*, 776).

88. Burns rejects that הילל is a name: "The monarch's fall is compared to that of Helel ben Shachar. This comparison (v 12a) is momentary and should not be understood as suggesting that the epithet is a title or alternative designation for the king—any more than Elyon in v 14b" (Burns, "Does Helel 'go to Hell?,'" 89). Burns must prove, however, that "Elyon" is not a name. Burns does correctly recognize that there is a comparison in Isaiah 14:12, but he seems to regard it as an instance of hypocatastasis which does not fit the larger context. Bullinger explains hypocatastasis, "As a figure, it differs from *Metaphor*, because in a metaphor the two nouns are *both* named and given; while, in *Hypocatastasis*, only *one* is named and the other is implied, or as it were, is *put down underneath* out of sight" (Bullinger, *Figures of Speech*, 744; emphasis his). Thus, according to Burns, הילל is the stated referent, and the king of Babylon is the implied one.

89. Rose, *ABD* 4:1002.

90. Hassler, "Isaiah 13:1—14:27," 130 (emphasis his).

91. Hassler, "Isaiah 13:1—14:27," 131.

Israel's Eschatological Enemy

Isaiah uses the star metaphor to illustrate that the king of Babylon is a great ruler. In fact, he is the brightest star, greatest ruler, and, therefore, the king of mortal kings.

Theologically, there may be a connection between rulers and the supernatural powers which empower them (Ps 82; Dan 10:13; Eph 6:10–12). Even if Satan empowers the king of Babylon, Isaiah 14:12–14 is not about Satan. It is the king of Babylon whose "majesty" (גאון) is brought down to Sheol (14:11). It is the king of Babylon who conquered (חולש) the nations (14:12). It is the king of Babylon himself who is brought down to Sheol (14:15). It is upon the king of Babylon whom the public stares (14:16). The arrogance, actions, and fate all concern the king of Babylon, not the supernatural force which may empower him.[92]

The second view is the mythological view. Concerning the identity of "shining one" (הילל), Watson explains, "The search for a comparable myth in neighboring religions has led scholars to Babylonian, Ugaritic and Greek mythology."[93] Scholars have looked everywhere for the corresponding myth and have not found it. Poirier's claim that there are two mythological allusions is unconvincing.[94] The inability of scholars to find a corresponding myth mitigates against this view.[95] Oswalt correctly states, "The indications

---

92. C. S. Lewis communicated the ambiguity between the actual person and the force possessing the person through the satanically indwelt character of Weston in *Perelandra*: "[Ransom] did not know whether in the last few hours the spirit which had spoken to him was really Weston's or whether he had been the victim of a ruse. Indeed, it made little difference. There was, no doubt, a confusion of persons in damnation. . . . They were melted down into their Master, as a lead soldier slips down and loses his shape in the ladle held over the gas ring. The question whether Satan, or one whom Satan has digested, is acting on any given occasion, has in the long run no clear significance" (Lewis, *Perelandra*, 148). Just as the identity of Weston had become confused with the supernatural force which empowered him, so also may the identity of the king of Babylon be confused with the supernatural power which may empower him. However, in *Perelandra*, Ransom killed Weston. So also, it is the king of Babylon who physically perishes.

93. Watson, "HELEL," 393. Watson then explains why he believes Isaiah 14:12–15 reflects the Ugaritic myth. As Hassler also has pointed out, Watson had previously believed הילל referred to Utnapishtim in the Gilgamesh Epic (Watson, *Classical Hebrew Poetry*, 309–10).

94. Poirier, "Illuminating Parallel to Isaiah XIV 12," 371–89.

95. Burns claims, "While there are undoubted mythological references, they do not set forth a consistent scheme, nor were they ever intended to do so" (Burns, "Does Helel 'go to Hell?,'" 89). Keown states, "The numerous references to heavenly places and heavenly beings have helped to give a mythical identity to הילל בן־שחר. Modern scholars have compared him to deities from the mythologies of surrounding regions. Athtar of Ugarit, Athtar of South Arabia, Phaethon of Greece, Kumarbi of Hittite legend, and others are

are that the prophet was not dependent upon any one story, but used a number of current motifs to fit his own point."⁹⁶

Functionally, the mythological view still claims "shining one" (הילל) is the king of Babylon. Childs writes, "The prophetic writer has taken this old myth and reworked it into his taunt song. He compares the mighty king of Babylon to the upstart Helel. He also had a brilliant start, but then Yahweh hurled him down to become the laughing stock of the nations."⁹⁷ Hassler rejects the mythological view: "A mythological being does not possess the reality necessary to weaken real nations."⁹⁸ Hassler's criticism, however, does not correspond. The mythological view only claims that the myth carries illustrative force. Childs explains, "the myth carries only illustrative value as an extended figure of speech."⁹⁹ Thus, the mythological view claims the myth provides a comparative background, and "shining one" (הילל) is still the king of Babylon.

Most likely, Isaiah is personifying the king of Babylon as a star. There are three reasons why "shining one" (הילל) is the king of Babylon. First, the context of the *mashal* argues for it.¹⁰⁰ Second, the second-person singular pronoun consistently refers to the king of Babylon.¹⁰¹ Third, the immediate context supports personification. Isaiah first personified the talking trees (14:8). Then he personified the dead kings who talk (14:9–11). Now, he personifies Venus, the morning star, which talks (in his heart) in Isaiah 14:13–14. The personification of stars is not unprecedented. In Job 38:7, the morning stars sing (כוכבי בקר),¹⁰² and in Numbers 24:16, "A star will

---

examined for possible parallel traits. As in the case of the historical king, no mythical figure furnishes a convincing parallel to הילל בן־שחר" (Keown, "History of the Interpretation of Isaiah 14:12–15," 139).

96. Oswalt, *Book of Isaiah*, 322.

97. Childs, *Myth and Reality*, 71.

98. Hassler, "Isaiah 13:1—14:27," 123–24.

99. Childs, *Myth and Reality*, 72. The function of the text is the same though the referent is the deity Helel, not Venus.

100. Calvin writes, "The context plainly shows that these statements must be understood in reference to the king of the Babylonians" (Calvin, *Commentary on the Book of the Prophet Isaiah*, 442).

101. Youngblood explains, "The pronoun *you* links vv. 12–15 with the other verses of Isaiah's taunt song. Beginning in v. 8 and continuing almost without interruption through v. 20, it refers throughout to the king of Babylon" (Youngblood, "Fall of Lucifer," 172).

102. Bullinger, *Figures of Speech*, 865. See also Hartley, *Book of Job*, 495n21.

come out of Jacob."¹⁰³ "Shining one, son of the dawn" (הילל בן שחר) is a real person who thinks arrogant thoughts.

The Earth and Kingdoms Tremble

The king of Babylon makes surrounding kingdoms tremble.

16a. Ones who see you, they stare	רֹאֶיךָ אֵלֶיךָ יַשְׁגִּיחוּ	16a
16b. At you they contemplate,	אֵלֶיךָ יִתְבּוֹנָנוּ	16b
16c. "Is this the man who shook the earth,	הֲזֶה הָאִישׁ מַרְגִּיז הָאָרֶץ	16c
16d. The one who made kingdoms tremble?"	מַרְעִישׁ מַמְלָכוֹת׃	16d

The contrast that began in Isaiah 14:15 continues in 14:16 through the contemplation of onlookers. As these people observe the fall of the king of Babylon, the contrast is emphasized through the rhetorical question, "Is this the man . . . ?" The shaker of the earth and trembler of kingdoms has descended to Sheol.¹⁰⁴ The focus here is on his greatness. When the king of Babylon ruled on the earth, the earth shook and kingdoms (plural) quaked before him. These two metaphors emphasize his greatness because a lesser king would not create such a tumultuous situation on earth. Torrey, claiming the king of Babylon is Alexander the Great, correctly explains:

> The powerful and highly finished poem, 14 ₄ᵦ₋₂₁, celebrates *the death of a mighty king*, a great conqueror and oppressor, the greatest, apparently, that the world had ever seen. . . .
>
> Now the poem has been recognized by some modern scholars as having for its subject the death of Alexander, a far greater conqueror than any Assyrian or Babylonian ruler, a man who "shook the earth" as no other had shaken it. In comparison with *his* "yoke," that of Assyria was negligible.¹⁰⁵

---

103. Concerning Numbers 24:17, Budd writes, "כוכב 'a star' cf. Isa 14:12 where this is a metaphor for a king, as should probably be understood here" (Budd, *Numbers*, 270). Ashley connects Numbers 24:17 with Isaiah 14 as well, "Although it is relatively uncommon to use this image to refer to a royal figure in Israel (Isa. 14:12, which refers to the Babylonian king; cf. Ezek. 32:7; Rev. 22:16), it seems common in the ancient Near East" (Ashley, *Book of Numbers*, 500). See also Harrison, *Numbers*, 321; Cole, *Numbers*, 426.

104. The catchword function of רגז and רעש was highlighted in the "King of Mortal Kings" section above.

105. Torrey, "Some Important Editorial Operations," 116 (emphasis his).

Torrey has correctly recognized the magnanimity of the king of Babylon. But even Alexander is only arguably the greatest ruler of all time. Some contend Genghis Khan was the greatest conqueror of all time.[106] Lamb states, "We Americans, raised in the European tradition, have been taught the roster of the great that begins with Alexander of Macedon, continues through the Caesars, and ends with Napoleon. Genghis Khan was a conqueror of more gigantic stature than the well known actors of the European stage."[107] The breadth of Genghis Khan's kingdom and his military genius create at least an equal, if not a usurper, to Alexander.[108] The king of Babylon will be an even greater king than Alexander the Great or Genghis Khan.

Conclusion

The king of Babylon is the king of mortal kings. This was argued first by the breadth of his kingdom. Isaiah 14:6 states that "peoples" and "nations" were under the authority of the king of Babylon. Thus, the king of Babylon did not simply vie for the domain of Babylon in the way that Merodach-baladan did.

Second, this section demonstrated the greatness of the king of Babylon through the personification of Sheol and the dead in Sheol. Sheol raises dead leaders, Rephaim, and kings to greet the king of Babylon. It is presumed that the kings would pay homage to the king of Babylon, but the poem shifts. Instead of paying homage, the kings speak and explain that the king of Babylon is now just like them. In the land of the living, the king of Babylon was the king of kings, and these kings would have paid homage to him. But in the land of the dead, the king of Babylon is just another dead king. This personification of Sheol reveals the greatness of the king of Babylon. He is the king of mortal kings.

Third, the king of Babylon conquered nations and is the brightest star. As the brightest star, he is the greatest ruler of all the stars.

Fourth, surrounding kingdoms trembled before the king of Babylon. While Torrey's claim that the king of Babylon is Alexander the Great is

---

106. Weatherford, *Genghis Khan and the Quest for God*.

107. Lamb, *Genghis Khan*, 13.

108. Lamb compares the two, "Of necessity we must turn to Alexander of Macedon, that reckless and victorious youth, to find a conquering genius the equal of Genghis Khan—Alexander the god-like, marching with his phalanx toward the rising sun, bearing with him the blessing of Greek culture" (Lamb, *Genghis Khan*, 16).

rejected, his claim illustrates well the greatness of the future king of Babylon. Alexander was a mighty conqueror who conquered many nations and made kingdoms quake. Yet even Alexander the Great is only debatably the king of mortal kings.

Exposed Corpse

The one criterion that eliminates most prospective kings of Babylon is his exposed corpse.

18a. All the kings of the nations,	כָּל־מַלְכֵי גוֹיִם	18a
18b. All of them.	כֻּלָּם	18b
18c. They lie down in glory,	שָׁכְבוּ בְכָבוֹד	18c
18d. Each man in his house.	אִישׁ בְּבֵיתוֹ:	18d
19a. But you, you have been cast out from your grave,	וְאַתָּה הָשְׁלַכְתָּ מִקִּבְרְךָ	19a
19b. Like an abominable branch,	כְּנֵצֶר נִתְעָב	19b
19c. Covered by the slain,	לְבוּשׁ הֲרֻגִים	19c
19d. Ones pierced with a sword,	מְטֹעֲנֵי חָרֶב	19d
19e. Ones going down to the stones of the pit,	יוֹרְדֵי אֶל־אַבְנֵי־בוֹר	19e
19f. Like a trampled underfoot corpse.	כְּפֶגֶר מוּבָס:	19f
20a. You will not unite with them in burial,	לֹא־תֵחַד אִתָּם בִּקְבוּרָה	20a

The contrast between the king of Babylon and the kings of the nations is implicit in Isaiah 14:9–11, but here it is explicit.[109] In Isaiah 14:9–11, the kings of the nations are astonished that the king of Babylon is "like them," because they are both dead and inhabitants of Sheol. But in Isaiah 14:18–20a, the reader learns that the king of Babylon is actually *not* "like them." Those kings are still buried in their "houses," but the king of Babylon is not in a "house."[110]

---

109. "Introduced by ואתה, 'yet, you,' these verses set forth a contrast between a comforting and honorable end of life for 'all the kings of the earth' and the humiliating end of the tyrant: 'cast out, having no grave'" (Wildberger, *Isaiah 13–27*, 70).

110. Shipp notes this contrast as well, "The Rephaim say, 'You have become just like us,' even though they have retained royal status (thrones and titles, v. 9) and possess regal burial 'houses' (v. 18), while the tyrant possesses none of these things" (Shipp, *Of Dead*

To leave a corpse exposed was a great dishonor. Kaiser explains, "For the people of the ancient world there was no more terrible fate than to remain unburied, and no more sacred duty than that of giving burial to relatives or comrades in arms. For someone who remained unburied lacked even the little bit of peace which death can bring men."[111] After the Philistines exposed the bodies of Saul and his three sons, the men of Jabesh Gilead traveled through the night, took the bodies, burned them, and buried the remains.[112] The king of Babylon, however, receives no such privilege.

Exegetically, it is difficult to tell whether his corpse is exhumed (19a) or just never buried (19cde). First, this section argues that Isaiah 14:11 is an extended personification and the king of Babylon's body is not necessarily laid to rest in the ground. Second, the resurrection view is analyzed. Third, the unburied view is presented. Finally, the exhumed view is presented.

The reference to "bed of maggots" and "covers of worms" in Isaiah 14:11 could refer to an interred corpse. Wächter, however, explains that these phrases describe the king of Babylon's lowly status in Sheol, not his state in the ground: "Those who were denied a proper burial must lie down on maggots and be covered with worms (Isa. 14:11)."[113] Wächter correctly notices that the king of Babylon is lying on maggots and is covered by worms before the kings of the nations in Sheol. Thus, the kings are on their thrones, but the king of Babylon possesses a demoted position in Sheol because his corpse was not buried. Wildberger, however, disagrees: "It is the grave, not Sheol, that v. 11b is describing. The concepts connected with the grave and Sheol, which really need to be distinguished from each other, are often used in the OT without close attention to that distinction; instead of שאול (Sheol), v. 15 speaks of בור, 'the pit,' and v. 19 of קבר, 'the grave.'"[114] Wildberger is correct. "Grave" (קבר) can refer to Sheol and vice versa. In Psalm 88:11–12 [H: 12–13], "grave" (קבר) is parallel with the underworld (אבדון), darkness (חשך), and a land of forgetting (ארץ נשיה). Biblical Sheol is simply the realm of the dead and could refer to the grave, the place of departed souls, or both at the same time. Thus, the maggots and worms refer to the grave, not the place of departed souls.

Kings and Dirges, 150).

111. Kaiser, *Isaiah: 13–39*, 41.
112. See also 2 Kgs 23:16 and Jer 8:1–2.
113. Wächter, "שְׁאוֹל," *TDOT* 14:242.
114. Wildberger, *Isaiah 13–27*, 62.

Israel's Eschatological Enemy

Wildberger's analysis, however, raises a new possibility. If Sheol (שאול) means "grave" in Isaiah 14:11, קבר could mean "place of departed souls" in 14:19. Hassler agrees and claims the king of Babylon will be resurrected:

> The monstrous beast of Revelation and the despicable Babylonian despot appear to depict the same ruler. When this man dies, he experiences a stint in Sheol (Isa 14:9–10, 15). His visit to Sheol ends soon enough when he arguably ascend [sic] from the abyss to mortal life (Isa 14:19; Rev 11:7; 13:3, 12, 14; 17:8, 11), which amazes the unbelievers of the world (Isa 14:16; Rev 13:3, 8). The king's resurrection from the dead to mortal life is potentially what sets him apart from all the other kings of the nations (Isa 14:18–19). Not until the battle of Armageddon does the king experience his second and final earthly death, this time bypassing Sheol and going directly to the lake of fire (Isa 14:20; Rev 19:19–20).[115]

Thus, according to Hassler, for a king to be the king of Babylon, he must come back from the dead. Holladay similarly believes the kings of the nations expel the king of Babylon from Sheol: "Of course, on one level the description we have here is that of an ordinary desecration of a grave, the disinterment of a corpse, but in the context of this poem the 'grave' must specifically be *Sheol*."[116] While Hassler believes there is a physical expulsion from Sheol back to the land of the living, Holladay only sees the king expelled from Sheol to some other unspecified place of the dead.

Hassler's analysis is unlikely for three reasons. First, the broad context indicates the *mashal* is given *when* the Lord returns (13:2–13), Babylon is destroyed (13:14–22), and Israel is regathered (14:1–2). Hassler's interpretation goes back in time. According to Hassler, "Armageddon" has already happened (Isa 13?).[117] Second, the *mashal* itself indicates that the king of Babylon is dead. It is his permanent death which is being celebrated through the entire *mashal*, so it is out of context to have a resurrection of the tyrant in verse 19. Third, the near context mitigates against Hassler's view. When the onlookers gaze at the king of Babylon in Isaiah 14:16 and say, "Is this the man who made the earth tremble, kingdoms quake?," they are not marveling that he rose from the dead as Hassler proposes, but that he is a mortal man who has been defeated and "brought down to Sheol" (14:15). Contextually, Hassler's position is unlikely.

---

115. Hassler, "Isaiah 13:1—14:27," 97–98.
116. Holladay, "Text, Structure, and Irony," 642 (emphasis original).
117. Hassler, "Isaiah 13:1—14:27," 98.

Concerning Isaiah 14:9–11, it is likely that Isaiah employs an extended personification in Isaiah 14:9–11. Bullinger claims there are two cases of personification in Isaiah 14:9–11: "Dead people in the grave are represented as speaking. And *Sheol* is represented as being moved and stirred. That it is the grave is clear from the reference to the 'worms.'"[118] Thus, according to Bullinger, Sheol is personified by "doing" things, and the dead people are personified by "speaking" things.

The surrounding context seems to argue on behalf of Bullinger's position. The trees rejoice and speak (14:8). Having *observed* and *heard* (the trees talk) the activity above the earth, Isaiah *observes* under the earth where dead people are awakened and, likewise, *speak*. Just as the trees above the earth did not actually speak, neither do the deceased under the earth. Isaiah 14 is a *mashal*. It is not surprising that Isaiah would employ such literary devices to mock the king of Babylon without attempting to teach his audience something about the afterlife. Isaiah 14:9–11 does *not* teach that the king of Babylon was physically buried. Instead, Isaiah uses personification to mock the king of Babylon.[119]

Wildberger believes the king of Babylon's corpse remains unburied. He focuses on colon 19c, "covered by the slain," and 14:20a, "You will not unite with them in burial" (לא־תחד אתם בקבורה). He explains, "The continuation, v. 19aγ–bβ, shows that the author clearly has in mind a death in battle. The ruler lies underneath a pile of others who had been slain."[120]

Olyan, however, believes Isaiah 14:19a requires an exhumed corpse: "A close look at Isaiah 14,19 suggests . . . that he was interred and that his corpse was exhumed and exposed."[121] The only support for the exhumation

---

118. Bullinger, *Figures of Speech*, 866 (emphasis original).

119. If one rejects the personification of Sheol, then an explanation of the worms and maggots in verse 11 needs to be proferred. Wächter is at least consistent by developing a view of Sheol where unburied people have to sleep on maggots in Sheol.

von Nordheim-Diehl presents yet another unlikely possibility, that Sheol is a deity whom Yahweh deposes. Thus, Sheol is not only the "place of the dead" but also the ruler of the dead; and, in Isaiah 14:9, Sheol, the god, is not a case of personification but the one who performs these actions. See von Nordheim-Diehl, "Wer Herrscht in Der Scheol?," 81–91. The biblical picture of Sheol is more consistent with Wächter's explanation, "the OT Israelites conceived the world of the dead as a great space in the depths, as an underworld" (Wächter, "שְׁאוֹל," *TDOT* 14:241). The Old Testament reveals Sheol as a place, not a god. The only possible exception is Isaiah 14:9, and the personification of the trees in Isaiah 14:8 mitigates against von Nordheim-Diehl's view.

120. Wildberger, *Isaiah 13–27*, 70.

121. Olyan, "Was the 'King of Babylon' Buried?," 423.

of the king of Babylon's corpse is Isaiah 14:19a: "you are cast from your grave" (ואתה השלכת מקברך). Olyan accuses: "Interpreters and translators have generally ignored or finessed the wording of ואתה השלכת מקברך, apparently in order to maintain the interpretation that the king was never buried."[122] He speculates that the reason for "finessing" is "the desire to identify the king with a known ruler such as Sargon II."[123] Olyan boldly claims, "Though much of the rest of the verse is difficult, ואתה השלכת מקברך is not. It requires no emendation or finessing to make sense."[124] Olyan analyzes several references where שלך ("to throw out") is used with מן ("from, away from") and demonstrates that it consistently occurs "with the unambiguous meaning 'to cast/be cast from locus A {to locus B}.'"[125] Thus, according to Olyan, the king of Babylon must be exhumed and the rest of Isaiah 14:19 should be understood in this light.

While Olyan's exegesis of "you are cast from your grave" (ואתה השלכת מקברך) is compelling, this colon cannot be interpreted outside its context. The extended metaphor which follows is difficult to reconcile with the exhumed view.[126] Whoever the "slain" are, they are the king of Babylon's clothing.[127] Unfortunately, Olyan does not reconcile his

122. Olyan, "Was the 'King of Babylon' Buried?," 424.

123. Olyan, "Was the 'King of Babylon' Buried?," 424n12. See "Sargon II" below.

124. Olyan, "Was the 'King of Babylon' Buried?," 424.

125. Olyan, "Was the 'King of Babylon' Buried?," 425. van Keulen seems persuaded by Olyan, "On the whole, however, the view that v. 19a describes the disinterment of the corpse carries conviction" (van Keulen, "On the Identity of the Anonymous Ruler," 112). van Keulen "[does] not exclude the possibility that v. 19 merely describes the looting of the royal tomb" (van Keulen, "On the Identity of the Anonymous Ruler," 111).

126. הרג occurs only one other time in the *massa'* against Babylon, in 14:20 where the king of Babylon's fate is revealed *because* "you destroyed your land; you slew (הרג) your people." The "slain ones" could be the ones the king of Babylon slew, referenced in 14:20. The king of Babylon could be "clothed with the slain" *because* he slew his own people.

Concerning "ones pierced with a sword," this could hearken back to Isaiah 13:15 where "all the ones found (מצא) will be pierced (דקר); and all the ones captured (ספה) will fall by the sword (חרב)." While the words for "pierce" are different, the two references to "sword" may strengthen the connection. This is a description, not of the king of Babylon, but of those slain. While the Medes were the ones who actually slew the king of Babylon's people, he could be the one incriminated for it. Thus, Isaiah is not describing a literal pile of corpses, and the king of Babylon is among them as the NET translation implies, "You lie among the slain." Rather, the ones whom he slew (or allowed to be slain) incriminate him, and testify why he should not receive a proper burial.

This interpretation, however, is extremely unlikely. Isaiah 14:19 is focusing on the actual body of the king of Babylon in 19abf.

127. Roberts, *First Isaiah*, 212; Ginsberg, "Reflexes of Sargon in Isaiah," 50; Sweeney,

interpretation with the rest of verse 19. Smith recognizes the difficulty with these lines: "The idea of being 'cast out of your tomb' does not coincide very well with the rest of the verse."[128] The first simile describes the king of Babylon "like an abominable branch" (כנצר נתעב).[129] There seems to be an intentional contrast between the king of Babylon and the fruitful "branch" of Jesse (Isa 11:1).[130] This simile, while noteworthy, does not argue for an exhumed or unburied corpse.

The second description of the "slain" ones is that they are "ones going down to the stones of a pit." This likely hearkens back to the king of Babylon's assertion in Isaiah 14:13, "I will sit in the mount of the assembly; in the far reaches of the North (בירכתי צפון)," and 14:15, "Surely to Sheol you have been brought down; to the far reaches of the pit (אל־ירכתי־בור)." The "pit" refers to Sheol, and, as already evidenced, the references to "pit," "grave," and "Sheol" are only references to the realm of the dead.[131] Those "slain," however, only go down "to the *stones* of the pit." They are both relegated to the "pit," but the king of Babylon is sent "to the *far reaches* of the pit."[132]

Isaiah 1–39, 237; Shipp, *Of Dead Kings and Dirges*, 160; Oswalt, *Isaiah*, 210; Smith, *Isaiah 1–39*, 317; Wildberger, *Isaiah 13–27*, 70; Watts, *Isaiah 1–33*, 211.

128. Smith, *Isaiah 1–39*, 317.

129. There is a textual issue here. Gray dislikes the MT, presents a few options, but does not select one (Gray, *Isaiah I–XXXIX*, 259). Hassler provides five reasons why the MT should be upheld (Hassler, "Isaiah 13:1—14:27," 32–35). Oswalt prefers Gray's possible translation, "like an untimely birth" (Oswalt, *Book of Isaiah*, 324). Oswalt, however, explains, "'Rejected branch' (v. 19) is lit. 'abominable branch,' which must be a figure of speech. Two of the ancient versions translate it with 'miscarriage'" (Oswalt, *Isaiah*, 211n6). Hassler also notes that the ancient translators are being interpretive (Hassler, "Isaiah 13:1—14:27," 35). Thus, the MT is correct, Targum Jonathan and Symmachus are merely providing an interpretive translation.

130. Motyer, *Prophecy of Isaiah*, 145; Mackay, *Study Commentary on Isaiah*, 355; Wolf, *Interpreting Isaiah*, 114; Hassler, "Isaiah 13:1—14:27," 142.

131. Roberts hypothesizes a physical pit, "The prophet graphically describes his fate as being 'cast out from your grave like a loathsome miscarriage,' and then continues with imagery that well captures the picture of the dead king covered with the fallen corpses of his trampled and pierced body guards that littered the ground above and around the king's own corpse, all of these mutilated dead going down to the bottom stones of the pit with the corpse of Sargon" (Roberts, *First Isaiah*, 212). As articulated above, the distinction between the physical grave and Sheol is not clearly distinguished. Wildberger explains, "Since the fate of the ruler is described within the context of the underworld; one's fate on the field of battle leads to one's destiny in Sheol" (Wildberger, *Isaiah 13–27*, 71).

132. Motyer believes "far reaches of the pit" and "stones of the pit" are synonymous (Motyer, *Prophecy of Isaiah*, 145; emphasis original). Wildberger notes that the meanings of these phrases are a mystery (Wildberger, *Isaiah 13–27*, 71–72). The king of Babylon's

The verse ends with another simile, parallel with the "rejected branch" (כנצר נתעב). The king of Babylon is "like a trampled corpse." Oswalt writes, "Verses 16–20 show people staring at the mangled corpse of the tyrant lying in a heap of other corpses in a pit (see esp. verse 19)."[133] Oswalt errs, calling the king of Babylon a "mangled corpse" rather than *like* a mangled corpse. His body looks like a mangled corpse. Perhaps he has been resurrected and looks horrible, like a mangled corpse. Exegetically, strong arguments can be made for an exhumed corpse, resurrected body, or simply exposed corpse. Perhaps even all three have elements that are correct.[134] The text is too ambiguous to rule out any of these conclusions. However, the king of Babylon's body will at least be left exposed, even if only for a time.

ACTIVITIES OF THE KING OF BABYLON

The *mashal* also reveals six activities of the king of Babylon: (1) harvests Lebanon's trees (14:8); (2) makes the world a wilderness (14:17); (3) destroys cities (14:17); (4) puts Israel and Judah to forced labor (14:3, 17); (5) destroys his own land (14:20); and (6) kills his own people (14:20).

Harvests Lebanon's Trees

The first activity of the king of Babylon is that he harvests trees of Lebanon.

8a. Indeed, the cypress trees rejoice over you,	גַּם־בְּרוֹשִׁים שָׂמְחוּ לְךָ	8a
8b. The cedars of Lebanon.	אַרְזֵי לְבָנוֹן	8b
8c. Since you were laid down, he has not come up,	מֵאָז שָׁכַבְתָּ לֹא־יַעֲלֶה	8c
8d. The woodcutter against us.	הַכֹּרֵת עָלֵינוּ׃	8d

---

fate, however, seems worse than those around him.

133. Oswalt, *Isaiah*, 211.

134. Perhaps the Lord will slay the king of Babylon. In this way, the king of Babylon's corpse will be "clothed with the slain." Perhaps they will be buried together in a mass grave. Perhaps the Lord will then resurrect his corpse so that his body and soul are cast out of Sheol. In this way he is "cast from his grave." Perhaps then the Lord will send him "alive" to the lake of fire (Rev 19:19–20) as Hassler suggested. Or maybe Olyan is incorrect and the מן should just be taken in a privative sense, "you are cast away from your grave." There is simply not enough information available to make a clear exegetical decision concerning the nature of the king of Babylon's corpse's exposure.

The cypress trees rejoice in line 8a; the second colon intensifies the first by extending the rejoicing to the infamous cedars of Lebanon.[135] It was a common practice of ancient kings to harvest the cedars of Lebanon. Tiglath-pileser I stated, "I went to Lebanon (*Lab-na-a-ni*). I cut (there) timber of cedars."[136] The king of Babylon is a cedar harvester as well.

Makes the World a Wilderness

The second activity of the king of Babylon is that he makes the world a wilderness.

17a. He made the world like the wilderness,	שָׂם תֵּבֵל כַּמִּדְבָּר 17a

In Isaiah 14:16, the "ones who stare at you" "gaze" and "consider." Two rhetorical questions convey their astonishment at the king of Babylon's fall ("Is this the man who shook the earth; the one who made kingdoms tremble?").[137] The "gazers" continue "considering" through verse 17 by describing three atrocities of the king of Babylon.[138] The first atrocity is that he makes the world like the wilderness. Fry points out the correspondence with Isaiah 13:9, "As in 16cd the oppressor's actions are similar to Yahweh's. He made (שם) the world like a desert (מדבר, 14:17a) as Yahweh's day will make (שם) the land/earth a desolation (שמה, 13:9c)."[139] Thus, the king of Babylon is a wilderness maker.

Most conquering kings leave devastation in their wake, so possibly this criterion could apply to many kings. But the focus here is cosmic. Concerning תבל, Fabry explains, "When all is said and done, the primary meaning of *tēḇēl* appears to be '(dry) land,' usually with emphasis on solidity and

---

135. The cedars of Lebanon were coveted in the ancient world: Solomon (1 Kgs 5:6); Nebuchadnezzar (Pritchard, *ANET* 307); and the gods (Pritchard, *ANET* 134).

136. Pritchard, *ANET* 275.

137. See "Earth and Kingdoms Tremble" above. While Isaiah 14:16 does refer to "activities" of the king of Babylon, they are general descriptions which illustrate his greatness, and, therefore, are included above.

138. Concerning the speaker of Isaiah 14:17, Fry claims, "The public's reaction continues" (Fry, "'Oracle Concerning Babylon,'" 122). Several others claim the speaker continues into Isaiah 14:17: Sweeney, *Isaiah 1–39*, 220; Motyer, *Prophecy of Isaiah*, 145; Wildberger, *Isaiah 13–27*, 42; Roberts, *First Isaiah*, 212. The consideration of the onlookers ends with verse 17. The reference to "all the kings of the nations" in verse 18 points back to 14:9 and the scene in Sheol. Thus, Isaiah 14:18 marks a transition in the text.

139. Fry, "'Oracle Concerning Babylon,'" 122.

permanence. It is a term belonging to the lexical field of cosmology and can even mean 'cosmos.'"¹⁴⁰ תבל has the entire inhabited world in focus.¹⁴¹ Fabry analyzes several uses of תבל and concludes, "This survey leaves the impression that the translation 'dry (or) habitable land' is too narrow: *tēḇēl* refers to the solid earth of ancient Near Eastern cosmology."¹⁴² The entire land of earth is in view and the king of Babylon makes this land "like a wilderness."¹⁴³ No historic king can claim to "make the world like the wilderness."

Destroys Cities

Coming also from Isaiah 14:17, the king of Babylon destroys cities of the world.

17a. He made the world a wilderness,	שָׂם תֵּבֵל כַּמִּדְבָּר	17a
17b. And its cities he destroyed,	וְעָרָיו הָרָס	17b
17c. Its prisoners, he did not open to a house.	אֲסִירָיו לֹא־פָתַח בָּיְתָה	17c

The masculine suffix on וְעָרָיו ("and his/its cities") presents a problem because תבל ("world") in the previous colon is feminine. The Ethiopic translation changes the suffix to a 3fs (KJV translates, "thereof;" NKJV, ESV, NASB, HCSB translate the suffix as a 3fs with "its"). The LXX, Syriac, and Arabic translate it "cities" with no suffix. Wildberger claims it should be read either as the 3fs "her cities" or the pl. "cities."¹⁴⁴ Fry suggests these lines "were originally independent and have not been harmonized grammatically in their setting in the MT."¹⁴⁵ It is more likely that "world" (תבל) is functioning as a masculine here as Hitzig proposes: "The suffix in אסיריו could still relate to the King, but not in עריו: and since the latter cannot be traced back to מדבר, one would most likely say תֵבֵל here as a masculine."¹⁴⁶

---

140. Fabry, "תֵּבֵל," *TDOT* 15:558.

141. Alexander, *Prophecies of Isaiah*, 299.

142. Fabry, "תֵּבֵל," *TDOT* 15:559.

143. Oswalt explains, "[The king of Babylon] had not merely made the earth his home, he had made it his plaything. He had but to sneeze and the repercussions had reached the farthest kingdom; people lived in terror of his next move" (Oswalt, *Book of Isaiah*, 323).

144. Wildberger, *Isaiah 13–27*, 45–46.

145. Fry, "'Oracle Concerning Babylon,'" 122n64.

146. "Das Suffix in אסיריו könnte noch auf den König sich beziehn, nicht aber das in עריו: und da letzteres auch nicht wohl auf מדבר zurückgehn kann, so wird man am

If תבל is a masculine, then the two suffix pronouns create noun/pronoun parallelism.[147] Hitzig's quote also demonstrates the implications of this exegetical decision because it impacts the exegesis of the controversial succeeding colon as well.[148] Knobel explains that the masculine was substituted for the feminine because of the masculine "wilderness" (מדבר): "The masculine suffix is applied to תבל, whose feminine gender was substituted by the masculine מדבר. Cf. Hab. 1:10; Hos. 4:18."[149]

The second atrocity of the king of Babylon is that he destroyed the world's cities. Fry believes there is a correspondence here with God's overthrowing of Sodom and Gomorrah in Isaiah 13:19. He states, "He overthrew (חרס) cities as God overthrew (הפך) the cities Sodom and Gomorrah (13:19e)."[150] This "overthrowing" however is not a mere conquest but a demolition. Wildberger explains, "חרס (demolish), the opposite of בנה, 'build,' is a very strong word, one that describes the demolition of a city; cf. 2 Sam. 11:25; 2 Kgs. 3:25; Jer. 1:10; 24:6; 24:10; 45:4."[151] Thus, the king of Babylon is one who wipes out cities.

Put Israel and Judah to Forced Labor

Finally, from Isaiah 14:17, the king of Babylon puts Israel and Judah to forced labor.

| 17c. Its prisoners, he did not open the house | אֲסִירָיו לֹא־פָתַח בָּיְתָה | 17c |

There are two issues with Isaiah 14:17c: the delimitation of the text and the anticlimactic tricolon. Gray and Wildberger believe part of Isaiah

---

richtigsten תֵּבֵל hier als Maskulin fassen" (Hitzig, *Der Prophet Jesaia*, 170). Knobel agrees, Knobel, *Kurzgefasstes exegetisches Handbuch zum alten Testament*, 106.

147. Berlin explains, "This type of parallelism involves words from different parts of speech" (Berlin, *Dynamics of Biblical Parallelism*, 33). Berlin then lists "Noun // Pronoun" as one example.

148. See "Put Israel and Judah to Forced Labor" below.

149. "Die Suff. masc. gehen dem Sinne nach auf תבל, für welches femin. sich im Schreiben das dabei stehende masc. מדבר substituirte. Vgl. Hab. 1, 10. Hos 4, 18. פתח]" (Knobel, *Kurzgefasstes exegetisches Handbuch zum alten Testament*, 106). Habakkuk 1:10 and Hosea 4:18 contain textual issues just like Isaiah 14:17. Nevertheless, Knobel has produced a possible explanation of the pronoun gender problems in Isaiah 14:17.

150. Fry, "'Oracle Concerning Babylon,'" 122.

151. Wildberger, *Isaiah 13–27*, 69. See also Münderlein, "הָרַס," *TDOT* 3:461–63.

14:18a should be attached to 14:17c.¹⁵² Prospective textual corrections, however, lack textual support and have not produced a more promising solution.¹⁵³ The second issue concerns the tricolon which seems anticlimactic. Gray explains, "Unreadiness to release prisoners (ordinary, common captives, accord to [the MT]) is not the greatest of enormities; and therefore v.17c comes as a rather violent anti-climax after the preceding description of the king's creating world-wide desolation and terror."¹⁵⁴ Gray then emends the text: "If the main point were the *capture of the kings*, the anti-climax would be less; and this we could obtain in a slightly emended text from which ביתה is omitted as in [the LXX]."¹⁵⁵ Gray admits, however, "The capture of the kings" is still anticlimactic. Gray's understanding of the tricolon is correct. The tricolon develops from the general (the world), to the specific (mankind).

Because this crime does not seem very severe, commentators have read their interpretation of the historical context into the passage in an effort to heighten the severity. Kaiser, for example, explains, "The man . . . whose prisoners languished in his dungeons to the end of their lives . . . now lies among the bodies of the rabble."¹⁵⁶ Smith believes it is an example of his unmerciful rule.¹⁵⁷ Motyer claims, like Oswalt and Young, that the king of Babylon would not let his captives go home.¹⁵⁸ Mackay speculates, "Furthermore, 'he did not let his prisoners go home', but transported them elsewhere in his realm to work for him. The obsessive power-lust of this tyrant preferred all to be a ruined waste in his own grasp rather than for

---

152. Gray includes 18a with 17c and translates, "He fettered and released not; All the kings of the nations." He seems unsatisfied, however, with his emendation and concludes, "Not improbably v.17c is seriously corrupt" (Gray, *Isaiah I–XXXIX*, 258). Wildberger's reconstruction of 17c–18a is different from Gray's (Wildberger, *Isaiah 13–27*, 46). Holladay presents a slightly different emendation from Wildberger's (Holladay, "Text, Structure, and Irony," 637).

153. Neither Gray nor Wildberger agree on how the text should be emended. Wildberger's emendation seems less satisfactory than Gray's because it does not address the tricolon (Wildberger, *Isaiah 13–27*, 46). Furthermore, as Erlandsson points out, there is no textual support for an emendation (Erlandsson, *Burden of Babylon*, 36).

154. Gray, *Isaiah I–XXXIX*, 258.

155. Gray, *Isaiah I–XXXIX*, 258 (emphasis his).

156. Kaiser, *Isaiah: 13–39*, 41.

157. Smith, *Isaiah 1–39*, 316.

158. Motyer writes, "Did he really exercise such an inhumane grip on people that he would not let his captives go home? Yet this is what he did" (Motyer, *Prophecy of Isaiah*, 145).

it to be fruitful in the control of others."[159] God takes crimes against humanity seriously. For example, God judged Moab severely for abusing and desecrating the corpse of the king of Edom (Amos 2:1–3).[160] This section argues that the king of Babylon leads a worldwide imprisonment of Israel and Judah. This crime is not only a crime against humanity, but against God's chosen people, Israel. Because he refuses to let these prisoners out of the "house," his corpse will not be placed in a "house."[161]

The specific crime in Isaiah 14:17c has been allusive because of the misunderstanding of the masculine suffix on אסיריו ("his/its prisoners"). As argued above, the masculine suffix refers to the "world," thus the prisoners are the world's prisoners, not just the king of Babylon's.[162] The king of Babylon, however, is the subject of the verb פתח ("he opened"). Thus, the prisoners belong to the world, but the king of Babylon is the one responsible for their bondage. The king of Babylon appears to have organized a worldwide imprisonment in which every nation participates.

Another issue concerns "in a house" (ביתה). As stated above, Young, Motyer, and Oswalt claim the king of Babylon would not let his captives go home.[163] They believe "in a house" (ביתה) refers to one's homeland. Wildberger rejects this interpretation: "However, בית (house) never carries the

---

159. Mackay, *Study Commentary on Isaiah*, 354.

160. Niehaus explains, "Crimes against humanity bring God's punishment" (Niehaus, "Amos," 358). Concerning the atrocity of Moab, Wolff explains that "for lime" means they burnt the king of Edom to ashes from which "the Moabites had manufactured . . . some substance which could be used to whitewash stones (Dtn 27:2, 4) and houses" (Wolff, *Joel and Amos*, 162–63). Paul believes the bones were exhumed, burnt, and then used for lime (Paul, *Amos*, 72). According to Stuart, "This was, at any rate, an example of all-out vengeful war. Brother hated brother intensely and acted out the hatred" (Stuart, *Hosea–Jonah*, 315).

161. Fry explains, "The series of similarities between the oppressor and Yahweh alluded to in lines 16c–17b lead [sic] the reader to wonder whether there may be a similarity between the oppressor and Yahweh suggested in line 17c also. Is there a prisoner that Yahweh will not release to his home? In vv 18–20 the people of Israel answer the question posed by line 17c" (Fry, "'Oracle Concerning Babylon,'" 123).

162. See "Destroyed Cities" above.

163. Oswalt, *Book of Isaiah*, 323. Young agrees, "His prisoners he did not set free so that they could go to their own homes" (Young, *Book of Isaiah*, 3:444). Young later explains further, "The sentence continues with an anarthrous participle concluding with a finite verb, an additional clause being added, as in Isa. 44:26b. We may render: 'his prisoners he let not loose, nor sent them back to their home.' . . . Possibly there may be a reflection upon Babylon's refusal to allow the people of God to return home, whereas Cyrus did so permit them; cf. Jer. 50:33" (Young, *Book of Isaiah*, 3:444n81).

meaning of 'homeland,' and ביתה never means 'toward home' but always 'in the house.'"¹⁶⁴ Thus, "in a house" (ביתה) refers to the place from which the prisoners should be loosed, not the destination where they are going.

Finally, commentators have misapplied "prisoner" (אסיר). Four deductions can be made concerning the prisoners. First, the prisoners are imprisoned, not taken captive or deported.¹⁶⁵ According to HALOT, an אסיר is a "prisoner who is made to do all kinds of work."¹⁶⁶ Second, their imprisonment must be unlawful. If they were imprisoned lawfully, then it would not have been a crime. Third, the ones imprisoned must include Israel and Judah. The fall of the king of Babylon corresponds to the liberation of Israel and Judah (Isa 14:1–3). After the death of the king of Babylon, these Jewish prisoners are loosed and return to Israel with their captors as their captives (14:2). The prisoners may not be exclusively Israel and Judah, but the prisoners must include a significant portion of them to constitute a national regathering. The king of Babylon appears to have imprisoned Israel and Judah and put them to "hard bondage" (14:3). Knobel describes the severity of the crime and connects it to Jeremiah 50:33, "This nondischarge is cited as a sign of his power, and also his hardness just like Jer. 50:33."¹⁶⁷ Just as God redeems Israel from bondage in Jeremiah 50:33–34, so also does he liberate them in Isaiah 14:1–3, 17.

164. Wildberger, *Isaiah 13-27*, 46. "The he *locale* (or locative he) . . . indicate[s] the goal of a movement" (VanDerMerwe et al., *Biblical Hebrew Reference Grammar*, 227). The "goal" of the movement could refer to either the direction "toward" or "inside" the house. Both, "into" and "to, toward," are spatial which may be why Waltke and O'Connor do not make a distinction (Waltke and O'Connor, *Introduction to Biblical Hebrew Syntax*, 185). Hoffner, however, writes, "*bayith* occurs in the following constructions in the sense of 'the inside' . . . *bayethah* (with the *he*-locale: Ex. 28:26; 39:19; etc.)" (Hoffner, "בַּיִת," *TDOT* 2:113). Furthermore, there is considerable evidence which favors Wildberger's analysis, cf. Gen 19:10, 24:32, 39:11, 43:16, 17, 24, 26, 44:14; 47:14; Exod 8:20, 9:19; Josh 2:18; Judg 19:15, 18; 1 Sam 6:7; 2 Sam 13:7, 14:31, 17:20; 1 Kgs 6:15, 7:25, etc. While some of these passages could be understood as a direction toward the house, cf. Gen 24:32; Exod 9:19; 2 Sam 13:7, 14:31, most of them are clearly directed inside.

165. Contra Oswalt, *Book of Isaiah*, 323; Young, *Book of Isaiah*, 3:444; Motyer, *Prophecy of Isaiah*, 145. The imprisonment could include captivity or deportation, but a simple captive or deportee would not qualify as an אסיר.

166. HALOT, "אָסִיר," 1:72.

167. "Dies Nichtentlassen wird als Zeichen seiner Macht, zugleich auch Härte angeführt wie Jer. 50, 33" (Knobel, *Kurzgefasstes exegetisches Handbuch zum alten Testament*, 10). Erlandsson compares the Burden of Babylon with Jeremiah 50–51 (Erlandsson, *Burden of Babylon*, 154–59). Others have made this connection, e.g., Kaiser, *Isaiah: 13-39*, 10; Blenkinsopp, *Isaiah 1-39*, 277; Smith, *Isaiah 1-39*, 297; Allen, "Rebuilding and Destruction of Babylon," 19–27; Brangenberg III, "Re-Examination," 88. Concerning

The King of Babylon

Finally, the king of Babylon's imprisonment of Israel and Judah is brutal. The description of Isaiah 14:3 hearkens back to Israel's Egyptian bondage. Wildberger explains:

> In addition to the general sense of "work" and "service," עבדה can be used in a special sense, to describe "forced labor," more specifically, to describe Israel's bondage in Egypt (Exod. 1:14; 2:23; 5:9, 11; 6:9; see also 1 Kings 12:4). It is easy to insert the adjective קשה (hard) when speaking about this negative aspect of work. In this way, the deliverance from "Babylon" is promised to Israel here, set forth as a parallel to the deliverance from bondage in Egypt.[168]

The king of Babylon has put Israel to an Egyptian-like forced labor. God sent ten plagues upon Egypt to liberate his people. Isaiah 13–14 argue that the Lord does much more to the king of Babylon when he raises his hand against his chosen people.

Destroys His Own Land

The first reason why the king of Babylon will not be buried is because he destroys his own land.

| 20b. Because your land you destroyed | כִּי־אַרְצְךָ שִׁחַתָּ | 20b |

The LXX changes the pronouns from the second-person to the first-person in Isaiah 14:20b, "Because you destroyed *my* land and killed *my*

Jeremiah 50, Brueggemann explains, "Again, the demise of Babylon yields the liberation of Israel.... Verse 33 characterizes the oppression. Verse 34 counters the oppression with a strong first word: 'liberator' (*ga'al*; RSV 'Redeemer'), the one who ends oppression" (Brueggemann, *Commentary on Jeremiah*, 470). Thompson's comment on Jeremiah 50:33–34 could just as easily be a commentary on Isaiah 14: "It is all Israel that is in view, the people of Israel together with the people of Judah, emphasizing the concept of a united Israel that will enjoy the days of restoration. Taking up an ancient picture of the oppression of Israel in Egypt, the prophet describes Israel in Babylonia in similar terms. Neither in Egypt nor in Babylonia did there seem to be hope of release. Those who oppressed them refused to release them.... But as in the days of the first Exodus Yahweh had redeemed (*gā'al*) Israel from Egypt (Exod. 6:6; 15:13), so would he redeem them from Babylon" (Thompson, *Book of Jeremiah*, 743).

168. Wildberger, *Isaiah 13–27*, 50. See also Smith, *Isaiah 1–39*, 312; Oswalt, *Book of Isaiah*, 313; Roberts, *First Isaiah*, 203; Fry, "'Oracle Concerning Babylon,'" 95; Mackay, *Study Commentary on Isaiah*, 344; Motyer, *Prophecy of Isaiah*, 142. Clements agrees with this interpretation and applies it to the Babylonian exile, "[Isa 14:3] must be a reference to the period of the Babylonian exile in which the circumstances of those in Babylon appears [*sic*] to have been tantamount to a harsh form of slavery" (Clements, *Isaiah 1–39*, 140–41).

people."¹⁶⁹ The LXX appears to apply this text to Nebuchadnezzar.¹⁷⁰ Smith makes Merodach-baladan the indirect destroyer of his own land: "The king's selfish actions caused the destruction of his own nation and the deaths of thousands of his own people. Instead of blaming their destruction on their vile enemies, his own people will realize that the Babylonian king killed thousands of them by his foolish actions."¹⁷¹ Both the LXX and Smith illustrate the struggle of applying Isaiah 14:20b to a historic king. The king of Babylon is unique because he destroys *his own* land.

The subject of שחת ("destroy") is usually the one who is doing the action (cf. Gen 13:10, 38:9; Exod 32:7; Deut 9:12; 2 Kgs 19:12; Lam 2:6; Jer 5:10, 12:10, 48:18; Ezek 26:4, 28:17; Amos 1:11; Nah 2:2; Mal 2:8). If this was an indirect destroying, it would have to be ascertained from the context as in Numbers 32:15. The context does not argue for an indirect destruction, thus a direct destruction was likely intended. Concerning the extent of the destruction, Conrad writes concerning שחת, "The verb signifies an act of ruthless destruction subjecting the object to complete annihilation or decimating and corrupting it so thoroughly that its demise is certain."¹⁷² When a king went to war, he sometimes ruined the land he was invading (e.g., 1 Chr 20:1), but the king of Babylon ruins his own land.¹⁷³

169. "διότι τὴν γῆν μου ἀπώλεσας καὶ τὸν λαόν μου ἀπέκτεινας."

170. Gray, *Isaiah I-XXXIX*, 261; Clements, *Isaiah 1-39*, 144.

171. Smith, *Isaiah 1-39*, 318. Wildberger interprets this phrase indirectly as well, "One might argue that the poet thought that all the suffering he had inflicted on the other peoples was not, in the end, as horrible as the destruction he had inflicted on his own land, with his plans for conquering the world" (Wildberger, *Isaiah 13-27*, 72). Wildberger retains the indirect interpretation of שחת, but explains, "Instead, it is more likely that v. 20aβ simply furnishes the reason why the scoundrel would be refused admission to Sheol, in order to be reunited with his fellow citizens in the 'pit.' He had completely wrecked their land, brought his own fellow citizens (עמך, 'your people') to their death; this means that his single-minded arrogant lust for power was carried out at the expense of both land and people. Thus he is an outcast in the underworld, never to have the chance of associating even with his own people" (Wildberger, *Isaiah 13-27*, 72). Isaiah 14:20b, however, describes the king of Babylon destroying his own land.

172. Conrad, "שָׁחַת," *TDOT* 14:584. HALOT explains שחת means, "to ruin, destroy, annihilate" in the Piel, HALOT, "שׁחת," 4:1470.

173. Oswalt writes, "The judgment contained in this verse is a surprising one because it is expected. The reader expects to find the king judged for what he has done to the foreign lands which he has oppressed (so LXX '*my* land . . . *my* people'), but instead it is his own land and his own people he has destroyed and for which he is judged" (Oswalt, *Book of Isaiah*, 324). Roberts recognizes the validity of this interpretation but still applies it to Sargon, "According to the prophet, the reason for this frightening judgment was that Sargon had destroyed his own land and killed his own people (v. 20). Sargon did come to the Assyrian throne in a coup,

Kills His Own People

The king of Babylon not only destroys his own land, but he kills his own people.

| 20c. Your people, you slew | עַמְּךָ הָרָגְתָּ | 20c |

Fry claims, "His own people, he did not protect them, but killed them by using them in his schemes to rule the nations and by calling upon them the fate that belonged to him."[174]

Conclusion

This section presented five attributes and six activities of the king of Babylon. First, it was argued that the king of Babylon must be the king of *Babylon*. While some claim Babylon is symbolic, the reference to the Chaldeans in Isaiah 13:19 and the destruction of a city called "Babylon" in Isaiah 13:20–22 makes the case for a literal Babylon quite strong. Isaiah 14:6 provides two additional attributes of the king of Babylon: he is a brutal ruler and rules a vast domain. The fourth attribute is that the king of Babylon is the "greatest of all time" king. Four descriptions supported this claim: (1) the vastness of his kingdom (14:6); (2) the response of the dead kings in Sheol (14:9); (3) his status among the stars (14:12); and (4) the response of the earth and kingdoms (14:16). The exposure of the king of Babylon's corpse is the final attribute.

The *mashal* not only provides attributes concerning the king of Babylon, but also describes some of his activities. First, according to Isaiah 14:8, the king of Babylon is a cedar harvester. The next three activities are found in Isaiah 14:17. He makes the world a wilderness, destroys its cities, and unlawfully puts Israel and Judah to forced labor. The king of Babylon's ruthlessness extended not only to his enemies, but also to his own land and people. The last two activities are that he destroys his own land and kills his own people. These eleven characteristics build upon the four contextual criteria found outside the *mashal*. As a result of this study, the following analysis is proffered:

---

but since the text characterizes him as a king of Babylon, it is more likely that the reference is to his vigorous campaigning against Merodach-baladan in Babylonia that eventually led to Sargon's assuming the crown of Babylon" (Roberts, *First Isaiah*, 213). Similarly, Alexander explains, "But the only natural interpretation of the words is that which applies them to the Babylonian tyranny as generally exercised" (Alexander, *Prophecies of Isaiah*, 302).

174. Fry, "Oracle Concerning Babylon," 126. The exegetical discussion associated with this activity can be found in the "Destroyed His Own Land" section.

Contextual Criteria		
Cataclysmic Destruction (13:5–13)	Median Slaughter (13:17)	
Eternal Devastation of Babylon (13:9–22)	Israelite Regathering (14:1–2)	
Attributes of the King of Babylon		
King of Babylon (14:4a)	King of Kings (14:9–16)	
Brutal Ruler (14:6)	Exposed Corpse (14:18–20a)	
Ruler of Vast Kingdom (14:6)		
Activities of the King of Babylon		
Harvests Lebanon's Trees (14:8)	Puts Israel and Judah to Forced Labor (14:17c)	
Makes the World a Wilderness (14:17a)	Destroys His Own Land (14:20b)	
Destroys Cities (14:17b)	Kills His Own People (14:20c)	

THE KINGS OF BABYLON

This section argues that no historic king can accurately be called the Isaiah 14 king of Babylon. Each king is analyzed and evaluated in light of the criteria argued in the previous section. A summary table of the kings of Babylon can be found in Appendix 1. There are some methodological difficulties with identifying the king of Babylon. For example, a potential king may have "harvested Lebanon's trees," but no historic record exists that he did so. If a king ruled Lebanon, then it will be assumed that he was a cedar harvester. If there is insufficient or questionable evidence, then an arguable judgment will be made based upon the available evidence.

To reduce redundancy, a few statements are made here concerning some of the criteria. First, as presented in chapter 3, no historic king meets any of the contextual criteria; therefore, no king receives a mark in those categories.[175] Second, only one king can be labeled the "greatest of all time" king, and this title goes to Alexander the Great. Naturally, it is difficult to rank one king as greater than another. Cartledge, for example, refuses, "There are those who believe Alexander to be the world's greatest military conqueror ever. Full stop. I, on the other hand, don't think it's realistic to

---

175. A Persian army that consisted of Medes attacked Belshazzar and Nabonidus. See ch. 3 for more information.

try to make a global comparative judgement of that sort. Strictly noncomparable situations and contexts are involved."[176] Isaiah 14:9–12, however, describes the king of Babylon as greater than all others. That Alexander is only debatably the greatest king illustrates that even he falls short of this label. Nevertheless, among the kings presented, Alexander shines brighter than all the others and, therefore, warrants this label.

Alexander the Great

Alexander the Great ruled a vast kingdom, conquered Lebanon, and is arguably worthy of the title "king of kings." He was not an Isaiah 14:6 kind of brutal ruler.[177] He conquered Babylon but was never known as the "king of Babylon." The command to slaughter his children makes little sense because he had no children when he died.[178] His corpse was not exposed.[179] Concerning the activities of the king of Babylon, Brangeberg states, "Alexander hardly ruined his own land."[180] While he did destroy at least some cities (e.g., Tyre), he did not "make the world a wilderness." Generously, Alexander the Great meets only four of the fifteen criteria (see Table 4.1).

Table 4.1. Evaluation of Alexander the Great

Contextual Criteria			
Cataclysmic Destruction (13:5–13)		Median Slaughter (13:17)	
Eternal Devastation of Babylon (13:9–22)		Israelite Regathering (14:1–2)	
Attributes of the King of Babylon			
King of Babylon (14:4a)		King of Kings (14:9–16)	✓
Brutal Ruler (14:6)		Exposed Corpse (14:18–20a)	
Ruler of Vast Kingdom (14:6)	✓		

---

176. Cartledge, *Alexander the Great*, 50.

177. See "Brutal Ruler" above. Alexander's brutality is not comparable to the brutality described in Isaiah 14:6. For a description of Alexander's more brutal rule see Cartledge, *Alexander the Great*, 208–11.

178. Alexander IV was born after Alexander the Great's death, Cartledge, *Alexander the Great*, 231.

179. Cartledge, *Alexander the Great*, 216.

180. Brangenberg III, "Re-Examination," 87.

Activities of the King of Babylon			
Harvests Lebanon's Trees (14:8)	✓	Puts Israel and Judah to Forced Labor (14:17c)	
Makes the World a Wilderness (14:17a)		Destroys His Own Land (14:20b)	
Destroys Cities (14:17b)	✓	Kills His Own People (14:20c)	
✓ = Meets criterion			

Assur-uballit II

Auvray claims Assur-uballit II is the king of Babylon:

> If one refuses to descend to the time of nabuchodonosor for the reasons indicated, it remains to think of the last times of the Assyrian empire. In fact, Assourouballit, the last king of Assyria, who after the destruction of Nineveh (612) for some time remained in the country and died miserably (609). Everything fits well enough. If one thinks of the reverberation in Palestine of the fall of Nineveh attested by the prophet Nahum, one can consider this hypothesis quite plausible. Thirty years before Ezekiel, one understands a kinship of inspiration with the great prophet of Exile.[181]

According to Auvray, Babylon is really Nineveh and the kingdom is Assyria. Assur-uballit II lived for three years after the destruction of Nineveh, so he witnessed the destruction of "Babylon" (Nineveh) and was then destroyed himself. While there are no specific details concerning his death, it is plausible that his corpse was exposed and his progeny killed.[182] The problems, however, abound. Brangenberg explains, "He could hardly fit the mold of the great world conqueror described in verses 6–17. At best he was a lame-duck king of an already crippled kingdom fighting to

---

181. "Si l'on refuse de descendre à l'époque de nabuchodonosor pour les motifs indiqués, il reste à songer aux derniers temps de l'empire assyrien. On a pensé, en effet, à Assourouballit, dernier roi d'Assyrie, qui, après la destruction de Ninive (612) tint encore quelque temps la campagne et mourut misérablement (609). Tout correspond assez bien. Si l'on songe au retentissement qu'eut en Palestine la chute de Ninive, attesté par le prophète Nahum, on arrive à considérer cette hypothèse comme assez vraisemblable. Une trentaine d'années avant Ézéchiel, on comprend une parenté d'inspiration avec le grand prophète de l'Exil" (Auvray, *Isaïe 1–39*, 163).

182. Brangenberg states, "[He] died a pitiful death and was the last of his dynasty" (Brangenberg III, "Re-Examination," 88).

preserve what little remained of a formerly great empire."[183] The Babylonian Chronicle supports Brangenberg's analysis:

> 1180. In the month(?)......... [Assur-uballit] in Harran took his seat on the throne as king of Assyria....
>
> 1181. In the fifteenth year, the month of *Du'uzu* .... the king of Akkad (Babylon) .... against Assyria marched .... victoriously...
>
> 1182. In the sixteenth year, in the month of *Aiaru*, the king of Akkad mobilized his army and marched against the land of Assyria. In the month of *Arahsamnu*, the Ummanmanda .... came to the support of the king of Akkad and they united their armies and toward Harran, against Assur-uballit, who sat on the throne in Assyria, they marched. Assur-uballit and the army of Kullania(?), which had come to his aid,—fear of the enemy fell upon them and they forsook the city and .... they crossed. The king of Akkad reached Harran and .... he took the city....
>
> 1183. In the month of *Du'uzu* Assur-uballit, king of Assyria, the great army of Egypt ... marched against Harran to take it .... the garrison which the king of Akkad had stationed therein they defeated(?), they smote. Against Harran he encamped until the month of *Ululu*.[184]

This chronicle reveals a king trying to survive. He was a conquered king, not a conqueror. He may have harvested Lebanon's trees, but it is unlikely. It is even more unlikely that he was a brutal ruler, made the world a wilderness, destroyed cities, destroyed his own land, and killed his own people. Furthermore, he was not a king of *Babylon*, did not rule a vast domain, nor did he put Israel and Judah to forced labor. Assur-uballit II received only two questionable check marks and cannot be the king of Babylon (see Table 4.2).

---

183. Brangenberg III, "Re-Examination," 88.
184. Luckenbill, *Ancient Records of Assyria and Babylonia*, 2:420–21.

Table 4.2. Evaluation of Assur-uballit II

Contextual Criteria			
Cataclysmic Destruction (13:5–13)		Median Slaughter (13:17)	
Eternal Devastation of Babylon (13:9–22)		Israelite Regathering (14:1–2)	
Attributes of the King of Babylon			
King of Babylon (14:4a)		King of Kings (14:9–16)	
Brutal Ruler		Exposed Corpse (14:18–20a)	✓
Ruler of Vast Kingdom			
Activities of the King of Babylon			
Harvests Lebanon's Trees (14:8)	✓	Puts Israel and Judah to Forced Labor (14:17c)	
Makes the World a Wilderness (14:17a)		Destroys His Own Land (14:20b)	
Destroys Cities (14:17b)		Kills His Own People (14:20c)	
✓ = Meets criterion			

Belshazzar

Little historical information is available concerning Belshazzar. The only substantive criteria in his favor is that he is called "king of Babylon" in Daniel 5 and inherited the vast kingdom of his fathers. A Persian/Median force defeated him, but Babylon was not destroyed. He does not appear to be an Isaiah 14:6 kind of brutal ruler. His administration seems confined to Babylon, but it is possible that he harvested Lebanon's trees. Perhaps his corpse was exposed. It is very unlikely that he put Israel and Judah to forced labor, destroyed his own land, killed his own people, or destroyed cities. He did not make *the world* a wilderness. He was a nothing king; in fact, he was not even the real king, much less the conquering king of kings described in Isaiah 14:9–16. Cobb writes, "The old explanation, which connects [the *mashal*] with the violent overthrow of Babylon by Cyrus and the shameful death of Belshazzar the king, has at least two defects—no such overthrow took place, and Belshazzar was not the king."[185] Belshazzar received only four marks and cannot be the king of Babylon of Isaiah 14:4b–21 (see Table 4.3).

Table 4.3. Evaluation of Belshazzar

Contextual Criteria			
Cataclysmic Destruction (13:5–13)		Median Slaughter (13:17)	
Eternal Devastation of Babylon (13:9–22)		Israelite Regathering (14:1–2)	
Attributes of the King of Babylon			
King of Babylon (14:4a)	✓	King of Kings (14:9–16)	
Brutal Ruler (14:6)		Exposed Corpse (14:18–20a)	✓
Ruler of Vast Kingdom (14:6)	✓		
Activities of the King of Babylon			
Harvests Lebanon's Trees (14:8)	✓	Puts Israel and Judah to Forced Labor (14:17c)	
Makes the World a Wilderness (14:17a)		Destroys His Own Land (14:20b)	
Destroys Cities (14:17b)		Kills His Own People (14:20c)	
✓ = Meets criterion			

Merodach-baladan

Watts and Smith believe Merodach-baladan was the king of Babylon because he ruled Babylon during the days of Ahaz and Hezekiah.[186] His rebellion against Assyria did bring destruction to his land and city.[187] This destruction, however, only indirectly came by his hand and therefore does not constitute a fulfillment of the "destroyed his own land" and "killed his own people" activities.[188] Watts believes the destruction of Babylon took place in 710 BC by Sargon II or 703 BC by Sennacherib.[189] Smith points to

---

185. Cobb, "Ode in Isaiah XIV," 26.
186. Watts, *Isaiah 1–33*, 187–88; Smith, *Isaiah 1–39*, 310–11.
187. Brangenberg III, "Re-Examination," 88.
188. See "Destroyed His Own Land" above.
189. Watts, *Isaiah 1–33*, 188.

the 689 BC destruction.[190] All of these destructions, however, were temporary and could not be a fulfillment of Isaiah 13.

Merodach-baladan was a nuisance to Assyria, not a conqueror.[191] He capitalized on the political instability between the reigns of Shalmaneser V and Sargon II and became king of Babylon.[192] Sargon made a minor raid into Babylon during the first year of his reign, but this campaign failed to subjugate Merodach-baladan.[193] Sargon later wrote, "Twelve years [Merodach-baladan] ruled and governed Babylon."[194] Sargon finally defeated Merodach-baladan (c. 710 BC), but Merodach-baladan led a rebellion again in 703 BC after the death of Sargon. In Sennacherib's first campaign, he crushed Merodach-baladan's rebellion.[195] The annals of Sennacherib speak of Merodach-baladan being a regular foe, but he was a nuisance and regularly defeated.[196] Merodach-baladan was not a conqueror, much less the "king of mortal kings."

Most historical information concerning Merodach-baladan comes from his enemies. Smith interprets Isaiah 14:6 under the unlikely assumption that he was a brutal ruler.[197] If Merodach-baladan was a brutal ruler, one would think that the people of Babylon would have been more resistant to his rule. The fact that they returned to him after the death of Sargon II leads one to conclude he was not a brutal ruler.[198] Details concerning the death of Merodach-baladan are unknown, but it is unlikely his corpse was

---

190. Smith, *Isaiah 1–39*, 311.

191. Brangeberg states, "He was by no means a world-conqueror" (Brangenberg III, "Re-Examination," 88).

192. In the first year of Sargon's reign, Sargon wrote, "Merodachbaladan, king of Chaldea, who exercised the kingship over Babylon against the will of the gods" (Luckenbill, *Ancient Records of Assyria and Babylonia*, 2:2).

193. Luckenbill, *Ancient Records of Assyria and Babylonia*, 2:2. Elayi writes, "The outcome of the battle [against Elam and Babylon] seems to be clear: contrary to what he claimed Sargon was not victorious against the king of Elam alone" (Elayi, *Sargon II*, 184). Elayi comes to this conclusion because Sargon does not subjugate Babylon until 12 years later (Luckenbill, *Ancient Records of Assyria and Babylonia*, 2:33). For a full analysis of Sargon's interaction with Merodach-baladan see Elayi, *Sargon II*, 182–90.

194. Luckenbill, *Annals of Sennacherib*, 2:33.

195. Luckenbill, *Ancient Records of Assyria and Babylonia*, 2:153.

196. Luckenbill, *Ancient Records of Assyria and Babylonia*, 2:154–56.

197. Smith, *Isaiah 1–39*, 312–13.

198. Elayi explains, "Merodach-baladan survived and waited until Sargon's death to reconquer Babylonia in 703. Babylonians from cities and tribes were ready to flock to his side when he reappeared" (Elayi, *Sargon II*, 190).

exposed.[199] He did not rule a vast kingdom, make the world a wilderness, or destroy cities. He did not kill his own people or destroy his own land. He clearly did not put Israel and Judah to forced labor. Merodach-baladan received only one mark and cannot be the Isaiah 14 king of Babylon (see Table 4.4).

Table 4.4. Evaluation of Merodach-baladan

Contextual Criteria			
Cataclysmic Destruction (13:5–13)		Median Slaughter (13:17)	
Eternal Devastation of Babylon (13:9–22)		Israelite Regathering (14:1–2)	
Attributes of the King of Babylon			
King of Babylon (14:4a)	✓	King of Kings (14:9–16)	
Brutal Ruler (14:6)		Exposed Corpse (14:18–20a)	
Ruler of Vast Kingdom (14:6)			
Activities of the King of Babylon			
Harvests Lebanon's Trees (14:8)		Puts Israel and Judah to Forced Labor (14:17c)	
Makes the World a Wilderness (14:17a)		Destroys His Own Land (14:20b)	
Destroys Cities (14:17b)		Kills His Own People (14:20c)	
✓ = Meets criterion			

Nabonidus

Chisholm states, "The king of Babylon taunted here may be Nabonidus (the official last king of Babylon when it fell)."[200] Goldingay claims the curse, "Let him not be mentioned, offspring of evildoers" (Isa 14:20), suggests Nabonidus because "the Bible does not actually mention Nabonidus, Babylon's last king."[201] Applying the curse, however, to only the biblical revelation is not a restriction found in Isaiah 14:20. This curse failed because there is a

---

199. He seems to have died peacefully in Elam (Sack, *ABD* 4:704–5).
200. Chisholm, *Handbook on the Prophets*, 51.
201. Goldingay, *Isaiah*, 103.

record of Nabonidus, and his name is known.²⁰² A Persian/Median force conquered Babylon during his reign, but Babylon was not destroyed.

Clements claims Nabonidus's death corresponds to the harsh slavery in Isaiah 14:3: "[Isaiah 14:3] must be a reference to the period of the Babylonian exile in which the circumstances of those in Babylon appears [sic] to have been tantamount to a harsh form of slavery."²⁰³ Clements is careful with his words; he does not claim Nabonidus inflicted the harsh slavery, but lumps the harsh slavery into the entire Babylonian exile. Wilkie assumes Isaiah 14:3 refers to Nabonidus's rule and surmises that his rule must have been harsh.²⁰⁴ He examines various prophecies, primarily in Isaiah 40–66, and deduces the Babylonian captivity must have been a time of severe persecution. Wilkie even references Isaiah 13 as evidence of a severe persecution.²⁰⁵ Wilkie reads eschatological prophecies like Isaiah 13 into Nabonidus's rule. A brutal Nabonidus rule would promote a greater regathering to Israel which did not happen. The Babylonian captivity hardly corresponds to a time of harsh slavery and imprisonment described in Isaiah 14:3, 17.²⁰⁶

Lods presents additional evidence that Nabonidus is the king of Babylon: "The allusions which the satire contains fit in very well with what we know of Nabonidus, on the other hand, for he was the last king of Babylon, a great rebuilder of temples, he visited Lebanon himself, and, because of his repression of the revolt in Syria, might be accused of having 'destroyed thy land and slain thy people.'"²⁰⁷ Nabonidus was a cedar harvester, but the repression of a revolt hardly corresponds to the "destroys his own land" or "kills his own people" criteria. If they were in revolt, they were not his people.

---

202. See "Questionable Criteria" above.

203. Clements, *Isaiah 1–39*, 140–41.

204. Wilkie, "Nabonidus and the Later Jewish Exiles," 40. Wilkie argues that life appears to be favorable for the dispersed Jews at the beginning of their captivity and the "much later period of Persian ascendancy," but "no evidence is adduced from the intervening period to prove that these favourable conditions continued throughout" (Wilkie, "Nabonidus and the Later Jewish Exiles," 36).

205. Wilkie, "Nabonidus and the Later Jewish Exiles," 38n2. Chapter 3 argues these events cannot be applied to Nabonidus's rule.

206. Merrill writes, "The biblical literature offers hints here and there that life, on the whole, was pleasant and that the people adjusted remarkably well to their new locale" (Merrill, *Kingdom of Priests*, 483). Merrill references Jeremiah 29:4–7 and Ezekiel 33:30–32 as supporting passages.

207. Lods, *Prophets and the Rise of Judaism*, 237.

Wilkie provides additional proof asserting Nabonidus as the king of Babylon: "The king evidently claimed divine honours for himself, that he boasts in one of his inscriptions 'that the whole of Mesopotamia and the West, as far as Gaza on the Egyptian border, continued to acknowledge his authority.'"[208] Nabonidus did rule the vast domain of his predecessors, but he was not a conqueror and falls far short of the "king of kings." Cobb writes, "Nabonidus was a weak antiquarian, whose chief energy was expended in rebuilding ancient temples."[209] Because he was the last Babylonian ruler, his corpse may have been exposed and his progeny killed. It is unlikely he was an Isaiah 14:6 brutal ruler, nor did he make the world a wilderness, destroy cities, kill his own people, put Israel and Judah to forced labor, or destroy his own land. When considering the prospect of Nabonidus as the king of Babylon, Cobb humorously states, "The satire of our ode, 'Is this the man that made the earth to tremble, that did shake kingdoms?' if meant of Nabonidus, would have made its author immortal—as a laughing-stock."[210] Nabonidus meets only four of the fifteen criteria to be identified as the Isaiah 14 king of Babylon (see Table 4.5).

Table 4.5. Evaluation of Nabonidus

Contextual Criteria			
Cataclysmic Destruction (13:5–13)		Median Slaughter (13:17)	
Eternal Devastation of Babylon (13:9–22)		Israelite Regathering (14:1–2)	
Attributes of the King of Babylon			
King of Babylon (14:4a)	✓	King of Kings (14:9–16)	
Brutal Ruler (14:6)		Exposed Corpse (14:18–20a)	✓
Ruler of Vast Kingdom (14:6)	✓		
Activities of the King of Babylon			
Harvests Lebanon's Trees (14:8)	✓	Puts Israel and Judah to Forced Labor (14:17c)	
Makes the World a Wilderness (14:17a)		Destroys His Own Land (14:20b)	
Destroys Cities (14:17b)		Kills His Own People (14:20c)	
✓ = Meets criterion			

---

208. Wilkie, "Nabonidus and the Later Jewish Exiles," 41.
209. Cobb, "Ode in Isaiah XIV," 26.
210. Cobb, "Ode in Isaiah XIV," 27.

Israel's Eschatological Enemy

Nebuchadnezzar

Nebuchadnezzar has historically been identified as the Isaiah 14 king of Babylon. He was the king of *Babylon*. In his expedition to Syria, Nebuchadnezzar explains how he made a road by which he could harvest cedar trees.[211] He made Ashkelon "a ruin heap,"[212] razed Jerusalem, and deported Judah, so one could claim he destroyed cities.

Nebuchadnezzar was a conqueror and ruled a vast kingdom, but his kingdom and generalship pales in comparison to Alexander the Great.[213] He killed and deported many of the Jewish people, but he did not "imprison" them. No doubt some slaves were made of the Jewish captives, but overall their captivity was known as a pleasant time, not one of "harsh labor."[214] Nebuchadnezzar was not an Isaiah 14:6 kind of brutal ruler; he definitely did not make the world a wilderness, destroy his own land, or kill his own people.[215] Not much is known about Nebuchadnezzar's death, but his son Amel-marduk ruled after him, and, as van Keulen writes, "there is no indication that his body was ever cast out from his grave."[216] Nebuchadnezzar meets only four of the fifteen criteria specified in Isaiah 13–14 (see Table 4.6).

---

211. "I organized [my army] for a[n expedition] to the Lebanon. I made that country happy by eradicating its enemy everywhere (lit.: below and above). . . . I cut through steep mountains, I split rocks, opened passages and (thus) I constructed a straight road for the (transport of the) cedars" (Pritchard, *ANET* 307).

212. Grayson, *Assyrian and Babylonian Chronicles*, 100.

213. While Nebuchadnezzar decisively defeated Egypt in 605 BC, he suffered heavy losses in 601 BC, "They fought one another in the battlefield and both sides suffered severe losses (lit. they inflicted a major defeat upon one another). The king of Akkad and his army turned and [went back] to Babylon" (Grayson, *Assyrian and Babylonian Chronicles*, 101). The losses were so severe that it says of his fifth year, "The king of Akkad stayed home (and) refitted his numerous horses and chariotry" (Grayson, *Assyrian and Babylonian Chronicles*, 101). Unfortunately, the Babylonian chronicle is broken so there is no information after 594 BC (Grayson, *Assyrian and Babylonian Chronicles*, 19). In 595 BC, he even had to put down a rebellion.

214. See "Nabonidus" above.

215. Cobb agrees, "As for Nebuchadnezzar, he was a master-builder, both in the literal and the political sense; and very far from being a cruel oppressor. 'Thou hast destroyed thy land, thou hast slain thy people,' is utterly inapplicable to him" (Cobb, "Ode in Isaiah XIV," 26).

216. van Keulen, "On the Identity of the Anonymous Ruler." 115. Sweeney explains, "[Nebuchadnezzar] is rejected because his son Amel-Merodach succeeded him to the throne after his death in 562. Furthermore, there is no indication that his body was ever desecrated in the manner described in vv. 18–19" (Sweeney, *Isaiah 1–39*, 232).

Table 4.6. Evaluation of Nebuchadnezzar

Contextual Criteria			
Cataclysmic Destruction (13:5–13)		Median Slaughter (13:17)	
Eternal Devastation of Babylon (13:9–22)		Israelite Regathering (14:1–2)	
Attributes of the King of Babylon			
King of Babylon (14:4a)	✓	King of Kings (14:9–16)	
Brutal Ruler (14:6)		Exposed Corpse (14:18–20a)	
Ruler of Vast Kingdom (14:6)	✓		
Activities of the King of Babylon			
Harvests Lebanon's Trees (14:8)	✓	Puts Israel and Judah to Forced Labor (14:17c)	
Makes the World a Wilderness (14:17a)		Destroys His Own Land (14:20b)	
Destroys Cities (14:17b)	✓	Kills His Own People (14:20c)	
✓ = Meets criterion			

Sargon II

Sargon II meets several criteria but misses others. Shipp explains methodologically why so many scholars believe Sargon II was the king of Babylon, "Most scholars have adopted this position [that the king of Babylon has already died] and then looked for evidence of an Assyrian or Babylonian king who dies in the manner apparently depicted in the poem."[217] Roberts follows this formula: "The particular king whose death is being celebrated in this taunt song is presumably the Assyrian Sargon II, since he is the only king of Babylon during the relevant periods known to have died in the manner reflected in the poem."[218] Shipp even acknowledges, "The king who comes most readily to mind in this regard is Sargon II, who was slain on the field of battle and left unburied."[219] Blenkinsopp casts doubt on this claim, "We hear that Sargon II (+ 705) was not buried in his own house

---

217. Shipp, *Of Dead Kings and Dirges*, 159.
218. Roberts, *First Isaiah*, 207. See also Gallagher, *Sennacherib's Campaign to Judah*, 87.
219. Shipp, *Of Dead Kings and Dirges*, 159.

(*ina bitišu*) but that does not mean he remained unburied."²²⁰ Tadmor reconstructs the death of Sargon II using multiple sources:

> Sargon's politics came to an abrubt and tragic end with his death on a battlefield, against a certain Ešpai the Kulummean (ᴵ*Ešpai*ᴸᵁ *Ku-lum-ma-a-a*), referred to in the Eponym Chronicle (K. 4446 in Ungnad, *RLA* II, p.433, see Tadmor, *JCS* 12 [1958], p.97n311). It is suggested that this last campaign of Sargon had been conducted against Tabal (thus according to the entry in the Babylonian Chronicle II:6' [*JCS* 12 p.97n312 and now Grayson, *ABC*, p.76]) and it was often believed (e.g., Olmstead, *Sargon*, p. 15, Diakonoff, *Istoriya Midii*, p.236) that Sargon's enemies were the Cimmerians. In the course of that battle the king was killed (*šarru dēk*) and the royal camp was captured and looted (*ma-dak-tú ša šar* KUR *Aš-šur*ᴷᴵ <x> [. . . . . .], C♭ 6:10). From K.4730 obv. 20' one learns that Sargon's body was not buried according to the law, either because it fell into the hands of the enemy or because it was lost on the battlefield; alternatively it may have been cremated in the absence of the means of embalmment. The burying of the king "at home," that is, in his own palace, may reflect the custom of the kings of Assyria [p.158]. A similar practice is attested in Babylonia, where it is stated that certain kings were "buried in the palace of Sargon (of Akkad)" (thus King, *Chronicles* I, pp. 52:4; 56:14 [now in Grayson, *ABC*, pp. 142:4; 143:14]).²²¹

It is likely that Sargon's body was exposed and meets the criteria specified in Isaiah 14:19.

Sargon II was a conqueror and did rule a vast domain, though not on par with Alexander the Great.²²² He destroyed cities but did not make the *world* a wilderness.²²³ There are several problems with Sargon II; first, he was the king of *Assyria*, not the king of Babylon. Ginsberg responds:

---

220. Blenkinsopp, *Isaiah 1–39*, 287. Nielsen is not convinced either (Nielsen, *There is Hope for a Tree*, 160–61).

221. Tadmor, "Sin of Sargon and Sennacherib's Last Will," 28–29. See also Roberts, *First Isaiah*, 207–8.

222. Gallagher explains, "Sargon and Sennacherib really made the earth tremble and the kingdoms shake (Is. 14:16)" (Gallagher, *Sennacherib's Campaign to Judah*, 88).

223. Sargon claimed in his eighth campaign, "[Metattati of Zikirtu's] brave warriors who were stationed in the passes of Mount Uashdirikka, to guard (them), I slew and I captured Ishtaippa, Saktatush, Nanzu, Aukanê, Kâbani, Gurrusupa, Raksi, Gimdakrikka, Barunakka, Ubabara, Sitera, Tashtami, Tesammia,—twelve cities, strong and walled, together with 84 cities of their neighborhood,—all (of these). I destroyed their walls, I set fire to the houses inside them, I destroyed them like a flood, I battered them into

In view of Sargon's notorious Babylonism, whose manifestations included a three years' residence in Babylon and the stressing of both his Babylonian titles and of his benefactions to the inhabitants and temples of the southern metropolises in an account intended for foreigners (the Cyprus Stela), it would not be remarkable if Isaiah regarded Babylon (a city whose name was presumably far more familiar to him [see Genesis 10:10; 11:1–9] than Calah [see Genesis 10:11, 12] let alone Dūr-Sharrukīn, of which he probably never heard), as the center of the Assyrian empire.[224]

But Babylon was not considered the "center of the Assyrian empire." Claiming Isaianic ignorance is unlikely. In Isaiah 20:1, Isaiah acknowledges, "Sargon, king of Assyria," and years later the Babylonian envoy comes from Merodach-baladan, the king of Babylon (Isa 39). While Sargon did conquer Babylon, ascend the throne, and take Bel's hands, he was known as an Assyrian king.[225] Machinist explains why Sargon II took the title "king of Babylon":

> What, then, was the "Babylonian problem" for these Sargonids? At minimum, modern scholarship agrees, it was a political and military issue: how to govern a Babylonia which shortly before the Sargonids, under Tiglath-pileser III, had been incorporated into the Assyrian empire, only to prove a highly troublesome vassal. Thanks to a number of recent studies, we can follow in some detail how the Sargonids met this challenge: ruling Babylonia now by loyal natives, by Assyrian deputies, including royal heirs, *or directly by taking the Babylonian throne themselves*; then by setting native Babylonians in the older cities against "tribal" groups of Chaldeans and Arameans also in the area; lastly, by large-scale

---

heaps of ruins" (Luckenbill, *Ancient Records of Assyria and Babylonia*, 2:79). On the same campaign he also states concerning cities and fields, "The city of Ushkaia, the mainstay of his land, together with the cities round about, they turned into ruins; they abandoned their possessions and took the road that has no turning. With the advance of my mighty arms, I went up into that fortress, carried off its overflowing wealth, and brought it into my camp. . . . 115 cities of its neighborhood I burned like brush (?) and covered the face of heaven with their smoke, like a cyclone. As if destroyed by a flood, I made its fields, like heaps I made (*lit.*, poured out) their settlements" (Luckenbill, *Ancient Records of Assyria and Babylonia*, 85). Sargon's destruction of the land, however, does not constitute a worldwide devastation described in Isaiah 14:17.

224. Ginsberg, "Reflexes of Sargon in Isaiah," 49.

225. "Sargon (II) ascended the throne in Babylon. The thirteenth year: Sargon (II) took Bel's hand." (Grayson, *Assyrian and Babylonian Chronicles*, 75).

[construction] measures toward the capital and most important city of Babylonia, Babylon.[226]

When Sargon identified himself as the king of Babylon and "took Bel's hands," he was identifying himself as the ruler of Babylon in an effort to rule over and appease a troublesome vassal. Sargon II was always first and foremost the king Assyria. His grandson, Esarhaddon, did not call him the "king of Babylon," but "viceroy of Babylon": "son of Sennacherib, king of the universe, king of Assyria, (grand)son of Sargon, king of Assyria, viceroy of Babylon, king of Sumer and Akkad."[227] Furthermore, Sargon II's own inscriptions describe him as the "viceroy of Babylon" on several occasions.[228] Whether he was the "viceroy" or the "king" of Babylon depended on the governmental system which was enforced at the time of writing. Sargon II was the king of Assyria, and there was no reason for Isaiah to identify him as the king of Babylon. van Keulen agrees, "It is difficult to explain, however, why the author of the poem would designate an Assyrian king as 'King of Babylon.'"[229]

There are additional problems with Sargon II. He was not an Isaiah 14:6 kind of brutal ruler, and he did not kill his own people or destroy his own land. Blenkinsopp agrees, "There is no evidence that he warred against his own people."[230] Sweeney prefers Sargon II as the king of Babylon, but admits, "One difficulty with this proposal is that it seems to require that verses 3–4a be an editorial addition."[231] One cannot harmonize a harsh imprisonment of Israel *and Judah* and a subsequent regathering of Israel with a Sargonic kingship. Sargon II cannot be the Isaiah 14 king of Babylon for eleven reasons (see Table 4.7).

---

226. Machinist, "Assyrians and Their Babylonian Problem," 354 (emphasis mine).

227. Luckenbill, *Ancient Records of Assyria and Babylonia*, 2:282.

228. Luckenbill, *Ancient Records of Assyria and Babylonia*, 2:48, 50–51, 66–67, 101, 112.

229. van Keulen, "On the Identity of the Anonymous Ruler," 116.

230. Blenkinsopp, *Isaiah 1–39*, 287. Sargon built Dûr-Sharrukîn (Luckenbill, *Ancient Records of Assyria and Babylonia*, 2:56–59, 62–66).

231. Sweeney, *Isaiah 1–39*, 232.

Table 4.7. Evaluation of Sargon II

Contextual Criteria			
Cataclysmic Destruction (13:5-13)		Median Slaughter (13:17)	
Eternal Devastation of Babylon (13:9-22)		Israelite Regathering (14:1-2)	
Attributes of the King of Babylon			
King of Babylon (14:4a)		King of Kings (14:9-16)	
Brutal Ruler (14:6)		Exposed Corpse (14:18-20a)	✓
Ruler of Vast Kingdom (14:6)	✓		
Activities of the King of Babylon			
Harvests Lebanon's Trees (14:8)	✓	Puts Israel and Judah to Forced Labor (14:17c)	
Makes the World a Wilderness (14:17a)		Destroys His Own Land (14:20b)	
Destroys Cities (14:17b)	✓	Kills His Own People (14:20c)	
✓ = Meets criterion			

Sennacherib

Blenkinsopp prefers identifying Sennacherib as the king of Babylon: "Sennacherib (+ 682) looks more promising since we know he was murdered by members of his own family, and the biblical text elsewhere confirms his overbearing attitude (Isa 37:23-29). He also destroyed many cities, including Babylon, but we do not know that his corpse was dishonored."[232] van Keulen notes Sennacherib is the most promising candidate "within the literary framework of the Hebrew Bible."[233] These authors make too much of Sennacherib's boasting in Isaiah 36-37. While Sennacherib was an arrogant conqueror and he destroyed cities,[234] he still was not as great of a king as Alexander the Great.

---

232. Blenkinsopp, *Isaiah 1-39*, 287.

233. van Keulen, "On the Identity of the Anonymous Ruler," 120.

234. "The cities which were in those provinces I destroyed, I devastated, I burned with fire. To mounds and ruins I turned (them)" (Luckenbill, *Ancient Records of Assyria and Babylonia*, 2:123). See also Luckenbill, *Ancient Records of Assyria and Babylonia*, 2:131-32.

Sennacherib was a cedar harvester. Concerning the construction of his palace he states, "I had them build a palace of ivory, ebony(?), boxwood(?), *musukannu*-wood, cedar, cypress and spruce, the 'Palace without a Rival,' for my royal abode. Beams of cedar, the product of Mt. Amanus, which they dragged with difficulty out of (those) distant mountains, I stretched across their ceilings(?)."[235]

Sennacherib was never king of Babylon. Cobb responds, "For Sennacherib, as well as Sargon and Tiglath-Pileser, repeatedly calls himself *šarri Babili*, and this may have been as well known to Isaiah as to us."[236] He never acquired the title "King of Babylon."[237] Tiglath-pileser III became the "king of Babylon," Sargon II "ascended the throne" of Babylon and "took Bel's hands," but Sennacherib only conquered the city.[238] He destroyed Babylon because they refused to submit to his *Assyrian* dominance.[239] While Sennacherib did die a violent death, it is unlikely his body was ever exposed.[240] Sennacherib was not an Isaiah 14:6 kind of brutal ruler; he did not make the world a wilderness, put Israel and Judah to forced labor, destroy his own land, or kill his own people.[241] Sennacherib meets only three of the fifteen criteria demonstrating that he cannot be the king of Babylon (see Table 4.8).

---

235. Luckenbill, *Annals of Sennacherib*, 96. Sennacherib's intention to cut down the cedars of Lebanon is also found in Isaiah 37:24.

236. Cobb, "Ode in Isaiah XIV," 31.

237. Brangenberg III, "Re-Examination," 89.

238. Brangenberg writes, "Sennacherib, though he conquered Babylon on at least three occasions, never took the throne himself.... His son, Esarhaddon, in describing his father's titles and accomplishments, made no mention of Sennacherib ever having ruled over Babylon as king" (Brangenberg III, "Re-Examination," 90).

239. Brinkman, "Sennacherib's Babylonian Problem," 89–95.

240. Shipp agrees, "He also died violently, apparently at the hand of his sons, but did not die in battle and apparently his body was not exposed" (Shipp, *Of Dead Kings and Dirges*, 160).

241. Vanderburgh claims, "The sentence in the ode which says 'he destroyed his land' might be taken as referring to his wars with the Babylonians and the destruction of Babylon" (Vanderburgh, "Ode on the King of Babylon," 120). A land/people rebelling against him, however, would not be called "his own" land/people.

Table 4.8. Evaluation of Sennacherib

Contextual Criteria			
Cataclysmic Destruction (13:5–13)		Median Slaughter (13:17)	
Eternal Devastation of Babylon (13:9–22)		Israelite Regathering (14:1–2)	
Attributes of the King of Babylon			
King of Babylon (14:4a)		King of Kings (14:9–16)	
Brutal Ruler (14:6)		Exposed Corpse (14:18–20a)	
Ruler of Vast Kingdom (14:6)	✓		
Activities of the King of Babylon			
Harvests Lebanon's Trees (14:8)	✓	Puts Israel and Judah to Forced Labor (14:17c)	
Makes the World a Wilderness (14:17a)		Destroys His Own Land (14:20b)	
Destroys Cities (14:17b)	✓	Kills His Own People (14:20c)	
✓ = Meets criterion			

Tiglath-pileser III

Hayes and Irvine claim, "The king of Babylon, whose death is announced in the form of a celebrative eulogy, is Tiglath-pileser."[242] Brangenberg claims Tiglath-pileser III was a brutal ruler: "[Tiglath-pileser III] could be described as '[one] smiting the peoples with fury' and 'one ruling nations in anger, a persecution unhindered.' [He] exacted heavy tribute from *[his] subject kingdoms* and kept the masses under control by massive deportations and

---

242. Hayes and Irvine, *Isaiah*, 227. Brangenberg also identifies Tiglath-pileser III as the king of Babylon, Brangenberg III, "Re-Examination," 91.

Israel's Eschatological Enemy

exchange of populations."[243] Brangenberg misapplies Isaiah 14:6 to Assyrian conquests rather than Tiglath-pileser III's manner of rule.

Brangenberg's claim that Tiglath-pileser III destroyed his own land and killed his own people is speculative and unconvincing.[244] Brangenberg even acknowledges that Tiglath-pileser III participated in "massive building projects."[245] One who partakes in "massive building projects" hardly sounds like someone who "destroyed his own land."

He did conquer Lebanon and rule a vast domain though it does not compare to Alexander the Great's. Tiglath-pileser III destroyed cities but hardly "made the world a wilderness."[246] His death is a mystery, so his body may have been exposed.[247]

Tiglath-pileser III was a king of Assyria, not Babylon. Brangenberg, Hayes, and Irvine make much of the Neo-Babylonian Chronicle I where it states that Tiglath-pileser III "ascended the throne in Babylon."[248] They also note that the Nimrûd tablet states, "Palace of Tiglath-pileser, the great

---

243. Brangenberg III, "Re-Examination," 89 (emphasis mine).

244. "Layard observed during his excavations at Nimrud that the inscriptions and bas-reliefs in the palace of Tiglath-Pileser III had been treated with great irreverence. They had been deliberately erased and had often been re-used by Esarhaddon in building his own palace.... Such mistreatment of inscriptions and bas-reliefs was deemed to bring a curse upon the person performing such a misdeed. Thus Esarhaddon must have been given good reason to deface the monuments and inscriptions of his predecessors. Boutflower suggested that perhaps the clue to this destruction is found in 14:20 'You have destroyed your land, you have slain your people'" (Brangenberg III, "Re-Examination," 91–92).

245. Brangenberg III, "Re-Examination," 89.

246. Luckenbill, *Ancient Records of Assyria and Babylonia*, 1:271, 278, 284. According to the annals of Tiglath-pileser's conquests, he was known for destroying cities, but he did not devastate the land as his successors.

247. Brangenberg writes, "The details concerning the death of Tiglath-Pileser III are obscured by a lacuna in the text of the Eponym Canon for 727 B.C. However it appears that he had been campaigning against one of the rebellious territories, probably against Damascus, when he died. He was immediately succeeded on the throne by his son Shalmaneser. There are no details of how he died or of his burial or lack thereof" (Brangenberg III, "Re-Examination," 91). The Babylonian chronicle, however, implies a regular death and burial of a king (Grayson, *Assyrian and Babylonian Chronicles*, 72–73). Based on the Babylonian chronicle, Roberts surmises, "Both Tiglath-pileser III and Shalmaneser V apparently died natural deaths and received normal burials" (Roberts, *First Isaiah*, 208). Brangenberg then unconvincingly argues that Tiglath-pileser's dynasty was extinguished five years later, c. 722 BC, with the death of Shalmaneser V (Brangenberg III, "Re-Examination," 91).

248. Grayson, *Assyrian and Babylonian Chronicles*, 72.

king, the mighty king, king of the universe, king of Assyria, *king of Babylon*, king of Sumer and Akkad, king of the four regions (of the world)."[249] Hayes and Irvine then claim the historical setting of the *massa'* "suggest[s] a date after spring 729, when Tiglath-pileser assumed the throne in Babylon, but before 727, when he died."[250] Tiglath-pileser III, however, did not relinquish his Assyrian title and "ruled" Babylon for only the last two years of his life. There is no reason for Isaiah to call Tiglath-pileser the king of *Babylon*.[251]

Two of the most challenging obstacles for the Tiglath-pileser III view are the destruction of Babylon and regathering of Israel. Brangenberg claims the destruction of Babylon refers to the 689 BC destruction, over thirty years removed from the life of Tiglath-pileser III.[252] Concerning the regathering of Israel he states:

> The names given to the captives who are returning and the name given to the land to which they were returning (her [Israel's] soil, house of Jacob, the soil of Yahweh) strongly suggest that 14:1–2 refers to an Assyrian exile of the Israelites rather than the Babylonian Exile of the Jews. . . . The mention in verse 2 of the nations escorting the exiles home and then becoming their slaves, sounds very much akin to the eschatological expectations of the post-exilic community. However in this context, the events referred to in verse 2 may simply be an expansion of what it means for Yahweh to choose Israel once again.[253]

Brangenberg's three explanations concerning the regathering argues against Tiglath-pileser III being the king of Babylon. The Assyrian antagonization of Israel persisted after the death of Tiglath-pileser III, even after

---

249. Luckenbill, *Ancient Records of Assyria and Babylonia*, 1:282–83 (emphasis mine). Brangenberg III, "Re-Examination," 89–90; Hayes and Irvine, *Isaiah*, 227–28.

250. Hayes and Irvine, *Isaiah*, 229. Brangenberg agrees with this dating, "The date of this oracle has been fixed at or shortly before the time of the death of Tiglath-Pileser III in 727 B.C." (Brangenberg III, "Re-Examination," 92).

251. See "Sargon II" above for additional responses to this claim.

252. Brangenberg III, "Re-Examination," 94.

253. Brangenberg explains, "The names given to the captives who are returning and the name given to the land to which they were returning (her [Israel's] soil, house of Jacob, the soil of Yahweh) strongly suggest that 14:1–2 refers to an Assyrian exile of the Israelites rather than the Babylonian Exile of the Jews. . . . The mention in verse 2 of the nations escorting the exiles home and then becoming their slaves, sounds very much akin to the eschatological expectations of the post-exilic community. However in this context, the events referred to in verse 2 may simply be an expansion of what it means for Yahweh to choose Israel once again" (Brangenberg III, "Re-Examination," 93).

the fall of Samaria in 722 BC. According to Isaiah 14:1–4, the death of the king ushers in a time of blessing for Israel and Judah. Brangenberg's explanation cannot be harmonized with Isaiah 14:1–4.

Brangenberg, Hayes, and Irvine attempt to reconcile the text with the life of Tiglath-pileser III, but it simply does not correspond. He was not king *of Babylon*, nor was there a corresponding regathering of Israel and Judah at his death. Tiglath-pileser III meets only four of the criteria of the Isaiah 14 king of Babylon (see Table 4.9).

Table 4.9. Evaluation of Tiglath-pileser III

Contextual Criteria			
Cataclysmic Destruction (13:5–13)		Median Slaughter (13:17)	
Eternal Devastation of Babylon (13:9–22)		Israelite Regathering (14:1–2)	
Attributes of the King of Babylon			
King of Babylon (14:4a)		King of Kings (14:9–16)	
Brutal Ruler (14:6)		Exposed Corpse (14:18–20a)	✓
Ruler of Vast Kingdom (14:6)	✓		
Activities of the King of Babylon			
Harvests Lebanon's Trees (14:8)	✓	Puts Israel and Judah to Forced Labor (14:17c)	
Makes the World a Wilderness (14:17a)		Destroys His Own Land (14:20b)	
Destroys Cities (14:17b)	✓	Kills His Own People (14:20c)	
✓ = Meets criterion			

CONCLUSION

This chapter argued for eleven additional criteria by which one may identify the king of Babylon. These eleven criteria built off the four contextual criteria found in chapter 3. Nine kings were evaluated based upon these fifteen criteria. A summary of the analysis presented in this chapter can be found in Appendix 1. Given the analysis presented in this chapter, it is difficult to see how these kings could be the Isaiah 14 king of Babylon.

Chapter 5

Conclusion

THE INTRODUCTION DEMONSTRATED THAT Hippolytus of Rome, Newton, and Pink believed Isaiah 14:4b–21 referred to the antichrist, an eschatolotical enemy of Israel, but did not develop this view exegetically. This dissertation has argued that the genre of Isaiah 14, content and structure of Isaiah 13, and content of Isaiah 14 support an eschatological interpretation. The events described and characteristics of the king of Babylon cannot find any historical correspondence and, therefore, must be eschatological.

The genre of Isaiah 14 argues against a symbolic, ideal, eclectic, or representative king. Chapter 2 explained a *mashal* makes a statement concerning the function of the text, not the content. The primary idea of a *mashal* is a comparison. Some comparisons are explicit (Gen 10:9), others are implicit (1 Kgs 20:11), but every *mashal* is a comparison. Isaiah 14 is a prophetic, human *mashal* (cf. Ezek 14:7–8) and makes an implicit comparison. While some *meshalim* may use representative individuals, two reasons were proffered why Isaiah 14 refers to a real person. First, a human *mashal* refers to a real person. Just as the idolater in Ezekiel 14:7–8 must be a physical individual for the *mashal* to function correctly, so also must the king of Babylon be a physical individual. Second, the construct chain "of Babylon" specifies which "king," thus referring to a specific individual (rather than some indefinite king [cf. Prov 20:8, 22:29]). If Isaiah was referring to a general, representative king, then there would be no purpose for him to add the phrase "of Babylon."

The *mashal* in Isaiah 14 is part of the larger *massa'* against Babylon which starts in Isaiah 13. Chapter 3 analyzed the structure and content of the *massa'*. Isaiah 14:22–23 concludes the *massa'* against Babylon, and Isaiah 14:24–27 is a short-term sign (annihilation of Sennacherib's army) to validate the long-term prophecy (deliverance from eschatological Babylon).

This chapter also argued that the content of Isaiah 13:2—14:2 is eschatological. An analysis of the battles, armies, leaders, and destructions reveals there are two different battles, and both are eschatological. Four reasons were proffered why the Isaiah 13:2-13 battle is eschatological: (1) the Lord is leading the armies into battle (13:4); (2) the armies are angelic (13:3, 5); (3) the battle encompasses the entire earth (13:5); and (4) there are accompanying cosmological signs (13:13). The Isaiah 13:14—14:2 battle and Israelite regathering could, in theory, be historical, but there are no corresponding historic battles or Israelite regatherings. Therefore, Isaiah 13:2—14:2 describes two eschatological battles. One battle is between the Lord and a united nations force composed of kingdoms of nations. The other battle is between the Medes and Babylonians which results in the eternal desolation of Babylon. After the destruction of Babylon and its king, Israel will be regathered back to the land of Israel where they will be at "rest." Chapter 3 presented four criteria by which the king of Babylon can be identified. There must be cosmic signs, a destruction of Babylon by Median attackers, and a subsequent Israelite regathering. When Israel is regathered, they will "lift up this *mashal* against the king of Babylon."

Chapter 4 argued for eleven additional criteria for identifying the king of Babylon. The eleven criteria in the *mashal* were divided into attributes and activities. The five attributes of the king of Babylon are the following: (1) king of *Babylon* (14:4); (2) brutal ruler of nations (14:6); (3) vast kingdom (14:6); (4) king of kings (14:6, 9–14, 16); and (5) exposed corpse (14:18–20). The six activities of the king of Babylon include: (1) harvests Lebanon's trees (14:8); (2) makes the world a wilderness (14:17); (3) destroys cities (14:17); (4) puts Israel and Judah to forced labor (14:3, 17); (5) destroys his own land (14:20); and (6) kills his own people (14:20).

Chapter 4 then analyzed nine historic kings whom scholars have claimed could be the Isaiah 14 king of Babylon. It was argued that not only do these historic kings not meet the criteria described in Isaiah 13–14, but they do not even come close. Isaiah 13–14 prophesies a future Egyptian-like captivity of Israel by a "king of Babylon." The Lord himself will annihilate the armies of the king of Babylon and regather Israel where they will truly have "rest." At this time, Israel will mock the king of Babylon by speaking Isaiah 14:4b–21 against their defeated foe.

THEOLOGICAL IMPLICATIONS

There are several theological implications of this study. First, concerning Satan, Isaiah 14:12–14 does not describe the fall of Satan. Second, concerning life after death, Isaiah 14:9–11 is an extended personification and does not explain the nature of the afterlife.

Several eschatological implications are apparent as well. A portrait of Israel's eschatological enemy is deduced. He will rule from Babylon, conquer other nations, and rule a vast kingdom. He will be a brutal ruler; not only making the world a wilderness and destroying its cities but killing his own people and destoying his own land. His greatness and majesty will supersede all kings who have gone before him, even Alexander the Great. He will be feared throughout the entire world, making the earth shake, and kingdoms tremble. He will lead a worldwide imprisonment and persecution of the Jewish people.

The Lord himself will battle and annihilate the kingdoms and nations of the earth. The Medes will attack Babylon which will then be made a perpetual desolation. The Lord will liberate Israel, and the remnant will be regathered to Jerusalem where their captors will become their captives. The corpse of the king of Babylon will be abused, his descendants will be slaughtered, and the king of Babylon will be forgotten forever.

AREAS FOR FURTHER STUDY

This dissertation analyzed Isaiah 13–14 and provided an exegetical explanation of the identity of the king of Babylon. A detailed exegetical study is needed which argues for or against identifying the king of Tyre as Satan, a historic king, or an eschatological ruler in any portion of Ezekiel 28.

Additional study is also needed on the *mashal*. This dissertation argued that when a *mashal* is definite, it must refer to a specific individual and cannot be a general *mashal*. An analysis of all definite *meshalim* is needed to confirm this finding.

Finally, the fifteen criteria argued in this dissertation presents a fuller understanding of the identity and activities of this eschatological enemy of Israel. One could synthesize this information with what the rest of Scripture reveals about the end times.

Appendix 1

Summary of the Kings of Babylon

	Alexander the Great	Assur-uballit II	Belshazzar	Merodach-baladan	Nabonidus	Nebuchadnezzar	Sargon II	Sennacherib	Tiglath-pileser III
Contextual Criteria									
Cataclysmic Destruction (13:5–13)									
Median Slaughter (13:17)									
Eternal Devastation of Babylon (13:9–22)									
Israelite Regathering (14:1–2)									
Attributes of the King of Babylon									
Ruler of Babylon (14:4a)			✓	✓	✓	✓			
Brutal Ruler (14:6)									
Vast Kingdom (14:6)	✓		✓		✓	✓	✓	✓	✓
King of Kings (14:9–16)	✓								
Exposed Corpse (14:18–20a)		✓	✓		✓			✓	✓

Appendix 1

Activities of the King of Babylon									
Harvests Lebanon's Trees (14:8)	✓	✓	✓		✓	✓	✓	✓	✓
Makes the World a Wilderness (14:17a)									
Destroys Cities (14:17b)	✓					✓	✓	✓	✓
Puts Israel and Judah to Forced Labor (14:17c)									
Destroys His Own Land (14:20b)									
Kills His Own People (14:20c)									

✓ = Meets criterion

Bibliography

Abrams, Meyer, and Geoffrey Harpham. *A Glossary of Literary Terms*. 11th ed. Stamford, CT: Wadsworth, 2014.
Akin, Daniel L., ed. *A Theology for the Church*. Revised. Nashville: Broadman & Holman, 2014.
Albani, Matthias. "Herrschaft Will Ewigkeit: Das Spottlied Vom Aufstieg Und Fall Des 'Sohnes Der Morgenröte' (Jes 14,12ff) Und Sein Königsideologischer Hintergrund." In *Mensch Und König: Studien Zur Anthropologie Des Alten Testaments: Rüdiger Lux Zum 60. Geburtstag*, edited by Angelika Berlejung and Raik Heckl, 141–56. Freiburg im Breisgau: Herder, 2008.
Albright, William F. *Yahweh and the Gods of Canaan: A Historical Analysis of Two Contrasting Faiths*. Winona Lake, IN: Eisenbrauns, 1994.
Alden, Robert L. "Lucifer, Who or What?" *Bulletin of the Evangelical Theological Society* 11.1 (1968) 35–39.
Alexander, Joseph A. *The Prophecies of Isaiah*. Grand Rapids: Zondervan, 1980.
Allen, Kenneth W. "Rebuilding and Destruction of Babylon." *Bibliotheca Sacra* 133.529 (1976) 19–27.
Allen, Leslie C. *Ezekiel 20–48*. Word Biblical Commentary 29. Dallas: Word, 1995.
Alonso Schökel, Luis. "Traducción de Textos Poéticos Hebreos I (Isa 13)." *Cultura Biblica* 17 (1960) 170–76.
———. "Traducción de Textos Poéticos Hebreos I (Isa 14)." *Cultura Biblica* 17 (1960) 257–65.
Alter, Robert. *The Art of Biblical Poetry*. Revised and updated. New York: Basic, 2011.
Amzallag, Gérard Nissim, and Mikhal Avriel. "The Cryptic Meaning of the Isaiah 14 Māšāl." *Journal of Biblical Literature* 131.4 (2012) 643–62.
Anderson, George W. "Isaiah XXIV-XXVII Reconsidered." In *Congress Volume Bonn 1962*, edited by George W. Anderson et al., 9:118–26. Supplements to Vetus Testamentum. Leiden: Brill, 1963.
Anselm of Canterbury. *Complete Philosophical and Theological Treatises of Anselm of Canterbury*. Translated by Jasper Hopkins and Herbert Richardson. Minneapolis: Arthur J. Banning, 2000.
Archer, Gleason. "Isaiah." In *The Wycliffe Bible Commentary*, edited by Charles F. Pfeiffer, 605–54. Nashville: Southwestern, 1964.
Arnold, Bill T. *Who Were the Babylonians?* Archaeology and Biblical Studies 10. Atlanta: Society of Biblical Literature, 2004.
Arrian. *Arrian: Anabasis of Alexander, Books I-IV*. Translated by Peter A. Brunt. Loeb Classical Library. Cambridge, MA: Harvard University Press, 1976.

Bibliography

Ashley, Timothy R. *The Book of Numbers*. The New International Commentary on the Old Testament. Grand Rapids: Eerdmans, 2009.

Aune, David E. *Revelation 6-16*. Edited by Bruce M. Metzger. Word Biblical Commentary 52B. Nashville: Thomas Nelson, 1998.

Auvray, Paul. *Isaïe 1-39*. Sources Bibliques. Paris: J. Gabalda, 1972.

Bailey, Lloyd. "Expository Articles: Isaiah 14:24-27." *Interpretation* 36.2 (1982) 171-76.

Baker, David W. *Isaiah*. Edited by John H. Walton. Zondervan Illustrated Bible Backgrounds Commentary. Grand Rapids: Zondervan, 2013.

Bandstra, Barry. *Genesis 1-11: A Handbook on the Hebrew Text*. Baylor Handbook on the Hebrew Bible. Waco, TX: Baylor University Press, 2008.

Barackman, Floyd. *Practical Christian Theology: Examining the Great Doctrines of the Faith*. 4th ed. Grand Rapids: Kregel, 2012.

Barrick, William D. "The Eschatological Significance of Leviticus 26." *The Master's Seminary Journal* 16.1 (2005) 95-126.

Bavinck, Herman. *Reformed Dogmatics*. Edited by John Bolt. Grand Rapids: Baker Academic, 2011.

Beale, G. K. *The Book of Revelation*. New International Greek Testament Commentary. Grand Rapids: Eerdmans, 1999.

Begg, Christopher T. "Babylon in the Book of Isaiah." In *The Book of Isaiah—Le Livre de Isaïe: Les Oracles et Leurs Relecture*, edited by J. Vermeylen, 121-25. Leuven: Peeters/Leuven University Press, n.d.

Berlin, Adele. *The Dynamics of Biblical Parallelism*. Revised and expanded. Grand Rapids: Eerdmans, 2008.

———. *Lamentations*. Old Testament Library. Louisville: Westminster John Knox, 2002.

Bertoluci, Jose Maria. "The Son of the Morning and the Guardian Cherub in the Context of the Controversy between Good and Evil." ThD diss., Andrews University, 1985.

Beuken, Willem. "Common and Different Phrases for Babylon's Fall and its Aftermath in Isaiah 13-14 and Jeremiah 50-51." In *Concerning the Nations: Essays on the Oracles against the Nations in Isaiah, Jeremiah and Ezekiel*, edited by Andrew Mein et al., 53-73. New York: T. & T. Clark, 2016.

Bewer, Julius. "Text Critical Suggestions on Hosea Xii.1, Iv.4, Iv.8; Isaiah Xiv.12; Xi.1." *Journal of Biblical Literature* 21.1 (1902) 108-14.

Blenkinsopp, Joseph, ed. *Isaiah 1-39: A New Translation with Introduction and Commentary*. Anchor Bible. New York: Doubleday, 2000.

Block, Daniel. *The Book of Ezekiel: Chapters 25-48*. New International Commentary on the Old Testament. Grand Rapids: Eerdmans, 1997.

———. "The Old Testament on Hell." In *Hell Under Fire: Modern Scholarship Reinvents Eternal Punishment*, edited by Christopher W. Morgan and Robert A. Peterson, 43-65. Grand Rapids: Zondervan, 2004.

Blomberg, Craig L. *Interpreting the Parables*. Downers Grove, IL: InterVarsity, 1990.

Bordjadze, Karlo V., and R. Walter L. Moberly. *Darkness Visible: A Study of Isaiah 14:3-23 as Christian Scripture*. Eugene, OR: Pickwick, 2017.

Bost, Hubert. "Le Chant Sur La Chute d'un Tyran En Esaïe 14." *Études théologiques et religieuses* 59.1 (1984) 3-14.

Botterweck, G. Johannes, et al., eds. *Theological Dictionary of the Old Testament*. 15 vols. Grand Rapids: Eerdmans, 2012.

Boutflower, Charles. *The Book of Isaiah, Chapters [I-XXXIX] in the Light of the Assyrian Monuments*. New York: Society for Promoting Christian Knowledge, 1930.

Bibliography

Brangenberg III, John. "A Re-Examination of the Date, Authorship, Unity and Function of Isaiah 13–23." PhD diss., Golden Gate Baptist Theological Seminary, 1989.
Bredenkamp, Conrad Justus. *Der Prophet Jesaia*. 2 vols. Erlangen, Germany: Andreas Deichert, 1887.
Brinkman, John A. "Sennacherib's Babylonian Problem: An Interpretation." *Journal of Cuneiform Studies* 25.2 (April 1973) 89–95.
Bruce, F. F. *1 and 2 Thessalonians*. Edited by Bruce M. Metzger. Word Biblical Commentary 45. Waco, TX: Word, 1982.
Brueggemann, Walter. *A Commentary on Jeremiah: Exile and Homecoming*. Grand Rapids: Eerdmans, 1998.
———. *Isaiah*. Westminster Bible Companion. Louisville: Westminster John Knox, 1998.
Budd, Philip J. *Numbers*. Word Biblical Commentary 5. Waco, TX: Word, 1984.
Budde, Karl. "Das Hebräische Klagelied." *Zeitschrift für die alttestamentliche Wissenschaft* 2 (1882) 1–52.
———. "Jesaja 13." In *Abhandlungen zur semitischen Religionskunde und Sprachwissenschaft: Wolf Wilhelm Grafen von Baudissin*, edited by Wilhelm Frankenberg et al., 55–70. Giessen: Töpelmann, 1918.
Buksbazen, Victor. *The Prophet Isaiah: Original Translation and Commentary*. Collingswood, NJ: Spearhead, 1971.
Bullinger, E. W. *Figures of Speech Used in the Bible: Explained and Illustrated*. Reprint. Grand Rapids: Baker, 1991.
Bultema, Harry. *Commentary on Isaiah*. Grand Rapids: Kregel, 1981.
Burns, John Barclay. "Does Helel 'go to Hell?' Isaiah 14:12–15." *Proceedings, Eastern Great Lakes and Midwest Biblical Societies* 9 (1989) 89–97.
———. "'hôlēš Al' in Isaiah 14:12: A New Proposal." *Zeitschrift für Althebräistik* 2.2 (1989) 199–204.
Calvin, John. *Commentary on the Book of the Prophet Isaiah*. Translated by William Pringle. 4 vols. Grand Rapids: Eerdmans, 1958.
Carman, Jon. "The Falling Star and the Rising Son: Luke 10:17–24 and Second Temple 'Satan' Traditions." *Stone-Campbell Journal* 17.2 (2014) 221–31.
Cartledge, Paul. *Alexander the Great: The Hunt for a New Past*. New York: Vintage, 2005.
Chafer, Lewis Sperry. *Satan, His Motive and Methods*. Grand Rapids: Zondervan, 1981.
———. *Systematic Theology*. 8 vols. Grand Rapids: Kregel, 1993.
Cheyne, Thomas Kelly. *The Prophecies of Isaiah*. 5th ed. 2 vols. London: Kegan Paul, Trench, 1889.
Childs, Brevard. *Isaiah*. Old Testament Library. Louisville: Westminster John Knox, 2001.
———. *Isaiah and the Assyrian Crisis*. Studies in Biblical Theology. London: SCM, 1967.
———. *Myth and Reality in the Old Testament*. Studies in Biblical Theology 27. Reprint. Eugene, OR: Wipf & Stock, 2009.
Chilton, Bruce. *The Isaiah Targum*. Edited by Kevin Cathcart, et al. Vol. 11. *The Aramaic Bible: The Targums*. Collegeville, MN: Liturgical, 1990.
Chisholm, Robert. *From Exegesis to Exposition: A Practical Guide to Using Biblical Hebrew*. Grand Rapids: Baker, 1998.
———. *Handbook on the Prophets: Isaiah, Jeremiah, Lamentations, Ezekiel, Daniel, Minor Prophets*. Grand Rapids: Baker Academic, 2009.
Chung, Tae Whoe. "The Development of the Concept of Satan in Old Testament and Intertestamental Literature." PhD diss., Southwestern Baptist Theological Seminary, 2000.

Bibliography

Clarke, Adam. *Isaiah—Minor Prophets.* Clarke's Commentary on the Old Testament. London: Joseph Butterworth and Son, 1825.

Clements, Ronald E. *Isaiah 1–39.* New Century Bible Commentary. Grand Rapids: Eerdmans, 1980.

———. "Isaiah 14:22–27: A Central Passage Reconsidered." In *The Book of Isaiah—Le Livre de Isaïe: Les Oracles et Leurs Relecture,* edited by Jacques Vermeylen, 253–62. Leuven: Peeters/Leuven University Press, n.d.

Cobb, William Henry. "The Ode in Isaiah XIV." *Journal of Biblical Literature* 15 (1896) 18–35.

Cole, R. Dennis. *Numbers.* The New American Commentary. Nashville: Broadman & Holman, 2000.

Cooper, Lamar Eugene. *Ezekiel.* New American Commentary. Nashville: Broadman & Holman, 1994.

Couey, J. Blake. *Reading the Poetry of First Isaiah: The Most Perfect Model of the Prophetic Poetry.* Oxford: Oxford University Press, 2015.

Craigie, Peter C. *The Book of Deuteronomy.* New International Commentary on the Old Testament. Grand Rapids: Eerdmans, 1976.

———. "Helel Athtar and Phaethon, Jes 14:12–15." *Zeitschrift für die alttestamentliche Wissenschaft* 85.2 (1973) 223–25.

Criswell, Wallie A. *Isaiah: An Exposition.* Grand Rapids: Zondervan, 1977.

Cross, Frank Moore. *Canaanite Myth and Hebrew Epic: Essays in the History of the Religion of Israel.* Cambridge, MA: Harvard University Press, 1997.

Curkpatrick, Stephen. "Between Mashal and Parable: 'Likeness' as a Metonymic Enigma." *Horizons in Biblical Theology* 24.1 (2002) 58–71.

Cushman, Beverly W. "The Politics of the Royal Harem and the Case of Bat-Sheba." *Journal for the Study of the Old Testament* 30.3 (2006) 327–43.

Damon, Arwa. "Bringing Babylon Back from the Dead." *CNN.* April 4, 2013. http://www.cnn.com/2013/04/04/world/meast/iraq-babylon-tourism/index.html.

Davidson, Israel. "Parody in Jewish Literature." PhD diss., Columbia University, 1907.

Davis, Andrew M. *Exalting Jesus in Isaiah.* Christ-Centered Exposition Commentary. Nashville: B&H, 2017.

Day, John. *Yahweh and the Gods and Goddesses of Canaan.* Sheffield: Sheffield Academic, 2000.

Delitzsch, Franz. *Biblical Commentary on the Prophecies of Isaiah.* Translated by James Martin. Grand Rapids: Eerdmans, 1969.

Dickason, C. Fred. *Angels: Elect & Evil.* Chicago: Moody, 1995.

Dietrich, Manfried, et al., eds. *The Cuneiform Alphabetic Texts from Ugarit, Ras Ibn Hani and Other Places.* 2nd ed. Abhandlungen zur Literatur Alt-Syrien-Palästinas und Mesopotamiens. Münster: Ugarit-Verlag, 1995.

Dijkstra, Meindert. "Astral Myth of the Birth of Shahar and Shalim (KTU 1:23)." In *"Und Mose Schrieb Dieses Lied Auf": Studien Zum Alten Testament Und Zum Alten Orient: Festschrift Für Oswald Loretz Zur Vollendung Seines 70 Lebensjahres Mit Beiträgen von Freunden, Schülern Und Kollegen,* edited by Manfried Dietrich and Ingo Kottsieper, 265–87. Münster: Ugarit-Verlag, 1998.

Dillmann, August. *Der Prophet Jesaia.* 5th ed. Kurzgefasstes exegetisches Handbuch zum Alten Testament. Leipzig: S. Hirzel, 1890.

Dodge, Theodore Ayrault. *Alexander: A History of the Origin and Growth of the Art of War from the Earliest Times to the Battle of Ipsus, 301 BC, with a Detailed Account of the Campaigns of the Great Macedonian*. Cambridge, MA: Da Capo, 2004.

Drechsler, Moritz. *Der Prophet Jesaja*. Stuttgart: Gustav Schlawitz, 1849.

Duguid, Iain. *Ezekiel*. NIV Application Commentary. Grand Rapids: Zondervan, 1999.

Duke, Paul D. *Irony in the Fourth Gospel*. Atlanta: John Knox, 1985.

Dyer, Charles H. "The Biblical Argument for the Rebuilding of Babylon." Kansas City: Pre-Trib Research Center, n.d.

———. *Future Babylon: The Biblical Arguments for Rebuilding Babylon*. Taos, NM: Dispensational, 2016.

———. "The Identity of Babylon in Revelation 17–18: Part 1." *Bibliotheca Sacra* 144.575 (July 1987) 305–16.

———. "The Identity of Babylon in Revelation 17–18: Part 2." *Bibliotheca Sacra* 144.576 (October 1987) 433–49.

———. *The Rise of Babylon*. Updated. Chicago: Moody, 2003.

Eissfeldt, Otto. *Der Maschal im Alten Testament*. Gießen: Töpelmann, 1913.

———. *The Old Testament: An Introduction*. New York: Harper and Row, 1965.

Eitan, Israel. "Two Unknown Verbs: Etymological Studies." *Journal of Biblical Literature* 42.1–2 (1923) 22–28.

Elayi, Josette. *Sargon II, King of Assyria*. Archaeology and Biblical Studies 22. Atlanta: Society for Biblical Literature, 2017.

Elliger, Karl, and Wilhelm Rudolph, eds. *Biblia Hebraica Stuttgartensia*. 5th ed. Stuttgart: Deutsche Bibelstiftung, 1997.

Enns, Paul. *The Moody Handbook of Theology*. Chicago: Moody, 2014.

Epstein, Isidore, ed. *The Babylonian Talmud*. 18 vols. London: Soncino, 1978.

Erdman, Charles R. *The Book of Isaiah: An Exposition*. Grand Rapids: Baker, 1982.

Erickson, Millard. *Christian Theology*. 3rd ed. Grand Rapids: Baker Academic, 2013.

Erlandsson, Seth. "Burden of Babylon: A Study of Isaiah 13:2—14:23." *Springfielder* 38.1 (June 1974) 1–12.

———. *The Burden of Babylon: A Study of Isaiah 13:2—14:23*. Translated by George Houser. Lund: Gleerup, 1970.

Etz, Donald V. "Isaiah 14:12–15 a Reference to Comet Halley." *Vetus Testamentum* 36.3 (July 1986) 289–301.

Fee, Gordon D. *The First and Second Letters to the Thessalonians*. New International Commentary on the New Testament. Grand Rapids: Eerdmans, 2009.

Finley, Thomas John. *Joel, Amos, Obadiah*. The Wycliffe Exegetical Commentary. Chicago: Moody, 1990.

Fischer, Johann. *Das Buch Isaias. I. Teil: Kapitel 1–39*. Bonn: Hanstein, 1937.

Fokkelman, Jan P. *Reading Biblical Poetry: An Introductory Guide*. Translated by Ineke Smit. Louisville: Westminster John Knox, 2001.

Frame, John. *Systematic Theology: An Introduction to Christian Belief*. Phillipsburg, NJ: P&R, 2013.

Franke, Chris. "The Function of the Oracles against Babylon in Isaiah 14 and 47." *Society of Biblical Literature Seminar Papers* 32 (1993) 250–59.

———. "The Function of the Satiric Lament over Babylon in Second Isaiah (47)." *Vetus Testamentum* 41.4 (October 1991) 408–18.

Freedman, David Noel, ed. *The Anchor Bible Dictionary*. New Haven: Yale University Press, 2008.

Bibliography

Fruchtenbaum, Arnold G. *The Footsteps of the Messiah: A Study of the Sequence of Prophetic Events*. Revised. Tustin, CA: Ariel Ministries, 2003.

Fry, Mervin John. "The 'Oracle Concerning Babylon': An Exegetical Study of Isaiah 13:1—14:27." PhD diss., Union Theological Seminary, 1992.

Gallagher, William R. "On the Identity of Hêlēl Ben Šaḥar of Is 14:12–15." *Ugarit-Forschungen* 26 (1994) 131–46.

———. *Sennacherib's Campaign to Judah: New Studies*. Studies in the History and Culture of the Ancient Near East. Leiden: Brill, 1999.

Garr, W. Randall. "The Qinah: A Study of Poetic Meter, Syntax and Style." *Zeitschrift für die alttestamentliche Wissenschaft* 95.1 (1983) 54–75.

Gehman, Henry S. "The 'Burden' of the Prophets." *Jewish Quarterly Review* 31.2 (1940) 107–21.

Geisler, Norman L. *Systematic Theology: In One Volume*. Condensed ed. Minneapolis: Bethany House, 2011.

Gesenius, Wilhelm. *Der Prophet Jesaia*. 3 vols. Leipzig: Vogel, 1821.

Geyer, John B. "Twisting Tiamat's Tail: A Mythological Interpretation of Isaiah 13:5 and 8." *Vetus Testamentum* 37.2 (April 1987) 164–79.

Gibson, John C. L. *Canaanite Myths and Legends*. Edinburgh: T. & T. Clark, 1978.

Ginsberg, Harold Louis. "Reflexes of Sargon in Isaiah after 715 BCE." In *Essays in Memory of E. A. Speiser*, edited by William W. Hallo, 47–53. New Haven: American Oriental Society, 1968.

Goehring, Harry. "The Fall of Babylon-Historical or Future? A Critical Monograph on Isaiah 13:19–20." *Grace Journal* 2.1 (1961) 23–34.

Goering, Greg Schmidt. "Proleptic Fulfillment of the Prophetic Word: Ezekiel's Dirges over Tyre and its Ruler." *Journal for the Study of the Old Testament* 36.4 (June 2012) 483–505.

Goldingay, John. *Isaiah*. New International Biblical Commentary. Peabody, MA: Hendrickson, 2001.

———. *Psalms 42–89*. Baker Commentary on the Old Testament. Grand Rapids: Baker Academic, 2006.

———. *The Theology of the Book of Isaiah*. Downers Grove, IL: IVP, 2014.

Good, Edwin M. *Irony in the Old Testament*. 2nd ed. Bible and Literature Series. Sheffield: Almond, 1981.

Gōšen-Gōṭštayn, Mošeh. *The Book of Isaiah*. Jerusalem: Magnes, 1995.

Gosse, Bernard. *Isaïe 13,1–14,23: Dans la Tradition Littéraire du Livre d'Isaïe et dans la Tradition des Oracles contre les Nations*. Orbis Biblicus et Orientalis 78. Freiburg: Vandenhoeck & Ruprecht, 1988.

———. *Isaïe: Le Livre de La Contestation*. Supplément à Transeuphratène 17. Pendé, France: Gabalda, 2012.

Gowan, Donald E. *When Man Becomes God: Humanism and Hybris in the Old Testament*. Pittsburgh Theological Monograph 6. Pittsburgh: Pickwick, 1975.

Gray, George Buchanan. *A Critical and Exegetical Commentary on the Book of Isaiah: I–XXXIX*. International Critical Commentary. Edinburgh: T. & T. Clark, 1912.

Gray, John. "The Rephaim." *Palestine Exploration Quarterly* 81 (July 1949) 127–39.

Grayson, Albert Kirk. *Assyrian and Babylonian Chronicles*. Warsaw, IN: Eisenbrauns, 1975.

Green, Gene L. *The Letters to the Thessalonians*. Pillar New Testament Commentary. Grand Rapids: Eerdmans, 2002.

Gregory the Great, Pope. *Morals on the Book of Job*. Translated by Members of the English Church. 3 vols. Oxford, UK: Parker, 1845.

Grelot, Pierre. "Isaïe 14:12–15 et Son Arrière-Plan Mythologique." *Revue de l'histoire des religions* 149.1 (January 1956) 18–48.

———. "Sur La Vocalisation de היללּ (IS. XIV 12)." *Vetus Testamentum* 6.3 (July 1956) 303–4.

Grogan, Geoffrey W. "Isaiah." In *The Expositor's Bible Commentary*, edited by Frank E. Gaebelein, 3–354. Grand Rapids: Zondervan, 1986.

Grudem, Wayne. *Systematic Theology: An Introduction to Biblical Doctrine*. Grand Rapids: Zondervan, 1994.

Habel, Norman C. *The Book of Job: A Commentary*. Philadelphia: Westminster, 1985.

Hamilton, Victor. *The Book of Genesis: Chapters 1–17*. New International Commentary on the Old Testament. Grand Rapids: Eerdmans, 1990.

Hammond, Nicholas G. L. *The Genius of Alexander the Great*. Chapel Hill, NC: University of North Carolina Press, 1997.

Hannoosh, Michele. "The Reflexive Function of Parody." *Comparative Literature* 41.2 (1989) 113–27.

Harris, Gregory H. "Can Satan Raise the Dead?: Toward a Biblical View of the Beast's Wound." *Masters Seminary Journal* (April 2007) 23–41.

Harris, Scott L. "'Figure' and 'Riddle': Prov 1:8–19 and Inner-Biblical Interpretation." *Biblical Research* 41 (1996) 58–76.

Harrison, Roland K. *Numbers*. The Wycliffe Exegetical Commentary. Chicago: Moody, 1990.

Hartley, John E. *The Book of Job*. The New International Commentary on the Old Testament. Grand Rapids: Eerdmans, 2007.

Hassler, Mark. "Isaiah 13:1—14:27: The Babylonian Tyrant and the Morning Star." ThD diss., The Master's Seminary, 2013.

———. "Isaiah 14 and Habakkuk 2: Two Taunt Songs against the Same Tyrant?" *Master's Seminary Journal* 26.2 (September 2015) 221–29.

Haupt, Paul. "Hebrew MAŠÁL." *Journal of Biblical Literature* 36.1–2 (March 1917) 140–42.

Hayes, John H., and Stuart A. Irvine. *Isaiah: The Eighth Century Prophet: His Times and His Preaching*. Nashville: Abingdon, 1987.

Heater, Homer. "Do the Prophets Teach that Babylonia Will Be Rebuilt in the Eschaton?" *Journal of the Evangelical Theological Society* 41.1 (March 1998) 23–43.

Heiser, Michael S. "The Mythological Provenance of Isa. XIV 12–15: A Reconsideration of the Ugaritic Material." *Vetus Testamentum* 51.3 (2001) 354–69.

———. *Supernatural: What the Bible Teaches about the Unseen World and Why it Matters*. Bellingham, WA: Lexham, 2015.

———. *The Unseen Realm: Recovering the Supernatural Worldview of the Bible*. Bellingham, WA: Lexham, 2015.

Herbert, Arthur S. *The Book of the Prophet Isaiah: Chapters 1–39*. Cambridge Bible Commentary. Cambridge: Cambridge University Press, 1973.

———. "The 'Parable' (Māšāl) in the Old Testament." *Scottish Journal of Theology* 7.2 (June 1954) 180–96.

Hiebert, D. Edmond. *1 and 2 Thessalonians*. Revised. Winona Lake, IN: BMH, 1996.

Hitchcock, Mark. *Who is the Antichrist?* Eugene, OR: Harvest House, 2011.

Hitzig, Ferdinand. *Der Prophet Jesaia*. Heidelberg, Germany: C. F. Winter, 1833.

Bibliography

Hoffmann, Yair. "The Day of the Lord as a Concept and a Term in the Prophetic Literature." *Zeitschrift für die alttestamentliche Wissenschaft* 93.1 (1981) 37–50.

Holladay, William Lee. "Text, Structure, and Irony in the Poem on the Fall of the Tyrant, Isaiah 14." *The Catholic Biblical Quarterly* 61.4 (October 1999) 633–45.

Holmyard III, Harold. "Mosaic Eschatology in Isaiah, Especially Chapters 1, 28–33." ThD diss., Dallas Theological Seminary, 1992.

Hooke, Samuel H. *The Labyrinth: Further Studies in the Relation between Myth and Ritual in the Ancient World*. New York: Macmillan, 1980.

Hubbard, David A. "Antichrist." In *Evangelical Dictionary of Theology*, edited by Walter A. Elwell, 68–70. 2nd ed. Baker Reference Library. Grand Rapids: Baker, 2001.

Ice, Thomas. "Babylon in Bible Prophecy." Kansas City: Pre-Trib Research Center, May 2009.

Ironside, Harry A. *Expository Notes on the Prophet Isaiah*. New York: Loizeaux Brothers, 1952.

Jacobs, Jack. "The Eschatological Significance of Babylon." ThD diss., Grace Theological Seminary, 1971.

Jahnow, Hedwig. *Das hebräische Leichenlied im Rahmen der Völkerdichtung*. Giessen: Töpelmann, 1923.

Jennings, Frederick C. *Studies in Isaiah*. New York: Loizeaux Brothers, 1935.

Jensen, Joseph. "Helel Ben Shaḥar (Isaiah 14:12–15) in Bible and Tradition." In *Writing and Reading the Scroll of Isaiah: Studies of an Interpretive Tradition*, edited by Craig Boyles and Craig Evans, 1:339–56. Supplements to Vetus Testamentum. 2 vols. Leiden: Brill, 1997.

Jeremias, Joachim. *Parables of Jesus*. New York: Scribner, 1963.

Jervis, L. Ann. "Antichrist." In *Evangelical Dictionary of Biblical Theology*, edited by Walter A. Elwell, 27–28. Baker Reference Library. Grand Rapids: Baker, 1996.

Johnson, Aubrey R. "מָשָׁל." In *Wisdom in Israel and in the Ancient Near East*, edited by Martin Noth and D. Winton Thomas, 3:162–69. Supplements to Vetus Testamentum. Leiden: Brill, 1969.

Joüon, Paul, and Tamitsu Muraoka. *A Grammar of Biblical Hebrew*. Subsidia Biblica 27. Rome: Pontificio Istituto Biblico, 2006.

Kaiser, Otto. *Isaiah: 1–12: A Commentary*. Translated by John Bowden. 2nd ed. Old Testament Library. Philadelphia: Westminster, 1983.

———. *Isaiah: 13–39: A Commentary*. Translated by Robert Wilson. Old Testament Library. Philadelphia: Westminster, 1974.

Karrer, Martin. "Antichrist." In *The Encyclopedia of Christianity*, edited by Erwin Fahlbusch et al., 81–82. Translated by Geoffrey William Bromiley. Grand Rapids: Eerdmans, 1999.

Keil, Carl F. *Biblical Commentary on the Prophecies of Ezekiel: Volume 1*. Translated by James Martin. Biblical Commentary on the Old Testament. Grand Rapids: Eerdmans, 1968.

Keown, Gerald Lynwood. "A History of the Interpretation of Isaiah 14:12–15." PhD diss., Southern Baptist Theological Seminary, 1979.

van Keulen, Percy S. F. "On the Identity of the Anonymous Ruler in Isaiah 14:4b–21." In *Isaiah in Context: Studies in Honour of Arie van Der Kooij on the Occasion of His Sixty-Fifth Birthday*, edited by Michaël van der Meer et al., 109–23. Leiden: Brill, 2010.

BIBLIOGRAPHY

Khlevniuk, Oleg V. *Stalin: New Biography of a Dictator*. Translated by Nora Seligman Favorov. New Haven: Yale University Press, 2015.
Kim, Hyun Chul Paul. *Reading Isaiah: A Literary and Theological Commentary*. Macon, GA: Smyth & Helwys, 2016.
Kissane, Edward J. *The Book of Isaiah: Chapters I–XXXIX*. Translated by Richard R. Ottley. Dublin: Browne & Nolan, 1941.
Knobel, August. *Kurzgefasstes exegetisches Handbuch zum alten Testament*. 2d ed. Leipzig, Germany: S. Hirzel, 1854.
Knoblet, Gerald. "An Investigation of Isaiah Thirteen." ThM thesis, Denver Baptist Theological Seminary, 1983.
Koehler, Ludwig, et al., eds. *The Hebrew and Aramaic Lexicon of the Old Testament*. Translated by Mervyn E. J. Richardson. 5 vols. Leiden: Brill, 2000.
Koldewey, Robert. *The Excavations at Babylon*. Translated by Agnes Johns. London: Macmillan, 1914.
König, Eduard. *Historisch-comparative Syntax der hebräischen Sprache: Schlusstheil des historisch-kritischen Lehrgebäudes des Hebräischen*. Leipzig: J. C. Hinrichs'sche Buchhandlung, 1897.
van der Kooij, Arie, et al. *Isaiah in Context: Studies in Honour of Arie van Der Kooij on the Occasion of His Sixty-fifth Birthday*. Leiden: Brill, 2010.
Kőszeghy, Miklós. "Hybris Und Prophetie: Erwägungen Zum Hintergrund von Jesaja Xiv 12–15." *Vetus Testamentum* 44.4 (October 1994) 549–54.
Krüger, Thomas. *Qoheleth*. Translated by Orville C. Dean. Hermenia. Minneapolis: Fortress, 2004.
Kuenen, Abraham. *Historisch-kritische Einleitung in die Bücher des Alten Testaments*. 2 vols. Leipzig: Reisland, 1892.
Kugel, James L. *The Idea of Biblical Poetry: Parallelism and its History*. Baltimore: Johns Hopkins University Press, 1998.
Ladd, George Eldon. *A Commentary on the Revelation of John*. Grand Rapids: Eerdmans, 1984.
Lamb, Harold. *Genghis Khan: The Emperor of All Men*. Garden City, NY: International Collectors Library, 1927.
Landes, George. "Jonah: A Māsāl?" In *Israelite Wisdom: Theological and Literary Essays in Honor of Samuel Terrien*, edited by John Gammie et al., 137–58. Missoula, MT: Scholars, 1978.
Lang, George H. *The Histories and Prophecies of Daniel*. 4th ed. Grand Rapids: Kregel, 1973.
Lasch, Christopher. "Achieving Parody." *The Hastings Center Report* 3.1 (1973) 13–14.
Lelièvre, Frank J. "The Basis of Ancient Parody." *Greece & Rome* 1.2 (1954) 66–81.
Leupold, Herbert C. *Exposition of Isaiah: Chapters 1–39*. Grand Rapids: Baker, 1968.
Lewis, C. S. *Perelandra: A Novel*. Princeton: Simon and Schuster, 2005.
Lewis, Theodore J. *Cults of the Dead in Ancient Israel and Ugarit*. Harvard Semitic Monographs 39. Atlanta: Scholars, 1989.
L'Heureux, Conrad. "Ugaritic and Biblical Rephaim." *Harvard Theological Review* 67.3 (July 1974) 265–74.
Lieu, Judith. "Literary Strategies of Personification." In *Identity Formation in the New Testament*, 61–78. Tübingen: Mohr Siebeck, 2008.
Lindquist, Maria. "King Og's Iron Bed." *The Catholic Biblical Quarterly* 73.3 (July 2011) 477–92.

Bibliography

Lods, Adolphe. *Israel from its Beginnings to the Middle of the Eighth Century*. Translated by Samuel H. Hooke. London: Routledge & Kegan Paul, 1932.

———. *The Prophets and the Rise of Judaism*. Translated by Samuel H. Hooke. The History of Civilization. London: Routledge, 1996.

Long, Burke O. "The Divine Funeral Lament." *Journal of Biblical Literature* 85.1 (1966) 85–86.

Longman, Tremper. "Lament." In *Cracking Old Testament Codes: A Guide to Interpreting Literary Genres of the Old Testament*, edited by D. Brent Sandy and Ronald L. Giese, 197–215. Nashville: Broadman & Holman, 1995.

Lowth, Robert. *Isaiah: A New Translation; With a Preliminary Dissertation, and Notes, Critical, Philological, and Explanatory*. 3rd ed. Perth, UK: R. Morison Junior, 1793.

Luckenbill, Daniel David. *Ancient Records of Assyria and Babylonia*. 2 vols. London: Histories & Mysteries of Man, 1989.

———. *The Annals of Sennacherib*. Reprint. Eugene, OR: Wipf & Stock, 2005.

Lundbom, Jack R. *Deuteronomy: A Commentary*. Grand Rapids: Eerdmans, 2013.

Luther, Martin. *Lectures on Isaiah: Chapters 1–39*. Translated by Jaroslav Pelikan. Vol. 16. 55 vols. *Luther's Works*. St. Louis: Concordia, 1969.

MacArthur, John, and Richard Mayhue, eds. *Biblical Doctrine: A Systematic Summary of Bible Truth*. Wheaton, IL: Crossway, 2017.

Machinist, Peter. "The Assyrians and Their Babylonian Problem: Some Reflections." In *Wissenschaftskolleg Zu Berlin Jahrbuch*, edited by the Institute for Advanced Study, 353–64. Berlin: Siedler Verlag, 1985.

Mack, Robert L. *The Genius of Parody: Imitation and Originality in Seventeenth- and Eighteenth-Century English Literature*. New York: Palgrave Macmillan, 2007.

Mackay, John L. *A Study Commentary on Isaiah: Chapters 1–39*. An EP Study Commentary. Webster, NY: Evangelical, 2000.

Marti, Karl. *Das Buch Jesaja*. Tübingen: Mohr Siebeck, 1900.

Martin, John A. "Isaiah." In *The Bible Knowledge Commentary*, edited by John F. Walvoord and Roy B. Zuck, 1029–1121. Wheaton, IL: Victor, 1983.

Mathews, Kenneth. *Genesis 1—11:26*. New American Commentary. Nashville: Broadman & Holman, 1995.

May, Herbert Gordon. "Pattern and Myth in the Old Testament." *The Journal of Religion* 21.3 (1941) 285–99.

Mays, James Luther. *Amos: A Commentary*. Old Testament Library. Philadelphia: Westminster, 1969.

McClain, Alva J. *The Greatness of the Kingdom: An Inductive Study of the Kingdom of God*. Winona Lake, IN: BMH, 2007.

McCune, Rolland. *A Systematic Theology of Biblical Christianity: Volume 3*. 3 vols. Allen Park, MI: Detroit Baptist Theological Seminary, 2009.

McIntosh, Doug. *Deuteronomy*. Edited by Max E. Anders. Holman Old Testament Commentary. Nashville: Broadman & Holman, 2002.

McKane, William. *Proverbs: A New Approach*. Old Testament Library. Philadelphia: Westminster, 1970.

McKay, John W. "Helel and the Dawn-Goddess: A Re-Examination of the Myth in Isaiah 14:12–15." *Vetus Testamentum* 20.4 (October 1970) 451–64.

McKinion, Steven A., and Thomas C. Oden, eds. *Isaiah 1–39*. Vol. 10. 29 vols. Ancient Christian Commentary on Scripture. Downers Grove, IL: InterVarsity, 2004.

Merrill, Eugene H. *Kingdom of Priests: A History of Old Testament Israel*. 2nd ed. Grand Rapids: Baker Academic, 2008.
Miceli, Vincent P. *The Antichrist*. West Hanover, MA: Christopher, 1981.
Millard, Alan R. "Baladan, the Father of Merodach-Baladan." *Tyndale Bulletin* 22 (1971) 125–26.
Miller, Patrick D. "Divine Council and the Prophetic Call to War." *Vetus Testamentum* 18.1 (January 1968) 100–7.
Mizrahi, Noam. "The Linquistic History of מדהבה: From Textual Corruption to Lexical Innovation." *Revue de Qumran* 26.1 (2013) 91–114.
———. "The Textual History and Literary Background of Isa 14,4." *Zeitschrift für die alttestamentliche Wissenschaft* 125.3 (2013) 433–47.
Molnár-Hídvégi, Nora. "The Paths Not Taken: Novel Insights on the Function and the Use of Mashal (מָשָׁל) in the Old Testament." *Biblische Notizen* 169 (2016) 83–109.
Morgan, G. Campbell. *The Prophecy of Isaiah*. New York: Revell, 1910.
Morgenstern, Julian. "The Mythological Background of Psalm 82." *Hebrew Union College Annual* 14 (1939) 29–126.
Motyer, J. A. *Isaiah: An Introduction and Commentary*. Tyndale Old Testament Commentaries. Downers Grove, IL: InterVarsity, 1999.
———. *The Prophecy of Isaiah: An Introduction & Commentary*. Downers Grove, IL: InterVarsity, 1993.
Mounce, Robert H. *The Book of Revelation*. Revised. New International Commentary on the New Testament. Grand Rapids: Eerdmans, 1998.
Muilenburg, James. "The Linguistic and Rhetorical Usages of the Particle כי in the Old Testament." *Hebrew Union College Annual* 32 (1961) 135–60.
Munch, Peter Andreas. *The Expression Bajjôm Hāhū: Is it an Eschatological Terminus Technicus?* Oslo: I Kommisjon hos Jacob Dybwad, 1936.
Newton, Benjamin Wills. *Aids to Prophetic Enquiry*. 3rd ed. London: Houlston & Sons, 1881.
———. *Babylon, its Future History and Doom*. 3rd ed. London: Houlston & Sons, 1890.
———. *Babylon; its Revival and Final Desolation*. London: Houlston & Wright, 1859.
Niditch, Susan. *Folklore and the Hebrew Bible*. Edited by Gene M. Tucker. Guides to Biblical Scholarship: Old Testament. Minneapolis: Fortress, 1993.
Niehaus, Jeffrey H. "Amos." In *The Minor Prophets: An Exegetical and Expository Commentary: Volume 1*, edited by Thomas Edward McComiskey, 315–494. 3 vols. Grand Rapids: Baker, 1992.
Niehr, Herbert. "Zaphon." In *Dictionary of Deities and Demons in the Bible*, edited by Karel van der Toorn et al., 927–29. 2nd ed. Leiden: Brill, 1999.
Nielsen, Kirsten. *There is Hope for a Tree: The Tree as Metaphor in Isaiah*. Translated by Christine Crowley and Frederick Crowley. Sheffield: Sheffield Academic, 1989.
von Nordheim-Diehl, Miriam. "Wer Herrscht in Der Scheol?: Eine Untersuchung Zu Jes 14,9." *Biblische Notizen* 143 (2009) 81–91.
O'Connell, Robert H. "Isaiah 14:4b–23: Ironic Reversal through Concentric Structure and Mythic Allusion." *Vetus Testamentum* 38.4 (October 1988) 406–18.
van O'Connor, William. "Parody as Criticism." *College English* 25.4 (1964) 241–48.
Ogden, Graham S. *Qoheleth*. Vol. 2d. Sheffield: Sheffield Phoenix, 2007.
Ogden, Graham S., and Jan Sterk. *A Handbook on Isaiah: Volume One*. Ubs Handbook Series. New York: United Bible Societies, 2011.

Bibliography

Oldenburg, Ulf. "Above the Stars of El: El in Ancient South Arabic Religion." *Zeitschrift für die alttestamentliche Wissenschaft* 82.2 (1970) 187–208.

Olyan, Saul M. "Was the 'King of Babylon' Buried Before His Corpse Was Exposed?: Some Thoughts on Isa 14,19." *Zeitschrift für die alttestamentliche Wissenschaft* 118.3 (2006) 423–26.

Orlinsky, Harry Meyer. "Madhebah in Isaiah 14:4." *Vetus Testamentum* 7.2 (April 1957) 202–3.

Ortlund, Raymond. *Isaiah: God Saves Sinners*. Preaching the Word. Wheaton, IL: Crossway, 2012.

Osborne, William R. "Elements of Irony: History and Rhetoric in Ezekiel 20:1–44." *Criswell Theological Review* 9.1 (September 2011) 3–15.

Oswalt, John. *The Bible among the Myths: Unique Revelation or Just Ancient Literature?* Grand Rapids: Zondervan, 2009.

———. *The Book of Isaiah: Chapters 1–39*. New International Commentary on the Old Testament. Grand Rapids: Eerdmans, 1986.

———. *Isaiah*. NIV Application Commentary. Grand Rapids: Zondervan, 2003.

———. "Myth of the Dragon and Old Testament Faith." *Evangelical Quarterly* 49 (July 1977) 163–72.

Patmore, Hector M. *Adam, Satan, and the King of Tyre: The Interpretation of Ezekiel 28:11–19 in Late Antiquity*. Jewish and Christian Perspectives 20. Boston: Brill, 2012.

Patterson, Paige. *Revelation*. New American Commentary. Nashville: Broadman & Holman, 2012.

Paul, Shalom M. *Amos: A Commentary on the Book of Amos*. Edited by Frank Moore Cross. Hermeneia. Minneapolis: Fortress, 1991.

Pentecost, J. Dwight. *Things to Come: A Study in Biblical Eschatology*. Grand Rapids: Zondervan, 1964.

Peters, George N. H. *The Theocratic Kingdom*. 3 vols. Grand Rapids: Kregel, 1988.

Pink, Arthur. *The Antichrist*. Minneapolis: Klock & Klock, 1979.

Poirier, John C. "An Illuminating Parallel to Isaiah XIV 12." *Vetus Testamentum* 49.3 (July 1999) 371–89.

Polk, Timothy. "Paradigms, Parables, and Měšālîm: On Reading the Māšāl in Scripture." *The Catholic Biblical Quarterly* 45.4 (October 1983) 564–83.

Pope, Marvin H. "A Divine Banquet at Ugarit." In *The Use of the Old Testament in the New and Other Essays: Studies in Honor of William Franklin Stinespring*, edited by William F. Stinespring and James M. Efird, 170–203. Durham, NC: Duke University Press, 1972.

———. *EL in the Ugaritic Texts*. Leiden: Brill, 1955.

Price, Walter K. *The Coming Antichrist*. Chicago: Moody, 1974.

Prinsloo, Willem S. "Isaiah 14:12–15—Humiliation, Hubris, Humiliation." *Zeitschrift für die alttestamentliche Wissenschaft* 93.3 (1981) 432–38.

Pritchard, James B., ed. *Ancient Near Eastern Texts Relating to the Old Testament*. 3rd ed. Princeton: Princeton University Press, 1969.

von Rad, Gerhard. *Wisdom in Israel*. Nashville: Abingdon, 1972.

Radzinsky, Edvard. *Stalin: The First In-Depth Biography Based on Explosive New Documents from Russia's Secret Archives*. New York: Doubleday, 1996.

Riewald, Jacobus G. "Parody as Criticism." *Neophilologus* 50.1 (1966) 125–48.

Roberts, Alexander, and James Donaldson, eds. *The Ante-Nicene Fathers*. 10 vols. Reprint. Peabody, MA: Hendrickson, 1994.

Roberts, Jimmy J. M. *First Isaiah*. Edited by Peter Machinist. Hermenia. Minneapolis: Fortress, 2015.

Robertson, O. Palmer. *The Christ of Wisdom: A Redemptive-Historical Exploration of the Wisdom Books of the Old Testament*. Phillipsburg, NJ: P&R, 2017.

Roos, Deomar. "Babylon in the Book of Isaiah." PhD diss., University of Cambridge, 1998.

———. "Babylon in the Book of Isaiah." *Concordia Journal* 30.4 (October 2004) 350–75.

Ross, Allen P. *Commentary on the Psalms: Volume 2 (42–89)*. 3 vols. Grand Rapids: Kregel, 2013.

Rotz, Carol J., and Jan A. Du Rand. "The One Who Sits on the Throne: Towards a Theory of Theocentric Characterisation According to the Apocalypse of John." *Neotestamentica* 33.1 (1999) 91–111.

Rouillard-Bonraisin, Hedwige. "Rephaim." In *Dictionary of Deities and Demons in the Bible*, edited by Karel van der Toorn et al., 692–700. 2nd ed. Leiden: Brill, 1999.

Ruszkiewicz, John J. "Parody and Pedagogy: Explorations in Imitative Literature." *College English* 40.6 (1979) 693–701.

Ryken, Leland, et al., eds. *Dictionary of Biblical Imagery*. Downers Grove, IL: InterVarsity, 1998.

Ryrie, Charles C. *Basic Theology: A Popular Systemic Guide to Understanding Biblical Truth*. Chicago: Moody, 1999.

———. *Revelation*. Everyman's Bible Commentary. Chicago: Moody, 1996.

———. "Satan's Counterfeit." *Grace Theological Journal* 2.3 (Fall 1961) 15–18.

Schaff, Philip. ed. *The Nicene and Post-Nicene Fathers*, Series 1. 14 vols. Reprint. Peabody, MA: Hendrickson, 1994.

Schaff, Philip. ed. *The Nicene and Post-Nicene Fathers*, Series 2. 14 vols. Reprint. Peabody, MA: Hendrickson, 1994.

Schegg, Peter. *Der Prophet Jsaias*. 2 vols. München: Leutner, 1850.

Schmidt, Brian B. *Israel's Beneficent Dead: Ancestor Cult and Necromancy in Ancient Israelite Religion and Tradition*. Winona Lake, IN: Eisenbrauns, 1996.

Schmidt, Johannes. *Studien zur Stilistik der alttestamentlichen Spruchliteratur*. Alttestamentliche Abhandlungen 13. Münster: Aschendorffschen, 1936.

Schnabel, Eckhard J. "Israel, the People of God, and the Nations." *Journal of the Evangelical Theological Society* 45.1 (March 2002) 35–57.

Schöpflin, Karin. "משל—Ein Eigentümlicher Begriff Der Hebräischen Literatur." *Biblische Zeitschrift* 46.1 (2002) 1–24.

Scott, Robert B. Y. "The Book of Isaiah: Chapters 1–39." In *The Interpreter's Bible*, edited by George Arthur Buttrick, 5:149–381. 12 vols. Nashville: Abingdon, 1980.

———. "Oracles of God: The Prophetic Literature as a Medium of Revelation." *Interpretation* 2.2 (April 1948) 131–42.

Seitz, Christopher R. *Isaiah 1–39*. Interpretation. Louisville: John Knox, 1993.

Seow, Choon-Leong. *Ecclesiastes*. Anchor Bible. London: Yale University Press, 2008.

Sharp, Carolyn J. *Irony and Meaning in the Hebrew Bible*. Indiana Studies in Biblical Literature. Bloomington: Indiana University Press, 2009.

Shaw, Harry. *Concise Dictionary of Literary Terms*. New York: McGraw Hill, 1976.

Shipp, R. Mark. "Of Dead Kings and Dirges: Myth and Meaning in Isaiah 14:4b–21." PhD diss., Princeton Theological Seminary, 1998.

———. *Of Dead Kings and Dirges: Myth and Meaning in Isaiah 14:4b–21*. Academia Biblica 11. Leiden: Brill, 2002.

Bibliography

Skinner, John. *The Book of the Prophet Isaiah: Chapters I–XXXIX*. Edited by Alexander F. Kirkpatrick. Cambridge Bible for Schools and Colleges. Cambridge: Cambridge University Press, 1915.

Smith, Gary. *Isaiah 1–39*. New American Commentary. Nashville: Broadman & Holman, 2007.

Smith, George Adam. *The Book of Isaiah: Chapters I–XXXIX*. Revised. New York: Harper & Brothers, 1927.

Smith, Mark S. *The Origins of Biblical Monotheism: Israel's Polytheistic Background and the Ugaritic Texts*. Oxford: Oxford University Press, 2003.

Sorenson, David H. *Understanding the Bible: Proverbs through Isaiah*. Understanding the Bible. Duluth, MN: Northstar Ministries, 2005.

Sparks, Kenton. *Ancient Texts for the Study of the Hebrew Bible: A Guide to the Background Literature*. Peabody, MA: Hendrickson, 2005.

Spronk, Klaas. "Down with Hêlēl: The Assumed Mythological Background of Isa 14:12." In *"Und Mose Schrieb Dieses Lied Auf": Studien Zum Alten Testament Und Zum Alten Orient: Festschrift Für Oswald Loretz Zur Vollendung Seines 70 Lebensjahres Mit Beiträgen von Freunden, Schülern Und Kollegen*, edited by Manfried Dietrich and Ingo Kottsieper, 717–26. Münster: Ugarit-Verlag, 1998.

Stern, David. "The Alphabet of Ben Sira and the Early History of Parody." In *The Idea of Biblical Interpretation: Essays in Honor of James L. Kugel*, edited by Hindy Najman and Judith Newman, 423–48. Leiden: Brill, 2004.

Steuernagel, D. Carl. *Einleitung in das Alte Testament*. Tübingen: Mohr, 1912.

Steveson, Peter A. *A Commentary on Isaiah*. Greenville, SC: Bob Jones University Press, 2003.

Stuart, Douglas K. *Hosea–Jonah*. Word Biblical Commentary 31. Waco, TX: Thomas Nelson, 1987.

Suriano, Matthew J. *The Politics of Dead Kings: Dynastic Ancestors in the Book of Kings and Ancient Israel*. Tübingen: Mohr Siebeck, 2010.

Suter, David Winston. "Māšāl in the Similitudes of Enoch." *Journal of Biblical Literature* 100.2 (June 1981) 193–212.

Swartwood, Jana M. "'Babylon the Great, Mother of Prostitutes': Revelation 17–18 in an Isaianic Context." MA Thesis, Oral Roberts University, 2016.

Sweeney, Marvin A. *Isaiah 1–39: With an Introduction to Prophetic Literature*. Edited by Rolf Knierim and Gene M. Tucker. Forms of the Old Testament Literature. Grand Rapids: Eerdmans, 1996.

Tadmor, Hayim. "The Sin of Sargon and Sennacherib's Last Will." *State Archives of Assyrian Bulletin* 3.1 (1989) 3–51.

Talmon, Shemaryahu. "Biblical Rephā'îm and Ugaritic Rpu/i(M)." *Hebrew Annual Review* 7 (1983) 235–49.

Tarazi, Paul Nadim. "Israel and the Nations (According to Zechariah 14)." *St Vladimir's Theological Quarterly* 38.2 (1994) 181–92.

Tate, Marvin E. *Psalms 51–100*. Word Biblical Commentary 20. Waco, TX: Word, 2000.

———. "Satan in the Old Testament." *Review & Expositor* 89.4 (September 1992) 461–74.

Theodoret. *On Divine Providence*. Edited by Walter Burghardt and Thomas Lawler. Translated by Thomas P. Halton. Ancient Christian Writers 49. New York: Paulist, 1988.

Thiessen, Henry Clarence. *Lectures in Systematic Theology*. Revised. Grand Rapids: Eerdmans, 2006.

BIBLIOGRAPHY

Thomas, D. Winton. "Librum Jesaiae." In *Biblia Hebraica Stuttgartensia*, edited by Karl Elliger and Wilhelm Rudolph, 675-779. 5th ed. Stuttgart: Deutsche Bibelstiftung, 1997.

Thomas, Robert L. *Revelation 8-22: An Exegetical Commentary*. Chicago: Moody, 1995.

Thompson, John A. *The Book of Jeremiah*. The New International Commentary on the Old Testament. Grand Rapids: Eerdmans, 2007.

Tigay, Jeffrey H. *Deuteronomy*. Edited by Nahum M. Sarna. JPS Torah Commentary. Philadelphia: Jewish Publication Society, 1996.

Torrey, Charles Cutler. "Alexander the Great in the Old Testament Prophecies." In *Vom Alten Testament Karl Marti Zum Siebzigsten Geburtstage Gewidmet*, edited by Karl Budde, 281-86. Beihefte zur Zeitschrift für die alttestamentliche Wissenschaft 47. Giessen: Töpelmann, 1925.

———. "Some Important Editorial Operations in the Book of Isaiah." *Journal of Biblical Literature* 57.2 (1938) 109-39.

Tromp, Nicholas J. *Primitive Conceptions of Death and the Nether World in the Old Testament*. Rome: Pontifical Biblical Institute, 1969.

Tucker, Gene M. "The Book of Isaiah 1-39." In *The New Interpreter's Bible*, edited by Leander E. Keck, 6:25-305. 12 vols. Nashville: Abingdon, 2001.

Uzziel, Jonathan. *The Chaldee Paraphrase on the Prophet Isaiah*. Translated by Christian Pauli. London: London Society's House, 1871.

Vanderburgh, Frederick A. "The Ode on the King of Babylon, Isaiah XIV 4b-21." *The American Journal of Semitic Languages and Literatures* 29.2 (1913) 111-21.

VanDerMerwe, Christo H. J., et al. *A Biblical Hebrew Reference Grammar*. Reprinted with minor revisions. Biblical Languages: Hebrew 3. Sheffield: Sheffield Academic, 2002.

VanGemeren, Willem A., ed. *New International Dictionary of Old Testament Theology & Exegesis*. 5 vols. Grand Rapids: Zondervan, 1997.

Van Leeuwen, Raymond C. "Isa 14:12, Ḥôlēš Al Gwym and Gilgamesh XI, 6." *Journal of Biblical Literature* 99.2 (1980) 173-84.

Van Winkle, Daniel W. "The Relationship of the Nations to Yahweh and to Israel in Isaiah 40-55." *Vetus testamentum* 35.4 (October 1985) 446-58.

Van Wyk, Wouter C. "Isaiah 14:4b-21: A Poem of Contrast and Irony." In *Studies in Isaiah*, edited by W. C. Van Wyk, 240-247. Hercules, South Africa: NHW, 1982.

Vine, William E. *Isaiah: Prophecies, Promises, Warnings*. 3rd ed. Grand Rapids: Zondervan, 1953.

Walker, Larry L. *Isaiah, Jeremiah, Lamentations*. Edited by Philip W. Comfort. Cornerstone Biblical Commentary 8. Carol Stream, IL: Tyndale, 2006.

Waltke, Bruce. *The Book of Proverbs: Chapters 1-15*. New International Commentary on the Old Testament. Grand Rapids: Eerdmans, 2004.

Waltke, Bruce, and Michael O'Connor. *An Introduction to Biblical Hebrew Syntax*. Winona Lake, IN: Eisenbrauns, 1990.

Walvoord, John F. *The Revelation of Jesus Christ: A Commentary*. Chicago: Moody, 1989.

Wanamaker, Charles A. *The Epistles to the Thessalonians*. New International Greek Testament Commentary. Grand Rapids: Eerdmans, 1990.

Watson, Wilfred. *Classical Hebrew Poetry: A Guide to Its Techniques*. New York: T. & T. Clark, 2005.

———. "HELEL." In *Dictionary of Deities and Demons in the Bible*, edited by Karel van der Toorn et al., 392-94. 2nd ed. Leiden: Brill, 1999.

Bibliography

Watts, John D. W. *Isaiah 1–33*. Edited by Bruce M. Metzger. Word Biblical Commentary. Waco, TX: Word, 1985.

Weatherford, Jack. *Genghis Khan and the Quest for God: How the World's Greatest Conqueror Gave Us Religious Freedom*. New York: Penguin, 2017.

Weaver, Ann M. "The 'Sin of Sargon' and Esarhaddon's Reconception of Sennacherib: A Study in Divine Will, Human Politics and Royal Ideology." *Iraq* 66 (2004) 61–66.

Webb, Barry G. *The Message of Isaiah: On Eagles' Wings*. Bible Speaks Today. Downers Grove, IL: InterVarsity, 1996.

Weingreen, Jacob. "Construct-Genitive Relation in Hebrew Syntax." *Vetus Testamentum* 4.1 (January 1954) 50–59.

Weis, Richard D. "A Definition of the Genre Massa' in the Hebrew Bible." PhD diss., Claremont Graduate University, 1986.

Wenham, Gordon. *Genesis 1–15*. Word Biblical Commentary. Waco, TX: Word, 1987.

Werblowsky, R. J. Zwi. "Satan in the Old Testament." *Journal for the Scientific Study of Religion* 8.1 (1969) 169–72.

Westermann, Claus. *Lamentations: Issues and Interpretation*. Minneapolis: Fortress, 1994.

———. *Praise and Lament in the Psalms*. Atlanta: Westminster John Knox, 1981.

White, Ellen. *Yahweh's Council: Its Structure and Membership*. Tübingen: Mohr Siebeck, 2014.

Whybray, Roger N., ed. *The Book of Proverbs*. Cambridge Bible Commentary. Cambridge: Cambridge University Press, 1972.

———. *Proverbs*. New Century Bible Commentary. Grand Rapids: Eerdmans, 1994.

Wildberger, Hans. *Isaiah 1–12*. Translated by Thomas H. Trapp. Continental Commentaries. Minneapolis: Fortress, 1991.

———. *Isaiah 13–27*. Translated by Thomas H. Trapp. Continental Commentaries. Minneapolis: Fortress, 1991.

Wilken, Robert Louis, et al., eds. *Isaiah: Interpreted by Early Christian and Medieval Commentators*. Church's Bible. Grand Rapids: Eerdmans, 2007.

Wilkie, John M. "Nabonidus and the Later Jewish Exiles." *The Journal of Theological Studies* 2.1 (April 1951) 36–44.

Wolf, Herbert. *Interpreting Isaiah: The Suffering and Glory of the Messiah*. Grand Rapids: Zondervan, 1985.

Wolff, Hans Walter. *Joel and Amos: A Commentary on the Books of the Prophets Joel and Amos*. Edited by S. Dean McBride. Hermeneia. Philadelphia: Fortress, 1977.

Wyatt, Nicolas. "The Concept and Purpose of Hell: Its Nature and Development in West Semitic Thought." *Numen* 56.2–3 (2009) 161–84.

Yee, Gale. "The Anatomy of Biblical Parody: The Dirge Form in 2 Samuel 1 and Isaiah 14." *The Catholic Biblical Quarterly* 50.4 (October 1988) 565–86.

Young, Edward J. *The Book of Isaiah*. 3 vols. Grand Rapids: Eerdmans, 2000.

Youngblood, Kevin J. *Jonah: God's Scandalous Mercy*. Hearing the Message of Scripture. Grand Rapids: Zondervan, 2013.

Youngblood, Ronald F. "Fallen Star: The Evolution of Lucifer." *Bible Review* 14.6 (December 1998) 22–31.

———. "The Fall of Lucifer (in More Ways than One)." In *The Way of Wisdom: Essays in Honor of Bruce K. Waltke*, edited by Bruce K. Waltke et al., 168–79. Grand Rapids: Zondervan, 2000.

Younger, K. Lawson. "Recent Study on Sargon II, King of Assyria: Implications for Biblical Studies." In *Mesopotamia and the Bible: Comparative Explorations*, edited by Mark Chavalas, and K. Lawson Younger, 288–329. Grand Rapids: Baker Academic, 2002.

Zapff, Burkard M. *Schriftgelehrte Prophetie: Jes 13 und die Komposition des Jesajabuches : Ein Beitrag zur Erforschung der Redaktionsgeschichte des Jesajabuches*. Würzburg: Echter, 1995.

Zappia, Dominic. "Demythologizing the Satan Tradition of Historical-Criticism: A Reevaluation of the Old Testament Portrait of שָׂטָן in Light of the Old Testament Pseudepigrapha." *Scandinavian Journal of the Old Testament* 29.1 (2015) 117–34.

Zogbo, Lynell, and Ernst R. Wendland. *Hebrew Poetry in the Bible: A Guide for Understanding and for Translating*. New York: United Bible Societies, 2000.